P9-AQJ-630

Multicultural America

Volume VII
The Native Americans

Multicultural America

Volume VII

The Native Americans

Rodney P. Carlisle
GENERAL EDITOR

DISCARD

Facts On File
An imprint of Infobase Publishing

POQUOSON PUBLIC LIBRARY
500 CITY HALL AVENUE
POQUOSON, VIRGINIA 23662-19⁶

B. T 4/2011

Multicultural America: Volume VII: The Native Americans
Copyright © 2011 by Infobase Publishing

All rights reserved. No part of this book may be reproduced or utilized in any form or by any means, electronic or mechanical, including photocopying, recording, or by any information storage or retrieval systems, without permission in writing from the publisher. For information contact:

Facts On File, Inc.
An Imprint of Infobase Publishing
132 West 31st Street
New York, NY 10001

Library of Congress Cataloging-in-Publication Data
Multicultural America / Rodney P. Carlisle, general editor.
    v. cm.
  Includes bibliographical references and index.
  Contents: v. 1. The Hispanic Americans — v. 2. The Arab Americans —
v. 3. The African Americans — v. 4. The Asian Americans — v. 5. The
Jewish Americans — v. 6. The European Americans — v. 7. The Native Americans.
  ISBN 978-0-8160-7811-0 (v. 1 : hardcover : alk. paper) — ISBN
978-0-8160-7812-7 (v. 2 : hardcover : alk. paper) — ISBN
978-0-8160-7813-4 (v. 3 : hardcover : alk. paper) — ISBN
978-0-8160-7814-1 (v. 4 : hardcover : alk. paper) — ISBN
978-0-8160-7815-8 (v. 5 : hardcover : alk. paper) — ISBN
978-0-8160-7816-5 (v. 6 : hardcover : alk. paper) — ISBN
978-0-8160-7817-2 (v. 7 : hardcover : alk. paper) 1.
Minorities—United States—History—Juvenile literature. 2.
Ethnology—United States—History—Juvenile literature. 3. Cultural
pluralism—United States—History—Juvenile literature. 4. United
States—Ethnic relations—Juvenile literature. I. Carlisle, Rodney P.
  E184.A1M814 2011
  305.800973—dc22   2010012694

Facts On File books are available at special discounts when purchased in bulk quantities for businesses, associations, institutions, or sales promotions. Please call our Special Sales Department at (212) 967-8800 or (800) 322-8755.

You can find Facts On File on the World Wide Web at http://www.factsonfile.com

Text design and composition by Golson Media
Cover printed by Art Print, Taylor, PA
Book printed and bound by Maple Press, York, PA
Date Printed: March 2011
Printed in the United States of America

11 10 9 8 7 6 5 4 3 2 1

This book is printed on acid-free paper.

CONTENTS

Volume VII

The Native Americans

AMERICANS HAVE HAD a sense that they were a unique people, even before the American Revolution. In the 18th century, the settlers in the 13 colonies that became the United States of America began to call themselves Americans, recognizing that they were not simply British colonists living in North America. In addition to the English, other cultures and peoples had already begun to contribute to the rich tapestry that would become the American people.

Swedes and Finns in the Delaware River valley, Dutch in New York, Scots-Irish, and Welsh had all brought their different ways of life, dress, diet, housing, and religions, adding them to the mix of Puritan and Anglican Englishmen. Lower Rhine German groups of dissenting Amish and Mennonites, attracted by the religious toleration of Pennsylvania, settled in Germantown, Pennsylvania, as early as 1685. Located on the western edge of Philadelphia, the settlers and later German immigrants moved to the counties just further west in what would become Pennsylvania Dutch country.

The policies of the various other colonies tended to favor and encourage such group settlement to varying extents. In some cases, as in New Jersey, the fact that each community could decide what church would be supported by local taxes tended to attract coreligionists to specific communities. Thus in the colonial period, the counties of southern New Jersey (known in colonial times as West Jersey) tended to be dominated by Quakers, while townships in New Jersey closer to New York City were dominated by Lutheran, Dutch Reformed, and Anglican churches and settlers.

Ethnicity and religion divided the peoples of America, yet the official tolerance of religious diversity spawned a degree of mutual acceptance by one ethnic group of another. While crossreligious marriages were frowned upon, they were not prohibited, with individual families deciding which parents' church should be attended, if any. Modern descendants tracing their ancestry are sometimes astounded at the various strands of culture and religion that they find woven together.

To the south, Florida already had a rich Hispanic heritage, some of it filtered through Cuba. Smaller groups of immigrants from France and other countries in Europe were supplemented during the American Revolution by enthusiastic supporters of the idea of a republican experiment in the New World.

All of the 13 colonies had the institution of African slavery, and people of African ancestry, both slave and free, constituted as much as 40 percent of the population of colonies like Georgia and South Carolina. In a wave of acts of emancipation, slaves living in the New England colonies were freed in the years right after the Revolution, soon joined by those in Pennsylvania, New York, and New Jersey.

Although some African Americans in the south were free by birth or manumission, emancipation for 90 percent of those living south of Pennsylvania would have to wait until the years of the Civil War, 1861–65. Forcibly captured and transported under terrible conditions overland and across the ocean, Africans came from dozens of different linguistic stocks. Despite the disruptions of the middle passage, African Americans retained elements of their separate cultures, including some language and language patterns, and aspects of diet, religion, family, and music.

Native Americans, like African Americans, found themselves excluded from most of the rights of citizenship in the new Republic. In the Ohio and Mississippi Valley, many Native Americans resisted the advance of the European-descended settlers. In Florida, Creeks and Seminoles provided haven to escaped slaves, and together, they fought the encroachment of settlers. Some of the African Americans living with the Seminoles and other tribes moved west with them on the Trail of Tears to Indian Territory in what later became the state of Oklahoma. Other groups, like the Lumbees of North Carolina, stayed put, gradually adjusting to the new society around them. Throughout scattered rural communities, clusters of biracial and triracial descendents could trace their roots to Native-American and African ancestors, as well as to the English and Scotch-Irish.

The Louisiana Purchase brought the vast Mississippi Valley into the United States, along with the cosmopolitan city of New Orleans, where French exiles from Canada had already established a strong Creole culture. With the annexation of Texas, and following the Mexican-American War (1846–48), the United States incorporated as citizens hundreds of thousands of people of Hispanic ancestry. Individuals and communities in Texas and New Mexico preserve not only their religion, but also their language, cuisine, customs, and architecture.

As the United States expanded to the west, with vast opportunities for settlement, waves of European immigrants contributed to the growth of the country, with liberal naturalization laws allowing immigrants to establish themselves as citizens. Following the revolutions of 1848 in Europe, and famines in Ireland, new floods of immigrants from Central Europe, Ireland, and Scandinavia all settled in pockets.

As waves of immigrants continued to flow into the United States from the 1880s to World War I, the issue of immigration became even more politicized. On the one hand, older well-established ethnic communities sometimes resented the growing influence and political power of the new immigrants. Political machines in the larger cities made it a practice to incorporate the new settlers, providing them with some access to the politics and employment of city hall and at the same time expecting their votes and loyalty during election. The intricate interplay of ethnicity and politics through the late 19th century has been a rich field of historical research.

During the Progressive Era, American-born citizens of a liberal or progressive political inclination often had mixed feelings about immigrants. Some, with a more elitist set of values believed that crime, alcoholism, and a variety of vices running from drug abuse through prostitution, gambling, and underground sports such as cockfighting, all could be traced to the new immigrants. The solution, they believed, would be immigration reform: setting quotas that would restrict immigrants from all but Great Britain and northern Europe.

Other reformers took the position that the problems faced by new immigrants could be best dealt with through education, assistance, and social work. Still others approached the questions of poverty and adjustment of immigrants as part of the labor struggle, and believed that organizing through labor unions could bring pressure for better wages and working conditions. Meanwhile, immigrants continued to work through their churches, community organizations, and the complexities of American politics for recognition and rights.

Ultimately, two approaches emerged regarding how different ethnic groups would be viewed and how they would view themselves in America. For some, the idea of a "melting pot" had always held attraction. Under this way of thinking, all Americans would merge, with ethnic distinctions diminishing and the various cultures blending together to create a new American culture. Such a process of assimilation or integration appealed to many, both among American-born and immigrant groups. Others argued strongly that ethnic or racial identity should be preserved, with a sense of pride in heritage, so that America would continue to reflect its diversity, and so that particular groups would not forget their origins, traditions, and culture.

Whether an individual ethnic group should become homogenized, integrated, and assimilated into the total culture, or whether it should strive to maintain its own separate cultural identity, was often hotly debated. For some, like the Chinese, Native Americans, and African Americans, armed power of the state, law, and social discrimination tended to create and enforce separate communities and locales. For others, self-segregation and discrimination by other ethnic groups, and the natural process of settling near relatives and coreligionists led to definable ethnic regions and neighborhoods. Among such diverse groups as African Americans, Asians, Hispanics, Italians, Arab Americans, and Native Americans, leaders and spokesmen have debated the degree to which cultural identity should be sacrificed in the name of assimilation. In the 21st century, the debates have continued, sometimes with great controversy, at other times, the dialogues went on almost unnoticed by the rest of the country.

Armed conflict, race-wars, reservation policy, segregation, exclusion, and detention camps in time of war have shown the harsh and ugly side of enforced separation. Even though the multiethnic and multicultural heritage of the United States has been fraught with crisis and controversy, it has also been a source of strength. With roots in so many cultures and with the many struggles to establish and maintain social justice, America has also represented some of the best aspirations of humanity to live in peace with one another. The search for social equity has been difficult, but the fact that the effort has continued for more than two centuries is in itself an achievement.

In this series on Multicultural America, each volume is dedicated to the history of one ethnocultural group, tracing through time the struggles against discrimination and for fair play, as well as the effort to preserve and cherish an independent cultural heritage.

THE NATIVE AMERICANS

Much of the history of Native American–European American interaction in the United States is tragic, reflecting the great cultural and psychological gap between the two peoples. The interaction was viewed by European Americans in the colonial period as simply one of displacing a primitive or "savage" people and replacing them with "civilized" people of European ancestry. The Native-American people tended to regard the Europeans as invaders, but were sometimes willing to adapt parts of their technology or to make military alliances with European groups to fight against traditional enemies or to stave off other European invaders.

The great number of Native-American peoples, as defined by several hundred languages, made cooperation among them against the European invaders quite difficult, although, as detailed in this volume, several major alliances among different peoples emerged in the colonial and early national period. The English colonies, and later the states of the United States and the U.S.

federal government generally persisted in their view of the Native Americans as "uncivilized." Several aspects of Native-American life led to this view.

Generally, Native-American groups did not have regional or "national" governments, but instead, smaller bands or settlements, numbering up to a few hundred or few thousand individuals, that would operate quite independently of each other. Such communities or bands rarely had a formal process for selecting a chief; rather, councils of elders would agree on leaders and healers by consensus. Even after a chief or leader was selected, he (or she, in some cases), could not generally make major decisions such as those pertaining to war or peace, territorial boundaries, alliances, resettlement, or movement, without consulting councils (or whole communities) and obtaining a consensus. Agreements with colonial or U.S. governmental officials and such leaders were almost always subject to the approval of councils or subsidiary communities. Colonial and American government officials had difficulty understanding the cultural difference.

Other profound cultural differences troubled early contacts and relationships from the beginning. Native Americans did not practice private land ownership, and the concept was entirely foreign to them. While a band or community might share the land as a hunting range, and individual families might even raise crops on a plot, there was no legal or institutional concept among them that a particular piece of landscape "belonged" to an individual or family, to be sold, inherited, divided or otherwise treated as private property. Furthermore, in all of the British Colonies, the practice of chattel slavery had developed, and it persisted after the American Revolution in the states of the American south. The concept that one person could "own" another, with the right to buy, sell, or rent the person as property was unknown among Indians. Although captives in war might be held as prisoners and forced to do menial labor, or if children, raised as adopted members of a band, their status was not that of chattel slaves to be bought and sold.

More important than the cultural gulf in the early history of Native American–European conflict was the biological gulf. That is, Native-American peoples had no prior exposure to a wide range of diseases common among Europeans, including smallpox, influenza, and venereal diseases. As a consequence, vast numbers of Native Americans, from the far north of Canada, through Central and South America, rapidly fell victim to the imported diseases. The death of several million in the land that became the United States made the conquest of their territory all that much easier.

Despite the cultural differences and the biological disadvantage, Native Americans often picked and chose among the items of cultural heritage brought by the Europeans. Most notably and most importantly for the emerging military engagements between the peoples, the Native Americans quickly learned the use of horses, firearms, and metal weapons such as hatchets and metal arrow tips. Although early European firearms were fairly ineffective and inaccurate, they were extremely intimidating in battle. Furthermore, the armor worn by early European conquering armies offered some protection against obsidian-tipped arrows or battle-axes studded with the glass-like blades.

In the American Old Southwest (Georgia, Alabama, Mississippi), the so-called Five Civilized Tribes quickly adopted other imported technologies, including cattle raising, frame house construction, and wheeled vehicles. They came to understand European cash-based market systems. Even more remarkably, many understood the value of literacy. In the early 19th century, Cherokee leader Sequoya developed a writing system, a syllabary, rather than an alphabet, with 85 characters, and he printed books and newspapers in the language. Many European Americans recognized the Cherokee as "civilized," but that recognition did not prevent the implementation of the policy of Indian Removal that transported thousands of Creeks, Cherokees, Choctaws, Chickasaws, and Seminoles over the Trail of Tears to land in what later became Oklahoma.

The story of resistance to the invasion, conquest, removal and confinement to assigned lands is a complex one, spelled out in this volume in the early chapters. Later in the 19th century, after most Native Americans had been assigned to reservations, often located in inhospitable lands, the much reduced population was further demoralized by illness, starvation, failure of the U.S. government to provide promised support, and by continuing conception on the part of government officials that all aspects of Indian culture needed to be eliminated in order to civilize them. An effort in the late 19th century to disband the tribal structure and to allot lands to individuals was a general failure. In the 1920s, the Bureau of Indian Affairs revised its approach and worked to revive elements of Indian culture, particularly arts and crafts, as a means of providing a financial base. In the 1960s, some Native-American leaders, inspired by radical movements among African Americans and others, began to demand recognition of the injustices they had faced and restoration of lost properties.

In recent decades, the discovery of uranium, oil, and natural gas on some Native American–held lands has provided new financial resources, as has the development of policies allowing casinos (as well as lesser-known aspects of sovereignty, such as control over timber rights, and hunting and fishing licenses). These policies leading to new sources of revenue and improved health and social services have produced in recent decades, some increase in population figures and improvement in the economic status of Native Americans.

RODNEY CARLISLE
GENERAL EDITOR

CHAPTER 1

The Colonial Era: Beginnings to 1776

SCHOLARS DO NOT always agree on how Native Americans came to inhabit the land that became the United States of America. Some scholars believe that Native Americans immigrated across Beringia, an area near the Arctic that included parts of the Yukon, Alaska, and Siberia. According to legend, Native-American tribes have always inhabited American lands. Archaeological evidence indicates that Native Americans were present in what is now the United States as early as 15,000 to 10,000 B.C.E. The first signs of agricultural activity have been traced to 3500 B.C.E. Permanent Native-American villages appeared around 1000 B.C.E. By 800 B.C.E., the Adena culture was developing in the Ohio River Valley, where archaeologists have uncovered earthen burial grounds and fortifications.

By 100 B.C.E., the Hopewell culture had replaced the Adenans. Evidence of the Hopewell presence is still evident in thousands of mounds located in Ohio and Illinois. Trading was a major activity among the Hopewellians, and it is believed that they traded across a vast area. Along the cliff faces of the American west, ancestors of the Hopi tribe built stone and adobe pueblos. In modern-day New Mexico, the oldest continually occupied residence in the United States, containing more than 800 rooms, may be seen at Taos Pueblo. In Mesa Verde, Colorado, relics of a "cliff palace" containing more than 200 rooms are visible. By the first centuries C.E., the Hohokam tribes had begun to inhabit

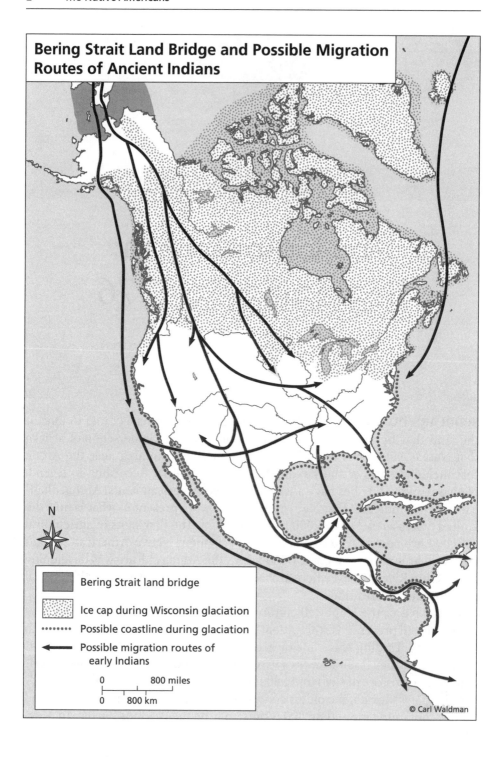

Bering Strait Land Bridge and Possible Migration Routes of Ancient Indians

N

Bering Strait land bridge

Ice cap during Wisconsin glaciation

Possible coastline during glaciation

Possible migration routes of early Indians

0   800 miles

0   800 km

© Carl Waldman

what became Phoenix, Arizona, erecting courts, pyramid-like mounds, canals, and irrigation systems.

From their earliest existence, Native Americans used the land to find materials for food, shelter, fuel, and tools. They hunted in wooded areas and fished in lakes and streams. Some 200 languages or dialects were used among the various tribes. Some employed sounds that could not be replicated in any European language. Before the Europeans arrived in America, Native Americans tended to be relatively healthy, suffering only from injuries, chills, fevers, infections, and diseases such as arthritis, rheumatism, and neuralgia. Interdisciplinary scholars have estimated that between 1492 and 1542, disease and famine coupled with internal and external wars wiped out 80 to 85 percent of the Native-American population. As European settlement expanded, the number of Native Americans declined still further, reducing a population of 1.4 million in 1700 to 770,000 by 1850.

By the 1500s, the Algonquian and the Iroquoian made up the two major groups of Native-American families. The Algonquian, who inhabited the valleys of the Hudson and Delaware Rivers, included the Micmac, the Abenaki, the Narragansett, the Wampanoag, and the Pequot. Tribes that lived in the Great Lakes area included the Algonkin, the Menominee, the Ottawa, and the Potawatom. Algonquian tribes of the western prairies included the Fox, the Illinois, the Kickapoo, the Miami, the Sauk, and the Shawnee.

Separate dwellings like these within the Taos Pueblo complex in New Mexico are still inhabited full time by about 150 Taos Native Americans.

Life among the Havasupai in the Southwest

Although most Native-American tribes shared many commonalities, there were also great differences in particular cultures. One of the most interesting tribes was the Havasupai, who inhabited land that became southern Utah, southern Colorado, New Mexico, Arizona, and the extreme western part of Texas. The western plains in which the Havasupai lived were characterized by canyons, jagged cliffs, cutting winds, and buttes. The gulches, washes, and arroyos that interspersed the plains were dry for much of the year. The Havasupai combined hunting and gathering with agriculture. Their farming practices were based on those of the neighboring Pueblo tribe that lived along the Rio Grande in New Mexico.

Unlike the Pueblo, who were often full-time farmers, the Havasupai were migratory. From early spring to early fall, the tribe lived in canyon villages where they planted, cultivated, and harvested. Entire families worked together in the fields. Using a planting stick to scratch a hole, the Havasupai prayed, "Grow good. When your stalk grows, grow tall. Grow like the mythic corn." They then chewed a kernel of corn and blew it toward two white marks on a canyon wall that represented the first two ears of corn that had been grown on Havasupai land. Between the rows of corn, farmers grew beans, squash, melons, and sunflowers.

The Havasupai used a system of ditches to irrigate crops. Water belonged to the entire tribe, but individual users were responsible for maintaining particular sections of the system. Irrigation of crops took place when corn grew to seven inches and again when it tasseled. Some green corn was picked and made into bread or roasted. After the rest of the crop ripened, it was set out on all available surfaces to dry. Seed corn was preserved for the following year, and foods not eaten were dried and stored for the winter.

Even with their hard work, the Havasupai enjoyed leisure time, which was spent in swimming, gossiping, athletics, horseracing, and gambling. Once crops were gathered, the Havasupai held a ritualistic harvest dance before departing for winter camps in the western plateaus. The harvest ritual, which lasted for several days, included the following prayer: "My ground, ground, hear me, let us always live. I want always to live well, ground hear me." At their winter camp, the Havasupai spent the interval before the first snow gathering wild plants and pinyon nuts and hunting game. Food was stored in granaries that had been protected from rodents with plaster made from guano and sand. Inside their homes, the Havasupai slept on depressions in the sand on cedar bark mats. They covered themselves with blankets made from rabbit pelts. Families retired early, even in summer, because they were supposedly afraid of ghosts.

Iroquoian tribes, including the Mohawk, Oneida, Seneca, and Huron, inhabited areas of New York State and Quebec and Ontario in Canada. A number of Iroquoian tribes united to form various confederations. The best known of these confederations was the League of the Hodenosaunee, often called the People of the Longhouse. The name later became Anglicized as the League of the Five Nations, consisting of a confederation of Mohawk, Oneida, Onondaga, Cayuga, and Seneca tribes. While 50 chiefs represented the various groups in the confederation, each tribe retained autonomy. According to Iroquoian legend, the league was founded by Hiawatha, an Onondaga brave who had been motivated by a peacemaker to look for ways to end intertribal fighting. Hiawatha was later immortalized in Henry Wadsworth Longfellow's *Song of Hiawatha* (1855), which was based on a collection of Native-American legends and stories. Longfellow depicted Hiawatha as a visionary:

From the brow of Hiawatha
Gone was every trace of sorrow,
As the fog from off the water,
As the mist from off the meadow.
With a smile of joy and triumph,
With a look of exultation,
As of one who in a vision
Sees what is to be, but is not.

INITIAL CONTACTS

By some accounts, Native Americans in what is now the United States first sighted European explorers in 1524, when Italian Giovanni da Verrazzano headed a French expedition to the New World, landing at what is now Cape Fear, North Carolina. Although he did trade with some natives, Verrazzano ignored them for the most part. His visit was followed by expeditions from other European countries. In 1584, Englishman Sir Walter Raleigh arrived at Roanoke Island on the North Carolina coast. He was welcomed by two Algonquian chiefs. When Raleigh set sail for England, he was accompanied by two Native Americans. It is believed that one volunteered for the trip, but the other may have been kidnapped. When the Delaware Indians sighted a Dutch ship for the first time, they believed it was a large floating house.

Around 500 Native-American tribes were resident in North America when British ships arrived in 1607 to establish the first permanent white settlement at Jamestown, Virginia. Estimates of the number of individuals within those tribes vary from 1 to 18 million. Traveling with the current European perspective, early settlers classified the Americas as *terra nullis* (empty land), with abundant resources inhabited by savages who needed to be civilized and Christianized. Contrary to images prevalent in popular culture, not all American land was

This 1645 etching shows a young Algonquian Indian man from Virginia.

taken from Native Americans by force. Much of it was bought for cash payment, as was the case with Manhattan. Other lands were negotiated away from Native Americans, sometimes by honest dealing, but often through chicanery. In Pennsylvania, William Penn became known for his honest dealing with the Delaware Indians.

Initially, Native Americans believed that white settlers had an amazing spiritual power to fashion objects from metal. Many individuals were willing to act as interpreters and mediators. While some Native Americans were afraid of close contact with Europeans, others saw the advantage of expanded trade. Fur trading proved to be a profitable enterprise for both Native Americans and whites because animal skins were used for a variety of purposes. The skin of the white tail deer, for instance, which was abundant in the southeast, was used in book binding, trousers, coats, trunk coverings, coach seats, buckets, hats, and tackle.

Although colonies, including South Carolina and Georgia, attempted to control trading practices by appointing commissions to oversee trading activities, the enterprise attracted large numbers of unscrupulous individuals who were intent only on serving their own interests. Some natives sold goods to the French and Spanish and to unfriendly tribes who made war on the English. A number of British traders purposely agitated tribes to pit them against one another in order to create a supply of Native-American slaves. Other Europeans spread rumors of imminent war to increase the demand for ammunition and war paint. One of the most common practices was for Europeans to overextend credit to Native Americans. When they were unable to pay their debts, merchants recouped their losses by kidnapping wives and children and holding them for ransom or selling them into slavery. Sometimes Native Americans resorted to making war on Europeans to avert retaliation for unpaid debts.

Native Americans were also willing to trade for European goods for their personal use, often preferring them because they made daily life easier than in the past. Native-American women began using needles, threads, scissors, and thimbles to sew lighter, more comfortable clothing. In the past, they had used bone needles and thread made of grass to make clothing from animal skins. European-style clothing could be washed easily, and it did not have to go through the tanning process.

To show their amicability, Native Americans often invited whites to smoke the calumet. This four-foot-long wood and stone pipe, which was decorated with paint and feathers, became known as the "peace pipe." To the Native Americans, smoking the calumet was a sacred ritual. They believed that prayers were lifted to heaven on tobacco smoke, and blowing smoke onto someone else was considered a great honor. If a visitor refused to take part in the ritual, it was viewed as a declaration of war. Music was a necessary part of many Native-American rituals, and Europeans found that music demonstrated a willingness to establish friendly relations. When English explorer John Davis arrived in North America in the late 16th century to search for the elusive Northwest Passage, he had musicians play while his crew danced ashore. The following day, Davis was able to trade European products for five kayaks, paddles, clothes, and seal skins.

Exchanging gifts was also considered a necessary part of the ritual of establishing friendly relations between Native Americans and visitors. In 1759,

Massasoit offering Governor John Carver a peace pipe as a way to communicate respect and friendship in Plymouth, Massachusetts, soon after the Pilgrims began their settlement.

Clothing

Before Europeans established permanent settlements in North America, native clothing was made entirely of natural materials. It was generally made of animal pelts embellished with bird feathers, reptile skins, and shells. Intricately executed tattoos were common. Clothing had to be replaced frequently because it was damaged by constant trips through wooded areas, and was difficult to clean.

Styles of clothing often varied among Native Americans who inhabited the United States before the Revolutionary War. The introduction of European clothing created greater diversity. Delaware (Lenapes) males, for instance, wore breech cloaks and leggings made of buckskin. A deerskin mantle was often worn over one shoulder. During the winter months, they added

A Native American with animal-skin clothing topped by a wool blanket.

robes made from the skins of beavers, bears, or wolves that had been sewn together. Delaware males often shaved their heads, leaving only a lock of hair at the back of their heads. Tools were carried in deerskin pouches. Once the Europeans arrived, some Delaware males traded traditional clothing for woolen trousers and long shirts that fell to their knees. Women of the tribe exchanged heavy animal-skin clothing for colorful calico dresses that were more comfortable and easier to clean. Woolen blankets around the shoulders replaced mantles and robes of fur. Even when Native Americans chose to wear European-style clothing, they sometimes managed to do it in a unique way. Some Native-American women, for example, wore hoops on top of their clothing rather than under full skirts, as white women did.

Native Americans of New England wore loose, sleeveless shirts made from bear, deer, or moose pelts with the fur next to the skin. Other hides, such as those of raccoons, were attached to the shoulder of the shirt to make them hang over one arm. Trousers and moccasins were also made from animal skins. In southern New England, some tribes wore clothes made from plant fiber in the hot summer months. Children often went naked in the summer until they reached their teens. Mary Rowlandson, who had been captured by the Wampanoag, described the ceremonial dress of her male captor as a "shirt with great laces sewed" at the shirttail worn with "silver buttons [and] white stockings." The captor's wife wore a "wool coat covered with girdles of wampum [shell beads]," and bracelets, necklaces, and earrings. The woman wore her hair powdered, and her face was painted red.

a boatload of Frenchmen arrived with gifts of 2,440 woodcutter knives, 1,200 clasp knives, 400 pairs of scissors, and 150 brass kettles. In exchange for European items, Native Americans often traded their own clothes and possessions. Because they had no idea of the value of their own products on the open market, Native Americans were often cheated by unscrupulous traders.

Close contact with European settlers frequently proved disastrous for natives, who had no immunity to European diseases that indiscriminately struck down friends and enemies, and epidemics spread from tribe to tribe. In the 1600s, a number of smallpox epidemics exacted heavy tolls on native populations. Between 1713 and 1715, large numbers of Native Americans were killed by a measles epidemic. Still reeling from that epidemic, natives from New England to Texas were felled by another smallpox epidemic that did not run its course until 1721. Eight years later, smallpox again ravaged native populations and was followed by a diphtheria epidemic in 1736. Europeans also

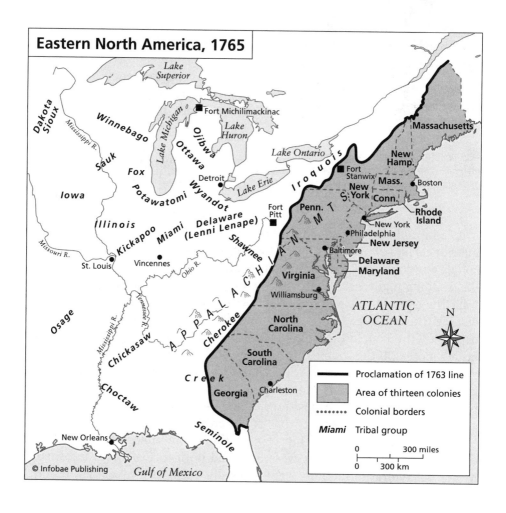

Eastern North America, 1765

This illustration of Native-American fishing methods on the west coast was made during one of Captain James Cook's expeditions in the 1770s.

transported venereal diseases into the Americas and created what became a persistent social problem among native populations by introducing them to alcohol.

DAILY LIFE AND CULTURE

There was great cultural diversity among early Native Americans, and vast differences existed in daily life, language, religion, and social, political, and economic systems. While some tribes were polygamous, many were monogamous. In some tribes, women moved into their husbands' villages, but in others, the husband took up residence in his wife's village. Among the Havasupai, fathers of boys negotiated marriage agreements with fathers of girls in neighboring clans. Braves who were shy might slip into a girl's home at night. If she let him stay, they were married. After the first child was born, the couple moved to the husband's village. The western Apache tribe followed a matrilineal line of descent. During the period immediately after a marriage, a couple was constantly in the company of another male and female. By custom, the wedding night was spent with the bride taking the position nearest the wall. The other female and male slept beside her, and the groom slept on the outside. The marriage was not consummated until the other male and female departed. The couple then moved to a wickiup that had been built by the bride's mother. If the couple divorced, the husband was expected to leave.

Government within each tribe tended to be democratic and decentralized. The power of chiefs ranged from absolute to advisory. Tribal headsman often inherited their positions, but some tribes bypassed a headman's close kin in favor of others who exhibited superior leadership qualities. Chiefs were generally male, but clan mothers sometimes had a great deal of power. Codes of behavior were enforced both formally and informally. Minor behavioral infractions were generally dealt with by gossip, teasing, or ostracism.

All tribes were dependent to some extent on the land, hunting, fishing, farming, and gathering what they needed to survive. Methods of performing such tasks frequently varied from tribe to tribe. Because Native-American farmers often moved their homes in response to seasonal cycles, European settlers sometimes mistakenly believed that they had no loyalty to particular lands. In general, Native-American women farmed the land and bore the responsibility for cooking, cleaning, and raising children while males hunted, traded, and fought battles against Europeans and enemy tribes. Europeans who viewed hunting as a leisure activity believed that Native-American males were lazy, deriding them for leaving the hard labor to females.

Among the Shawnee tribe, males hunted deer and turkey in the winter and fished during the summer. Shawnee women raised corn, beans, and squash. When winter approached, most of the tribe packed up their belongings and headed to winter quarters, leaving behind only a few elderly members to protect the village. Europeans were astounded at Native-American agricultural practices, which were viewed as primitive because natives used no plows, fertilizer, fences, or animal power. In 1585, Englishman Thomas Harriot expressed his astonishment that natives could grow great yields of corn that "reached prodigious heights" by using only crude hoes and handmade buckets.

In the past, Native Americans had been dependent on stone implements and weapons for performing daily tasks. European settlement introduced firearms that were usually less accurate, but more intimidating than bows and arrows, and metal pots proved more durable than traditional clay pots. Among the eastern tribes, brass and copper kettles, which were used to make arrow points and ornaments, were in great demand. Native Americans were often fascinated by even simple European items because they were unfamiliar. Buttons, bracelets, rings, and tubular beads were worn as jewelry or used to decorate clothing and headdresses.

Colorful European cloths and clothing were also sought after. Red and blue were the most popular colors among New England tribes. Males in southeastern tribes were quick to exchange buckskin shirts for colorful clothing that dried quickly after being washed. Native Americans, who had been used to wearing clothing made from animal skins that was worn with the fur on the inside, were delighted with loose-fitting European items. Other items popular among tribes in the southeast included awls, fire steels, tin pots, sewing supplies, razors, brass, and iron wire.

RELIGION AND FAMILY LIFE

Among Native-American tribes, religion was often interwoven with a love of the land. Some tribes believed that a god or creator resided in each tree, bird, animal, and plant. New England native Roger Williams counted 37 separate gods recognized by the Narragansett tribes. Native Americans believed that

Dwellings

In most Native-American villages, tribal members erected council houses for carrying out communal activities. Individual families lived in smaller dwellings. The most common dwelling was the teepee or wigwam, which was made of frames from small trees that had been bent together, leaving an opening big enough to allow smoke from the centrally placed fireplace to escape. Subsequent layers consisted of vertical saplings that were buried in the ground. The final layer was covered with pieces of bark that had been sewn together with thread made from roots of evergreen trees. A teepee might have one or several doorways, and flaps could be lifted to provide entry and exit and for ridding the residence of smoke. As the southwestern section of the United States became more settled, the teepee or wigwam became a popular architectural style among frontier homes.

New England tribes carefully chose village sites based on availability of water, elevations, and views. They looked for places that were protected from the elements and that could be easily defended. Each village was fortified with logs to shore up defenses. Some structures were either square with oblong or vertical sides, or round with domed roofs. In New York, the Seneca, Mohawk, Oneida, Onomdaga, and Cayuga tribes of the Iroquois Nation lived in longhouses that sometimes measured 200 feet long and 25 feet wide. In the longhouse, rooms were erected on either side of a central hallway for individual families. Platforms designated for specific activities such as sleeping, working, and eating were placed in each room. Platforms were covered with skins of seal and deer and grass mats. Supplies, which ranged from cooking vessels to sewing supplies and food, were stored underneath each platform. Animal skins were used for bedcovers and for wall decorations.

Among the southwestern tribes, the Havasupai erected either circular, dome-shaped dwellings that were thatched or covered with dirt, or rectangular residences with thatched sides and dirt roofs. Open-walled shades were built for common use. Men built the houses and shades, but women often helped with the thatching. The Havasupai also erected "sweat lodges," small conical structures that housed as many as four adults. During heavy rains, the tribe headed for caves and rock shelters. In camps where they spent the winter, the Havasupai built plateau homes in cedar thickets. These water-proofed homes always faced the south.

Thatched reed wigwams like this were one of the more common dwelling types.

particular powers were associated with the sun, moon, wind, and thunder and with bears, eagles, elk, snakes, and other animals. Dreams were considered a way of understanding the present and predicting the future.

Rituals and taboos were extremely important in the daily lives of Native Americans, and they were interwoven with social customs. Some tribes prohibited engaging in sexual intercourse for several days before hunting parties took place. Others fasted before battle. Taboos were often placed on both husband and wife when a couple expected a baby. Many Native Americans believed that viewing anything grotesque could cause a baby to be deformed at birth. Contact with quail or rabbit eggs was thought to cause freckles, and eating the leg muscle of game was likely to cause damage to a fetus.

Until they took their first steps, Native-American babies generally spent their days in cradle boards made by a grandmother. The grandparents and other tribal elders were responsible for naming a baby. Since a name was based on exhibited characteristics, the naming might not take place for several years, and additional names might be added later in life. Some tribes placed amulets in baby carriers to protect infants from accidents, falls, and illnesses. In general, Native-American children were granted more freedom than European children. A girl's first menstrual period marked her rite of passage and called for particular rituals. For boys, the right of passage was associated with killing the first deer alone. Death rituals were also observed rigidly, and corpses were placed in particular positions. In some tribes, the home and possessions of a male who died were destroyed.

Most Native-American tribes looked to shamans for spiritual guidance, but most Christian settlers viewed all Native Americans as barbarians who needed to be both civilized and Christianized. Upon arrival, Christian missionaries established schools and missions to make these tasks easier. They also imprisoned shamans. In turn, shamans were distrustful of Jesuit priests, believing they were witches who caused death when performing last rites. Native Americans were often offended by the black robes, short hair, and facial hair of the Jesuits and could not understand why vows of poverty prevented them from exchanging gifts of friendship. Catholic missionaries often brought death to Native Americans because they spread diseases when they came to live among the natives.

Family life generally focused on husbands, wives, and children. Extended family members lived nearby. Divorce was often simply a matter of a couple's deciding that they no longer wished to be married. Dogs, which had descended from wolves, were considered a sign of status among some tribes, and wealthy Native Americans were surrounded by large numbers of dogs. In addition to providing companionship, dogs were used in hunting and hauling. Native-American dogs were often expected to find their own food.

Among the Iroquois, a tribe was generally made up of three related clans. By contrast, eight clans made up a Seneca tribe. Intermarriage within a clan

The "Starving Time"

In the early years of European settlement, colonists were often dependent on Native Americans for survival because whites lacked the ability to live off the land like Native Americans had always done. The English settlers who landed in Jamestown, Virginia, in 1607, suffered from a shortage of food chiefly because they did not always understand how to find food in their new home. The worst of these shortages came to be known as the "starving time," a period in which some colonists managed to survive by eating corn kernels flavored with ants or boot leather. Others ate horses, dogs, cats, rats, snakes, and roots.

While the colonists had failed to store sufficient food for the winter months, much of the blame for the condition of the Jamestown settlers was assigned to Chief Powhatan, who incorrectly believed that the Europeans would leave the area if enough of them starved to death. As the leader of the Powhatan Confederation, which included 30 different tribes, Powhatan was extremely powerful. One starving colonist wrote that Powhatan "cut off some of our boats; he drove away all the deer; destroyed [600] hogs; he sent none of his Indians to trade with us but laid secret ambush in the woods."

Some colonists resorted to cannibalism. John Smith's diary describes an incident in which a colonist was executed after he killed his pregnant wife, ripping "the childe out of her wombe and [throwing] it in the River." Afterward, he "chopped the mother in pieces and salted her for his foode." The murderer was arrested before he finished eating his dead wife. Other desperate colonists dug up recent Native-American graves and dined on their corpses. Only 60 settlers survived the harsh conditions of the starving time, and some of those did so by deserting to Native-American villages. Supplies arrived along with Sir Thomas Gates in 1609. In early June, the remnants of the first settlers sailed back to England. While still on the way, they met Lord de la Warr, the newly appointed captain general, and 300 men who began repopulating Virginia.

was strictly forbidden. As disease and battles began diminishing the number of Native Americans, it became more difficult for young people to find mates. Some tribes were not averse to the intermarriage of Native-American women and white men because it was seen as a way to improve existing bloodlines. Members of the Iroquois Nation resorted to kidnapping wives and children during raiding parties to add new bloodlines. Within each clan, clan mothers were given the responsibility for overseeing daily life. These women often had considerable power and were responsible for choosing individuals to serve on the council, the tribe's all-male governing body.

POWHATAN AND THE VIRGINIA SETTLERS

The first European settlers who arrived early in the 17th century settled in the tidewaters of Virginia. They were initially unaware that the Iroquoian tribes to their north and south considered them enemies, as did the Siouan speakers to the south. Under the leadership of Captain John Smith, the colonists cleared land and erected shelters. Smith, who was well aware that the settlement needed to be protected from the powerful Powhatan Confederation, trained 100 soldiers in the ways of the natives, teaching them the language, customs, and fighting styles. When the Paspaheghs and Chickahominies attacked or refused to trade, Smith responded by destroying their villages and boats and taking members of the tribes prisoner.

Legends abound concerning Smith's relations with Powhatan, the chief of the Powhatan Confederation. According to the most popular version, Smith was twice saved from certain death by the actions of Pocahontas, the chief's daughter. Some modern scholars believe that Powhatan engineered the "rescues" to serve his own interests, asserting that he had no intention of killing Smith. When Smith left Virginia to explore New England, no other officer appeared capable of pulling the colonists together and teaching them survival skills. The period that followed his departure became known as the "starving time."

This 19th-century American print depicts the legendary confrontation in which Captain John Smith was said to have been saved by Chief Powhatan's daughter, Pocahontas. Powhatan is shown standing to the left behind Smith while Pocahontas protects him from Opechancanough.

A typical Algonquian village on the mid-Atlantic coast in an engraving from 1619.

In 1609, Virginians became embroiled in the First Anglo-Powhatan War. Conditions for the colonists were perilous because Powhatan set out to deliberately starve them to death. Conditions were made worse because of a drought that hit the area. Even though Powhatan was successful in driving survivors away from Jamestown, others took their place. The new settlers were well aware that Native Americans were more adept at surviving. To ensure a steady stream of supplies, they demanded that each chief supply the colony with baskets of food, dye, and animal skins at harvest time. They used native labor to plant their own crops. In return for these services, the colonists agreed not to attack the Powhatans and to protect them from attack by hostile tribes. Any tribe that refused to comply was subject to seizure of one-half of the next harvest and was threatened with kidnapping of the families of tribal leaders. Settlers also threatened to work with Powhatan enemies if they refused to cooperate.

On one occasion, 70 Englishmen, assisted by native prisoners, attacked a Paspahegh village, killing 16 members of the tribe and capturing the wife and children of the chief. They murdered children and burned the village to the ground. Powhatan responded by moving his capital from Jamestown to Orapales at the head of the Chickahominy River and dispatched war parties to harass the colonists.

An uneasy peace was reached in 1614, and Chief Powhatan died in 1618. The Second Anglo-Powhatan War broke out on March 22, 1622, after Powhatans unexpectedly attacked 1,240 colonists. The Powhatans killed 347 men, women, and children, and warriors desecrated their bodies. Powhatan's ostensible reason for the attack was that the servants of a Virginian had retaliated for the murder of their master by killing Native-American hero Jack-of-the-Feathers. The attack set off a series of plots and raids by the revenge-seeking colonists. In May 1623, Virginians murdered 200 natives with a poisoned sack of tobacco and killed 50 others in an ambush. The winter of 1622–23 was ultimately the bloodiest period since the English had arrived in 1607. In July 1624, an attack on the Pamunkey resulted in 800 Native-American deaths. Chief Opechancanough finally sued for peace in 1632 and withdrew from the area around Jamestown.

Hostilities broke out again on April 18, 1644. The Third Anglo-Powhatan War began with surprise attacks in which Powhatans killed approximately 500 of the 10,000 colonists who lived in Virginia. Two years later, Governor William Berkeley captured Opechancanough and placed him on public display. The once-powerful chief had aged and grown decrepit. By the time Virginia became the largest and wealthiest English colony, the once powerful Powhatan Empire was in ruins. Members of the tribe who remained either avoided the Europeans or began imitating their lifestyles.

NATIVE AMERICANS IN THE NORTHEAST

The Pilgrims who landed at Plymouth Rock, Massachusetts, in 1620 immediately set the stage for hostilities with Native Americans by stealing food supplies that had been stored in the ground. At the time, there were around 75,000 Native Americans residing in the New England area.

The most prominent tribes were the Pawtucket of Cape Ann; the Wampanoag of Cape Cod; the Massachusetts of the Boston area; and the Pequot, the Pauqusset, and the Mohegan of Connecticut; the Narragansett of Rhode Island; the Algonquin of Holyoke, Massachusetts; the Pocumtuck of Deerfield, Massachusetts; the Mohawk, who lived on the western frontiers of Massachusetts, New Hampshire, and Vermont; and the Penobscot and Abenaki of Maine.

A Great Sachem served as the leader of each tribe. In southern New England, this position was inherited through the female line. In the north, the Great Sachem was chosen because of leadership abilities. Southern sachems held absolute power, but northern sachems were considered advisers. Day-to-day government was carried out by a council of wise men and women, and debates sometimes went on for days. Peace was maintained among various tribes by recognizing natural boundaries such as lakes, streams, and mountains. Women had great freedom within New England tribes. White women captured by New England tribes were often surprised that rape was unknown. Couples tended to be openly affectionate. Divorce was rare, and remarriage was uncommon after a spouse died.

The settlers who arrived in America on the Mayflower were initially no more capable of wresting a living from the land than the Jamestown settlers had been. While some turned to fur trading, others learned survival skills from Native Americans, who taught them to fertilize crops by planting tiny fish with each corn kernel. Despite the help of friendly natives, the Pilgrims were constantly hungry. At the same time, Native Americans were enjoying wild rice, fruits, nuts, plums, berries, watermelon, salted meat, and breads and cakes that had been cooked over open fires.

Beginning in 1633, New England settlers became involved in conflicts with the Pequot and Narragansett tribes. By 1637, whites had succeeded in wiping out the Pequot, but expansion brought the settlers into contact with other tribes. In 1675, "King Philip," the chief of the Wampanoag tribe, joined forces with the French to attack the English. By the time open warfare ended in 1677, enormous losses had been suffered on both sides. Massacres continued despite the peace. The two most notorious massacres took place in 1690 in Schenectady, New York, and in Deerfield, Massachusetts, in 1704.

The Iroquois Nation had negotiated a peace settlement with both France and England in 1701. At that time the Cherokee Nation was waging a war, which lasted from 1759 to 1761, in the Carolinas and Tennessee. Beginning on May 28, 1754, the French and Indian War, also known as the Seven Years War, raged across the Ohio Valley and into New York. The peace of February 1763 gave the English control of Canada. In the Royal Proclamation of 1763, the British designated all lands between the Allegheny Mountains, Florida, the Mississippi River, and Quebec, Canada, for Native-American use. Outside of California and a few scattered outposts, most western lands were inhabited by Great Plains tribes that included the Sioux, Blackfoot, Pawnee, and Cheyenne tribes. The most prevalent cultures of the southwest were the Apache, Navajo, and Hopi.

NATIVE AMERICANS AND THE AMERICAN REVOLUTION

The American Revolution was a major turning point in the lives of most Native Americans. The natives used the word *indeb* ("we are dead now") to describe its effect. While the majority of tribes opted to remain neutral, others took on an active role in supporting the British, offering their services in exchange for rum, guns, and other products. Loyalties were generally decided according to which ally best served Native-American interests. As early as 1774, the Lenapes who lived along the Delaware River, the Shawnee who inhabited lands to the west of the Lenapes, and the Iroquois of western New York expressed their loyalty to the British. When the Paris Peace Treaty was signed on September 3, 1783, the British ignored their Native-American allies. Retaining posts only in Detroit and the Northwestern Territory to oversee restitution and compensation to Tory allies, the British yielded all lands between the Atlantic Ocean and the Mississippi River and between the Great Lakes and the Georgia/Florida border to the United States. The Iroquois Nation was in shambles after the war, and many tribal members moved to the Ohio Valley or to Canada. The governments of Virginia, North Carolina, South Carolina, and Georgia had claimed vast areas of Cherokee and Creek land during the war, and the federal government laid claim to additional lands after the war.

ELIZABETH R. PURDY
INDEPENDENT SCHOLAR

Further Reading

Access Genealogy: Indian Tribal History. "Havasupai Indian Tribe History." Available online, URL: http://www.accessgenealogy.com/native /tribes/havasupaiindianhist.htm. Accessed July 2008.

Axtell, James. *Natives and Newcomers: The Cultural Origins of North America*. New York: Oxford University Press, 2001.

Biography.com. "Sacagawea." Available online, URL: http://www.biography .com/search/article.do?id=9468731. Accessed July 2008.

Bradford, William. *Of Plymouth Plantation*. New York: Modern Library, 1981.

Crompton, Samuel Willard. *Illustrated Atlas of Native American History*. Edison, NJ: Chartwell Books, 1999.

Dunn, Walter S., Jr. *Choosing Sides on the Frontier in the American Revolution*. Westport, CT: Praeger, 2007.

Gibson, Arrell Morgan. *The American Indian: Prehistory to the Present*. Lexington, MA: D.C. Heath, 1980.

Haile, Edward Wright. *Jamestown Narratives: Eyewitness Accounts of the Virginia Colony, the First Decade, 1607–1617*. Champlain, VA: Round-House, 1998.

Hamby, Alonzo. *Outline of U.S. History*. New York: Nova Science, 2007.

Johnson, Claudia Durst. *Daily Life in Colonial New England*. Westport, CT: Greenwood, 2002.

Kehoe, Alice Beck. *North American Indians: A Comprehensive Account*. Englewood Cliffs, NJ: Prentice-Hall, 1981.

Kupfever, Harriet J. *Ancient Drums, Other Moccasins: Native North Americans Cultural Adaptation*. Englewood Cliffs, NJ: Prentice-Hall, 1988.

Longfellow, Henry Wadsworth. *Song of Hiawatha*. Available online, URL: http://www.hwlongfellow.org/poems_poem.php?pid=296. Accessed August 2008.

Mancall, Peter C. and James H. Merrell. *American Encounters: Natives and Newcomers from European Contact to Indian Removal, 1500–1850*. New York: Routledge, 2007.

Mann, Charles C. *1491: New Revelations of the Americans before Columbus*. New York: Alfred A. Knopf, 2005.

Miyares, Ines M. and Christopher A. Airriess, eds. *Contemporary Ethnic Geographies in America*. Lanham, MD: Rowman and Littlefield, 2007.

Nichols, Roger L. *American Indians in United States History*. Norman, OK: University of Oklahoma Press, 2003.

Page, Jake. *In the Hands of the Great Spirit: The 20,000-Year History of American Indians*. New York: Free Press, 2003.

Rogers, Ann. *Lewis and Clark in Missouri*. Columbia, MI: University of Missouri Press, 2002.

Rountree, Helen. *The Powhatan Indians of Virginia: Their Traditional Culture*. Norman, OK: University of Oklahoma Press, 1989.

Stevens, Laura M. *The Poor Indians: British Missionaries, Native Americans, and Colonial Sensibility*. Philadelphia, PA: University of Pennsylvania Press, 2004.

Virtual Jamestown. "Powhatan." Available online, URL: http://www.virtual jamestown.org/Powhat1.html. Accessed July 2008.

CHAPTER 2

The American Revolution: 1775 to 1783

THE ERUPTION OF hostilities between Great Britain and 13 of its mainland North American colonies in 1775 presented Native-American communities east of the Mississippi River with three poor options. They could attempt to remain neutral, or decide to join with either the British or the Americans. A host of factors determined which choice individual Native Americans might make during the conflict. Native Americans who had forged close ties with New England colonists enthusiastically joined the Patriot cause. In northern New England, Native Americans tried to remain neutral, but they were pressured by both sides. The Ohio River Valley had been the site of vicious interracial warfare in the 1750s and 1760s, and the onset of war in the 1770s gave both whites and Native Americans an opportunity to renew the violence.

Neutrality would prove almost impossible to maintain in the pressure-filled environment of the 1770s and 1780s; the British had a history of disreputable trade and land policies, and their American cousins were attempting to build a continental nation based, in part, on the notion that Native Americans were "merciless Indian savages." In the July 1776 Declaration of Independence, the Continental Congress accused King George III of England of "endeavour[ing] to bring on the inhabitants of our frontiers, the merciless Indian Savages, whose known rule of warfare, is an undistinguished destruction of all ages, sexes and conditions." George III's land policies also infuriated colonists,

21

since the British monarch had tried to prevent the appropriation of Native-American lands through the Proclamation of 1763 and the Quebec Act of the 1770s.

The War for Independence wreaked havoc on Native communities in the eastern half of North America, breaking alliances that had held for centuries and launching retaliatory violence that would continue to echo until the early 19th century. In the aftermath of the fighting, it mattered little which option a given Native group had chosen. In the words of one of the leading scholars of the period, the leaders of the United States envisioned a "world without Indians" who might oppose their nation's divinely sanctioned spread across North America.

NATIVE AMERICA IN 1775

Despite the catastrophic effect of the War for Independence on Native Americans in the east and northeast, Native America was extremely diverse in 1775, and the majority of Native Americans were not too profoundly affected by the fighting. Large swaths of Native North America, especially the vast region west of the Mississippi River, managed to escape the violence that ripped through eastern North America. However, all tribes within what is now the United States would come into contact with that nation as it expanded across the continent.

By 1775, most Native-American groups had experienced some sort of contact with strangers from Europe. West of the Mississippi, this contact usually came in the form of trade goods, scattered missionaries, and new diseases. East of the Mississippi, some groups had weathered two centuries of European colonization. Tribes living near the coast had suffered mightily over this time span, and by 1775 lived in small clusters on the margins of white settlements. Some of these were descended from the "praying town" reservations of Puritan New England. Though the trend was more pronounced closer to the East Coast, most Native-American communities exhibited a mix of indigenous and European cultural forms, from religion to architecture to ideas about trade. Death from European disease combined with the cultural pressure exerted by Europeans to bring increasing levels of violence to eastern Native America. As a result, military leaders gained prestige, while civil leaders took on lesser roles. Dealing with Europeans also brought about changes in Native-American gender relations, since Europeans refused to recognize female political leaders or influential women in Native-American communities.

In the areas between the almost exclusively non-Native east and the almost exclusively Native west, large polities had grown up around the same time that Europeans "discovered" and took an interest in colonizing the Americas. By 1775, the Iroquois Confederacy numbered six nations in upstate New York and southern Ontario. Though not numerous, the Iroquois were well armed, and had taken advantage of their position between English and French

America by playing the two empires against one another. In the south, the Creeks and the Cherokees resisted land-hungry white colonists, while at the same time relying on Europeans (and their descendants) for trade items such as firearms. Large Native-American nations would play a crucial role in the conflict that followed.

NEW ENGLAND

New England tribes had been in contact, and occasionally in conflict, with Europeans for a very long time by 1775. The Revolution brought out tensions in the Native villages of New England. In northern New England, the tribes struggled to remain neutral, hoping to avoid the consequences of allying completely with one side. The Abenakis are a useful case study. The Abenakis inhabited the border country between New France and New England, and their villages had been the site of Jesuit missionary activities. During the war, Abenakis participated on both sides, and there was no official "national" position among the several groups. This flexibility allowed individual communities and families to serve with the British when it was expedient to do so, and with the rebellious colonists when that option made more sense. Abenaki villages took in refugees fleeing the fighting farther south, too.

American and British forces stormed through Abenaki country in the late 1770s. British forces occupied villages and coerced Abenaki men to fight. Abenakis in Vermont and New Hampshire were more likely to offer their services as scouts and soldiers to the American cause. Unfortunately, such offers did not prevent some Abenakis from losing their homelands to land-hungry

This late 18th-century print published in Boston shows an Abenaki chief saving the life of an English officer from two other natives wielding axes.

Americans just after the fighting ended. The war divided Abenaki communities, but when the hostilities came to a close, the Abenakis had survived, and their homeland had escaped the devastation that affected so many Native-American communities.

Farther south, the town of Stockbridge in western Massachusetts had forged close ties with its white neighbors. It was an old "praying town," where a varied group of Native Americans—Mahicans, Housatonics, and Wappingers—eked out an existence on the margins of English Massachusetts. Like other parts of western Massachusetts, Stockbridge was gradually coming under white control, but there were still significant numbers of Native Americans living there. Once fighting broke out, Brothertown Indians from New York joined the community as well. As early as 1775, Stockbridge men had joined Patriot militia in Massachusetts as diplomats, riflemen, and scouts in the campaigns around Boston. In the next years, they would also see fighting around New York City and suffer heavy casualties at Kingsbridge (in today's Bronx).

In spite of their losses during the war, Stockbridges had a hard time holding onto their homeland in the years immediately following the conflict. As their Massachusetts land base was whittled away by white encroachment, they attempted to secure land in New York or Vermont. When these efforts failed, the Stockbridges accepted an offer of some land from another pro-American tribe, the Oneidas. Eventually, the Stockbridges removed to Wisconsin. For decades, the Stockbridges petitioned Congress for compensation for their heroic service during the War for Independence, but these petitions went largely unanswered.

THE IROQUOIS DILEMMA

The political and military alliance between the Iroquois Six Nations (Cayuga, Oneida, Mohawk, Seneca, Onondaga, and Tuscarora) existed long before extensive white colonization in North America, and it weathered the storm of European colonialism by playing imperial powers off one another. The evacuation of the French after that empire's defeat in the Seven Years' War (known in the later United States as the French and Indian War) removed one possible ally and trading partner and somewhat limited Iroquois options.

Though substantial variation occurred within the nations, and even within some villages, a pattern developed from east to west. In eastern Iroquoia, among the Mohawks and Oneidas, Christian missionaries exerted a heavy influence and the people were more likely to be dependent upon European trade goods. In western Iroquoia, home to the Senecas and Cayugas, Native peoples resisted these influences. To make matters worse, eastern Iroquois homelands had come under increasing pressure from land speculators and white settlers in the years leading up to the war. The pressure did not let up, even after the controversial Treaty of Fort Stanwix, signed in 1768.

Thayendanegea, or Joseph Brant, was a Mohawk war leader educated at Eleazar Wheelock's Indian school. After just two years at the school, he turned toward William Johnson—the leading British emissary to the Iroquois—and the world of British-Native diplomacy. By the 1770s, Brant was a respected figure in both the British and the Mohawk worlds. When fighting broke out between Britain and the colonies, Johnson moved from New York to Canada with a group of loyal Mohawks, and Brant traveled to London to voice Mohawk complaints about colonial land policy to the king.

As the Americans planned their invasion of Canada, they recognized that securing the assistance, or at least the non-

Joseph Brant, a leader of the Mohawks during the Revolution, in a portrait from around 1776.

interference, of the Iroquois would be essential to the effort. A contingent from the Continental Congress met some Iroquois leaders at Albany. Significantly, most Mohawks, Senecas, Cayugas, and Onondagas avoided the conference, leaving the white congressmen a more favorable assemblage of Oneidas, Tuscaroras, and Stockbridges. The Iroquois leaders were particularly concerned that the Americans replenish their supply of kettles, axes, hoes, and other valuable items, and looked to restore the fur trade to something approaching its former status. They also wanted the Americans to keep the fighting away from them.

In the negotiations, it often seemed as though both sides were talking past each other, and neither had much of a chance of living up to the agreement. Senecas, Cayugas, and Mohawks were more likely to support the British cause, since they had ties of kinship and commerce to the British Empire, which promised more, at least in terms of trade goods. To underscore this point, Joseph Brant returned from London in July 1776 and took part in the British victories around New York City before heading west to recruit Iroquois warriors to fight for the British.

By 1777, as war moved closer to the Iroquois heartland, the Onondagas—the central and oldest Iroquois nation and keepers of the centuries-old coun-

Joseph Brant on "Civilization"

In 1789, Thomas Eddy, a writer for the magazine *American Museum*, asked an aging Joseph Brant to describe the differences in European (or American) and Iroquois civilization. His response was telling:

In the government you call civilized, the happiness of the people is constantly sacrificed to the splendor of empire. Hence your codes of criminal and civil laws have had their origin; hence your dungeons and prisons. I will not enlarge on an idea so singular in civilized life, and perhaps disagreeable to you, and will only observe, that among us we have no prisons; we have no pompous parade of courts; we have no written laws; and yet judges are as highly revered amongst us as they are among you, and their decisions are as much regarded.

Property, to say the least, is as well guarded, and crimes are as impartially punished. We have among us no splendid villains above the control of our laws. Daring wickedness is here never suffered to triumph over helpless innocence. The states of widows and orphans are never devoured by enterprising sharpers. In a word, we have no robbery under the color of law. No person among us desires any other reward for performing a brave and worthy action, but the consciousness of having served his nation. Our wise men are called Fathers they truly sustain that character. They are always accessible. I will not say to the meanest of our people, for we have none mean but each as render themselves so by their vices. The palaces and prisons among you form a most dreadful contrast. Go to the former places, and you will see perhaps a deformed piece of earth assuming airs that become none but the Great Spirit above. Go to one of your prisons; here description utterly fails! Kill them, if you please; kill them, too, by tortures; but let the torture last no longer than a day. Those you call savages, relent the most furious of our tormentors exhausts his rage in a few hours, and dispatches his unhappy victim with a sudden stroke. Perhaps it is eligible that incorrigible offenders should sometimes be cut off. Let it be done in a way that is not degrading to human nature. Let such unhappy men have an opportunity, by their fortitude, of making an atonement in some measure for the crimes they have committed during their lives. But for what are many of your prisoners confined? For debt!—astonishing! and will you ever again call the Indian nations cruel? Liberty, to a rational creature, as much exceeds property as the light of the sun does that of the most twinkling star. . . . Great Maker of the world! And do you call yourselves Christians? Does then the religion of Him whom you call your Saviour, inspire this conduct and lead to this practice? Surely no. It was a sentence that once struck my mind with some force, that "A bruised reed he never broke." Cease then, while these practices continue among you, to call yourselves Christians, lest you publish to the world your hypocrisy. Cease, too, to call other nations savage, when you are tenfold more the children of cruelty than they.

During the 1777 battle of Oriskany, shown above, American militiamen commanded by General Nicholas Herkimer were ambushed by a combined force of Mohawks and Senecas and a smaller number of British soldiers and loyalists.

cil fire—remained neutral, but a serious rift continued to open in Iroquois country. The Mohawks heavily favored the British cause, and the Senecas and Cayugas were clearly heading in that direction. The Oneidas and Tuscaroras were leaning toward the Americans, thanks in part to the American presence and trade goods flowing from Fort Stanwix, but also because of their relationships with the missionary Samuel Kirkland. At precisely this moment, epidemic disease struck the Onondagas, killing scores of people including several leaders. It also killed the already-dim prospects for Iroquois neutrality. The battle at Oriska (Oriskany) in August 1777 reinforced the divisions among the Iroquois peoples.

The Oneidas joined American militia under General Nicholas Herkimer on a march to Fort Schuyler. Intelligence gathered by Molly Brant and sent to her brother Joseph ensured that the march would not go unopposed. Joseph Brant and Seneca chiefs (this particular "British" force was about 80 percent Native American) planned an ambush just where the road passed through a deep ravine. Herkimer's forces were caught totally unaware, and a bloody day-long battle ensued. Herkimer was wounded early in the fighting and did not play a significant role. Small clusters of Oneidas fought valiantly against Mohawk and Seneca attackers and managed to hold the field. Losses

Incident at Cherry Valley, New York: 32 noncombatants were killed, including women and children The engraving shows Jane Wells pleading for her life while a man tries to protect her from an attacking Native American.

were staggering on the Oneida and American side, with at least 200 dead (though accounts did not mention specific Oneida deaths, only casualties). The pro-British forces suffered scores of casualties as well, but withdrew before things could get much worse. Oneida warriors responded by attacking Mohawk villages and raiding the home of Molly Brant. Civil war had come to Iroquois country.

While the destruction of Iroquois warriors by other Iroquois warriors was a relatively rare occurrence, Iroquois on both sides of the Revolutionary War attacked each other's homes, camps, and towns in a cycle of revenge and retaliation. In 1778, Americans and allied Native Americans burned Oquaga village, and, in response, British and allied Native Americans under the leadership of Brant and Seneca chief Cornplanter destroyed the village of Cherry Valley. The situation became even worse in 1779, when George Washington ordered three armies to move through Seneca and Cayuga country to take Fort Niagara. None of the armies actually succeeded in taking the fort, but the campaign was brutal by design. Washington ordered his men to systematically destroy the Iroquois villages they came upon. Dwellings, crops, livestock, and all manner of property were confiscated or destroyed. Senecas managed to survive the assault by abandoning their towns.

The major fighting between the British and their former colonies came to an end in October 1781 after the British evacuation from Yorktown, but deep divisions remained in Iroquois country. The Six Nations Iroquois had lost approximately one-third of their population to disease and violence. Iroquois who had chosen the British side relocated to Montreal or to southern Ontario (where Joseph Brant received a sizeable grant of land, the Grand River reserve). Pro-American Iroquois settled in upstate New York, but their hold on their lands in the face of a new wave of white settlers was tenuous at best. Iroquois delegates were not invited to the peace conference at Paris that nearly doubled the size of the United States when the British gave up their claim to the entire Ohio River Valley.

THE WAR IN SHAWNEE COUNTRY

By the 1770s, Shawnee homelands in the Ohio River Valley were under pressure from white colonists and land speculators. The Treaty of Fort Stanwix, signed by Iroquois leaders in 1768, had given England's American colonists the idea that they could speculate and settle in lands currently occupied by Shawnees, and in the early 1770s they began to come to Shawnee country in increasing numbers. Prominent trespassers included Daniel Boone, who led a hunting party through the Cumberland Gap into what is now Kentucky in 1769.

The Shawnees were upset by continual and increasing white encroachment on their land, and they were exasperated by British and Iroquois attitudes that seemed to encourage such behavior. The Shawnees took the lead of a large, multitribal confederacy of western Indians and began holding regular meetings at a large council house on the Scioto River. Some Shawnee families began to feel hemmed in by the increasing white presence and removed to points west.

In 1774, the growing Shawnee frustration with white encroachment and white violence erupted into full-blown conflict, known to the colonists and later generations of Americans as Lord Dunmore's War, after the last colonial governor of Virginia. White colonists murdered the family of John Logan (Tachnedorus) in gruesome fashion: Logan's Shawnee wife was killed, and his pregnant sister was tied by her wrists and cut open, her unborn child impaled on a sharp stick nearby. After a series of frontier raids, Logan declared the

The Narrative of Mary Jemison

Mary Jemison was a white woman who was captured by Shawnees and adopted by Senecas in 1758, when she was 15 years old. She spent the rest of her life as a Seneca. Her life story was recorded and published in 1824 as *A Narrative of the Life of Mrs. Mary Jemison*, and is excerpted below.

I had then been with the Indians four summers and four winters, and had become so far accustomed to their mode of living, habits and dispositions, that my anxiety to get away, to be set at liberty, and leave them, had almost subsided. With them was my home; my family was there, and there I had many friends to whom I was warmly attached in consideration of the favors, affection and friendship with which they had uniformly treated me, from the time of my adoption. Our labor was not severe; and that of one year was exactly similar, in almost every respect, to that of the others, without that endless variety that is to be observed in the common labor of the white people. Notwithstanding the Indian women have all the fuel and bread to procure, and the cooking to perform, their task is probably not harder than that of white women, who have those articles provided for them; and their cares certainly are not half as numerous, nor as great. In the summer season, we planted, tended and harvested our corn, and generally had all our children with us; but had no master to oversee or drive us, so that we could work as leisurely as we pleased. We had no ploughs on the Ohio; but performed the whole process of planting and hoeing with a small tool that resembled, in some respects, a hoe with a very short handle.

Our cooking consisted in pounding our corn into samp or hommany, boiling the hommany, making now and then a cake and baking it in the ashes, and in boiling or roasting our venison. As our cooking and eating utensils consisted of a hommany block and pestle, a small kettle, a knife or two, and a few vessels of bark or wood, it required but little time to keep them in order for use.

. . . In the season of hunting, it was our business, in addition to our cooking, to bring home the game that was taken by the Indians, dress it, and carefully preserve the eatable meat, and prepare or dress the skins. Our clothing was fastened together with strings of deer skin, and tied on with the same.

In that manner we lived, without any of those jealousies, quarrels, and revengeful battles between families and individuals, which have been common in the Indian tribes since the introduction of ardent spirits amongst them.

. . . Notwithstanding all that has been said against the Indians, in consequence of their cruelties to their enemies—cruelties that I have witnessed, and had abundant proof of—it is a fact that they are naturally kind, tender and peaceable towards their friends, and strictly honest; and that those cruelties have been practised, only upon their enemies, according to their idea of justice.

matter finished, but Dunmore and white Virginians saw an opportunity in the violence. The Shawnees were diplomatically isolated in the conflict, and the Virginians hoped to use the fighting to bring peace to the Ohio River Valley (on their terms, of course, and always with more land cessions in mind). Two Anglo-American armies converged on Shawnee country, but Shawnee leaders, including Cornstalk, Blue Jacket, and Black Hoof, devised a plan to turn back one of the armies before they could join forces.

The October battle at Point Pleasant previewed some of the atrocities that would take place when the War for Independence came to Shawnee Country. After a daylong fight, the Shawnees ran short on ammunition and were forced to withdraw. Seventy-five white Virginians were dead, in comparison to between 20 and 30 Shawnee losses. The Virginians proceeded to scalp the corpses of the Shawnees. After Point Pleasant, Cornstalk negotiated a costly peace, agreeing to give up lands and to send four hostages, including his son, to Williamsburg.

As fighting erupted between the British and their American colonies, the Shawnees at first attempted to remain neutral. Shawnees were among the Native Americans assembled at Fort Pitt to declare neutrality with negotiators from the Continental Congress in the fall of 1775. Geographically, they were caught between American forces in western Virginia and the British stronghold at Detroit. In April 1776, some Shawnees traveled south to try to convince Cherokees to join the war effort against the Americans. At Fort Pitt, Cornstalk and other leaders met with Indian agent Henry Morgan to explain their dilemma. They believed in neutrality, but younger warriors were incensed by American land hunger, and they would prove difficult to placate. As Cornstalk put it:

When God created this World he gave this Island to the red people and placed your younger Brethren the Shawnese here in the Center. Now we and they see your people seated on our Lands which all Nations esteem as their and our heart. All our lands are covered by the white people, and we are jealous that you still intend to make larger strides. We never sold you our Lands which you now possess on the Ohio between the Great Kenhawa and the Cherokee River, and which you are settling without ever asking our leave, or obtaining our consent. Foolish people have desired you to do so, and you have taken their advice. We live by Hunting and cannot subsist in any other way. That was our hunting country and you have taken it from us. This is what sits heavy upon our Hearts and upon the Hearts of all Nations, and it is impossible for us to think as we ought whilst we are thus oppressed.

In the late 1770s, some Shawnee warriors had begun to fight with the British at Detroit and had joined raids on the western edge of Virginia. In November 1777, Cornstalk himself fell victim to the spreading violence. He was visiting Fort Randolph, on the Kanawha River, again trying to explain that he opposed

The Shawnee chief Black Hoof in a lithograph from the 1830s.

Shawnee participation in what he and other leaders saw as a white people's war, when he was murdered by white vigilantes seeking revenge for an earlier killing. The murder of Cornstalk drove even more moderate Shawnees toward war against the colonists and toward support of the British. In Delaware (Lenape) country, the 1778 murder of the chief White Eyes by white Americans had a similar effect, ending American hopes of Lenape neutrality.

In spite of the fact that Shawnees faced repeated depredations from American troops, they held their own on the battlefield and continued to resist American forces by relocating when that was possible. In 1779 and 1780, American forces struck Shawnee country, managing to destroy crops and villages, but failing to subdue Shawnee militants. In the winter of 1780, after burning Chillicothe to keep it from falling into American hands, hundreds of Shawnees approached Detroit in a desperate condition.

As mentioned earlier, British and American forces stopped fighting after Yorktown in 1781, but violence continued to plague Shawnee country. George Rogers Clark led regular incursions into the Shawnee heartland, conducting a "scorched earth" campaign much like the one General Washington had ordered to reduce Seneca resistance farther to the north. Still, the Shawnees refused to surrender, and they struck back under Black Hoof in 1782. In fact, it appeared that the Shawnees, at the head of a large confederacy of western Native Americans, had a chance of winning their war against the Americans, until the Treaty of Paris in 1783 removed the option of British assistance and transferred British claims to the Ohio River Valley to the newly independent United States.

THE CHEROKEES' STRUGGLE

The Cherokees, one of the largest and most powerful nations in the southeast, were torn apart by the American War for Independence. They had lost valuable lands in the 1768 Treaty of Fort Stanwix. Cherokees also faced frontier violence at the hands of white neighbors and increasing pressure

A Report from Cherokee Country

Henry Stuart, the British deputy superintendant of Indian affairs, attended the dramatic meeting at Chota in 1776. He described that event as follows:

[T]*he day being come for hearing the Grand Talk, we went to Chote where we could easily judge their different inclinations from their appearances; those from the Great Island except Otacite & two or three men were all black, also all the Chilhowie and Settico [Tellico] people and some from every Town were blacked. . . . The principal Deputy for the Mohawks and six Nations began. He produced a belt of white and purple Whampum with strings of white beads and purple whampum fixed to it; He said he supposed there was not a man present that could not read his Talk; the back settlers of the Northern Provinces whom he termed the Long Knife had without any provocation come into one of their Towns and murdered their people and the son of their Great Beloved Man; . . . That his Nation was fighting at this time and that he was sent by them to secure the friendship of all Nations for he considered their interests as one, and that at this time they should forget all their quarrels among themselves and turn their eyes and their thoughts one way. The Belt was delivered to Chincanacina.*

The principal Deputy of the Ottowas produced a white Belt with some purple figures; they expressed their desire of confirming a lasting bond of true friendship with all their red Brethren; that they were almost constantly at war one Nation against another, and reduced by degrees, while their common enemies were taking the advantage of their situation; that they were willing & they hoped every Nation would be the same to drop all their former quarrels and to join in one common cause, and that altho' the Trade to their Nation and all the other Northern Nations had been stopped, that their friends, the French in Canada, had found means to supply them and would assist them. . . .

The Belt was received by Chincanacina. It was some minutes before any one got up to give his Assent which was to be done by laying hold of the Belt. At last a Head man of Chilhowie who had lived long in the Mohawk Nation and whose wife had constantly lived in Sir William Johnson's house . . . rose up to take the Belt from Chincanacina. He sung the war song and all the Northern Indians joined in the chorus. Almost all the young warriors from the different parts of the Nation followed his example, though many of them expressed their uneasiness at being concerned in a war against the white people. But the principal Chiefs, who were averse to the measure and remembered the Calamities brought on their Nation by the last war, instead of opposing the rashness of the young people with spirit, sat down dejected and silent.

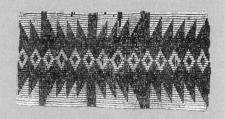

The pattern of diamonds in this wampum belt likely represented an alliance of towns.

from colonial governments to part with even more territory. The Treaty of Sycamore Shoals signed in 1775 between some Cherokees and the colonial government of North Carolina accomplished colonial goals by cutting off Cherokees from the Ohio River country and forcing the cession of vast tracts of land (about 27,000 square miles between the Kentucky and Tennessee Rivers). Attakullakulla and Oconosta, both aging war leaders, signed the agreement, but later Cherokee leaders argued that they had been deceived by the white negotiators. Attakullakulla's son, Dragging Canoe, was so incensed by the proceedings that he walked out on the negotiations, allegedly threatening violence against white settlers.

Near the outset of hostilities, in the spring of 1776, Mohawk, Shawnee, and Ottawa leaders journeyed south to the Cherokee town of Chota in an effort to influence the Cherokees to join the British war effort. Older leaders, perhaps remembering the awful bloodshed of the Anglo-Cherokee War of 1759–61, urged restraint. In one particularly dramatic moment, younger, more militant leaders accepted a war belt—nine feet in length and "strewn over with vermilion"—from the Shawnee representative. Dragging Canoe, Doublehead, and Young Tassel were among those who declared war against the Americans.

The Creeks refused to join the Cherokees in attacking the Americans, and this refusal spelled trouble for the Cherokees, leaving them exposed to white attacks. North and South Carolinians stepped up calls for a war of extermination or removal against the Cherokees that would leave their lands open to white settlement. In a few months in the summer and fall of 1776, several Cherokee towns had been destroyed by American forces (though Chota was saved, and tried to strike a neutral pose). Militant Cherokees like Dragging Canoe, meanwhile, moved west to the Chickamauga River country, rebuilt their towns, and began to draw young militants from many nations upset with American expansion.

Following a series of assaults in 1779, Dragging Canoe and others moved farther west and continued to resist American forces, even when food was scarce. The despair was heightened by the arrival of smallpox in Cherokee country in 1779 and 1780. American forces continued to rampage through Cherokee territory, destroying villages and crops as they invaded. When the British and Americans stopped fighting in 1781, white Americans swarmed over lands claimed by the Cherokees. Violence continued until the mid-1780s, at which point most Cherokees had been forced to sign treaties recognizing American rights to large portions of their lands.

CREEK DIVISIONS

The Creek Nation was divided by the War for Independence, and some individual Creeks favored neutrality or independence, but in the borderlands of the southeast, gunpowder was essential for warfare and for the trade in furs, and the British were far more generous with their supplies. In addition, as in

Mohawk country, some Musk-ogee (or Creek) families had developed ties of kinship and trade with the British. These factors influenced some Creeks to side with the British against their rebellious colonists. However, the Creeks also had some close ties to the American side (largely through South Carolina trader George Galphin) and a long history of trying to avoid entangling alliances with any outside powers, whether imperial or more regional.

Alexander McGillivray was one of the prominent Creeks with close connections to the British Empire, and he put forth a great effort in the late 1770s to sway his fellow Muskogees to support the British cause. McGillivray never obtained a "national" declaration of war against the Americans, but

This late 18th-century French print depicts a Native-American warrior from Louisiana bearing a snake in one hand and a scalp in the other.

he conducted trade and sponsored raids in a way that seriously hampered American war efforts in the Deep South. McGillivray's support was stronger in the Upper Towns. In the Lower Towns, leaders managed to maintain some semblance of neutrality until younger militants began to join anti-American Cherokees at Chickamauga.

Farther south, in Florida, the Creeks's Seminole cousins were divided by the conflict as well. As the Americans conquered some territory in Florida, northern Seminoles threw their support behind the British. Like all other Native-American nations, the Creeks and Seminoles were not present at the negotiations that led to the Treaty of Paris. In the years after 1783, McGillivray tried to carve out a Creek space between Spanish Florida and the emerging American empire, but the position became increasing untenable as some Creeks sold land to Americans, and McGillivray's rivals resented his actions.

SPANIARDS, APACHES, AND COLONIZATION IN THE FAR WEST

Events in the eastern half of North America between 1775 and 1783 far overshadowed events west of the Mississippi River. For many Native Americans, the American Revolution was not a defining feature of their lives. In much of western North America, and especially in California, tribes continued to interact primarily with the Spanish.

One narrative that began in the distant past, but took on new significance in the second half of the 18th century, was the rise of the Comanches to dominate the Apaches. Bands of Apaches—Lipan, Jicarilla, Mescalero, and Chiricahua—had long opposed Spanish encroachment, but they had been forced southward and westward by Spanish and Comanche raids in the 1760s and 1770s. They continued to resist the Spanish and the Comanches, mainly through raiding and trading, whenever the opportunity arose. The Spanish sought to gain allies against the Apaches by providing trade goods to the Comanches or by going to war with them to obtain peace treaties. Western Comanches signed just such a treaty with the Spanish after the death of their war leader Cuerno Verde in 1786. Under similar circumstances, the Navajos agreed to more or less peaceful coexistence with the Spanish colony of New Mexico in the 1780s.

Joint military and religious expeditions resulted in the founding of Spanish California in the 1760s and 1770s. Spanish missionaries, following the lead of Junipero Serra, who founded a chain of missions in California, attempted to convert California's Native Americans to Christianity and to teach them the value of European "civilization" in the missions between San Diego and San Francisco. If Native Californians attempted to resist mission activities, Spanish soldiers could be called in to pressure them through violence. Despite horrific numbers of deaths from venereal disease and some violence, the mission system of California continued to grow into the early 19th century. After violence erupted on the overland route between northern New Spain and California, near the confluence of the Gila and Colorado Rivers, Spanish officials decided to reinforce California by sea, leaving it somewhat isolated.

THE AFTERMATH OF THE REVOLUTION

Peace came between the colonists and England after the 1781 fall of Yorktown. This peace was cemented in the Treaty of Paris, which did not include Native-American representatives, and which ignored Native-American land claims. Violence continued to sweep through Native America in the years after the Peace of Paris, and the terms of the treaty paved the way for extensive conflicts over land, ranging even to the very heart of Native North America.

Violence of the most hideous sort enveloped the border country between the emerging United States and Native America. In 1782, American militia marched on Gnadhütten, a town of Lenape Moravians (who were pacifists), rounded up the nearly 100 parishioners, including men, women, and children, and clubbed them to death as they sang hymns. Elsewhere, other American armies raged through Cherokee, Shawnee, Cayuga, and Seneca country, conducting total warfare on Native-American civilian populations.

As they learned about the British decision to cede that empire's claims to the Ohio River Valley (doubling the size of the United States), Native-American leaders reacted with shock, disappointment, and fear for the future. Alexander McGillivray, who was trying to centralize Creek authority to ward off outside intrusions, remarked that "at the Close of it to ourselves & Country betrayed to our Enemies & divided between the Spaniards & Americans is Cruel & Ungenerous." Some southern Indians went so far as to suggest evacuating with the British, though few Native people chose this option. Joseph Brant and other Iroquois leaders were informed by American general Philip Schuyler that "We are now Masters of this Island, and can dispose of the lands as we think most proper or convenient to ourselves." Essentially, Native Americans would be treated as obstacles to American expansion and enemies of the American state.

In the Great Lakes region, which had formerly featured a multiethnic "middle ground," neither wholly European nor Native American in composition, violence became the order of the day. Hordes of white settlers streamed into the area, and the weak U.S. government was nowhere near powerful enough to stop them, even if it had desired to do so. Many of the states (including Virginia, New York, Massachusetts, the Carolinas, Connecticut, and Georgia) ceded their western land claims to the fledgling American state, and the federal government profited mightily from selling the lands to speculators and ordinary colonists alike. New rounds of treaty making between state governments, federal governments, and tribes left a confusing patchwork of conflicting land claims over Native-American homelands.

Perhaps most damagingly, the victorious Americans attempted to reduce the multifarious Native-American roles in the conflict to a single function. In the creation story of the United States, Native Americans acted as a foil to the virtuous Americans. The War for Independence presented Native-American communities with three bad options: a tenuous neutrality, siding with the British, or siding with the Americans. In the aftermath of the war, it did not matter which of the three options a given community had chosen. Neutral, pro-American, and pro-British tribes faced an aggressive, expansionist nation bent on expanding into Indian homelands.

MATTHEW JENNINGS
MACON STATE COLLEGE

Further Reading

Calloway, Colin. *The American Revolution in Indian Country: Crisis and Diversity in Native American Communities.* Cambridge: Cambridge University Press, 1995.

———. *The Shawnees and the War for America.* New York: Penguin, 2007.

Colonial Records of North Carolina. Available online, URL: http://docsouth .unc.edu/csr/index.html/document/csr10-0351#p10-767. Accessed March 2010.

Derounian-Stodola, Kathryn Zabelle, ed. *Women's Indian Captivity Narratives.* New York: Penguin, 1998.

Dowd, Gregory Evans. *A Spirited Resistance: The North American Indian Struggle for Unity, 1745–1815.* Baltimore, MD: Johns Hopkins University Press, 1992.

Edmunds, R. David, Frederick E. Hoxie, and Neal Salisbury. *The People: A History of Native America.* Boston, MA: Houghton Mifflin, 2007.

Glatthaar, Joseph T. and James Kirby Martin. *Forgotten Allies: The Oneida Indians and the American Revolution.* New York: Hill and Wang, 2006.

Green, Michael D. *The Politics of Indian Removal: Creek Government and Society in Crisis.* Lincoln, NE: University of Nebraska Press, 1985.

Hinderaker, Eric. *Elusive Empires: Constructing Colonialism in the Ohio Valley, 1673–1800.* Cambridge: Cambridge University Press, 1997.

Richter, Daniel K. *Facing East from Indian Country: A Native History of Early America.* Cambridge, MA: Harvard University Press, 2000.

Shannon, Timothy J. *Iroquois Diplomacy on the Early American Frontier.* New York: Penguin, 2008.

Sugden, John. *Blue Jacket: Warrior of the Shawnees.* Lincoln, NE: University of Nebraska Press, 2000.

Sword, Wiley. *President Washington's Indian War: The Struggle for the Old Northwest, 1790–1795.* Norman, OK: University of Oklahoma Press, 1985.

Taylor, Alan. *The Divided Ground: Indians, Settlers, and the Northern Borderland of the American Revolution.* New York: Vintage, 2006.

White, Richard. *The Middle Ground: Indians, Empires, and Republics in the Great Lakes Region, 1650–1815.* Cambridge: Cambridge University Press, 1991.

CHAPTER 3

The Early National Period and Expansion: 1783 to 1859

AFTER THE DELEGATES to the Constitutional Convention signed off on the new constitution on September 17, 1787, it was sent to the states for ratification. Two months before, the Northwest Ordinance had pledged that "utmost good faith shall always be observed toward the Indians; their land and property shall never be taken from them without their consent." Despite this promise, the U.S. government was already involved in transferring huge tracts of Native-American acreage to companies that were responsible for selling land to pioneers who migrated westward. Two years before Congress passed the Northwest Ordinance, a treaty signed at Fort McIntosh in Pennsylvania by representatives of the Delaware, Wyandot, Ottawa, and Chippewa tribes had ceded Native-American lands in southern and eastern Ohio. Some say the treaty was signed only after tribal representatives had been plied with alcohol. The British government had maintained control of outposts in the Northwest Territory after the American Revolution, and members of the Wyandot, Delaware, Shawnee, Miami, Ottawa, Chippewa, Potawatomi, Kickapoo, and remnants of the Six Nations living in the Northwestern Territory used British arms to attack settlers. One estimate places the number of settlers who died in the contested Ohio area between 1783 and 1790 at 1,500.

By 1789, the new American government was operational under the leadership of President George Washington. The Constitution had assigned control of

Indian affairs exclusively to the national government. Because the new government was struggling financially, government officials did not have the option of buying Native-American land. Instead, Washington and his adviser, General Philip Schuyler, promoted the notion of gradually taking over Native American lands through treaties. Washington issued a statement informing Native Americans that they were living on lands that had been won by right of conquest during the American Revolution. However, he promised that the government would be "merciful" and that a "reasonable" boundary would be drawn between lands occupied by settlers and those of Native Americans.

SHOWDOWN IN OHIO

When frontier wars continued, Washington asked Kentucky, Virginia, and Pennsylvania to dispatch militia to the Northwestern Territory. In the summer of 1790, General Josiah Harmer arrived with a motley force of 1,500 untrained and undisciplined men. On their way to a showdown on the Maumee River, Harmer's forces destroyed a number of Native-American villages. Snipers from the Miami, Shawnee, and Kickapoo tribes followed behind, keeping close track of troop movements. On September 10, the Americans were ambushed, and some 200 militiamen were slaughtered. The others broke rank and fled the scene. One retreating soldier shouted out at reinforcements, "For God's sake retreat. You will be all killed—there is Indians enough to eat you all up."

The following year, a second American force of 3,000 arrived under the command of Governor Arthur St. Clair. The untrained men managed to construct a series of forts before marching toward the Maumee River, but they could not withstand the ambush of November 3 in which 630 Americans died and another 300 were wounded. Convinced that they had driven the American military out of the area, Native-American warriors began forcing settlers to evacuate the Ohio River Valley.

A brilliant military strategist, President Washington was not inclined to repeat the mistake of sending in untrained troops. In the fall of 1793, General Anthony Wayne arrived in Ohio with a force of well-disciplined and highly trained men. After building Fort Greenville at Winford, the Americans set out for a third showdown. Under the command of Blue Jacket and Little Turtle, more than 2,000 warriors from confederated tribes had gathered at Fort Miami, a British fort. Wayne took his time, familiarizing his troops with the area and only engaging them in defensive battles. The major battle took place in August 1794, at Fallen Timbers near what is now Toledo. The British refused to become involved in the battle, partly because there were rumors that all British forces were to be withdrawn from the United States once negotiations on the Jay Treaty were completed. After winning a decisive victory, Wayne's forces built Fort Wayne at the head of the Maumee River. The Treaty of Greenville gave control of most of the Ohio River Valley to the United States. Native

Americans were offered $20,000 in goods and a $10,000 annuity to be shared among the Delaware, Potawatomi, Wyandot, Shawnee, Miami, Chippewa, Ottawa, and Kickapoo tribes.

SHIFTING LOYALTIES

In 1794, Eli Whitney invented the cotton gin, revolutionizing the economy of the American south. Cotton plantations increasingly needed large areas of land in order to meet the demands of the cotton export market. The Cherokee, the Creek, the Choctaw, the Chickasaw, and the Seminole, who were known as the "five civilized tribes," were pushed off tribal lands to free up large areas for planting cotton. Although early presidents expressed sympathy toward the plight of Native Americans, they did not altogether trust their loyalties. Supporters of the movement to push tribes westward often claimed that Native Americans should be considered enemies because so many had supported the British during the Revolution. They put forth the argument that all previous treaties with Native Americans had been nullified by their participation in the Revolutionary War, thereby rendering native lands liable to seizure. Many whites simply wanted to push natives off their ancestral lands because they were intolerant,or because they feared their lack of "civilization." The Six Nations continued to stand by their unified strategy for fighting encroachment, demanding that all future negotiations be brought before the confederacy, and insisting that individual chiefs could not sign treaties with Americans.

The Southern Confederation under the leadership of Alexander McGillivray, a Creek chief of mixed blood, had been negotiating with the Spanish in Florida and the French in Louisiana. The confederation was following a common strategy in which Native Americans played one nation against another. In this case, they wanted to use France and Spain to protect them from U.S. expansion. Spain and France were also protecting their own interests, expecting the Southern Confederation to protect them from invasion by American forces. American officials responded by inviting McGillivray to New York, where he was wined and dined and named brigadier general of the U.S. Army with an annual salary of $1,200. Despite being on the payroll of the U.S. government, McGillivray continued to work with the Spanish.

When the partnerships between the Southern Confederation and the French and the Spanish governments ultimately fell apart in the 1790s, Native Americans in the south were left on their own. The Chickamaugas left the south for less-populated areas in the western United States. The Chickasaw Nation had refused to join the confederation, opting instead to ally themselves with the United States. In retaliation, the Creeks waged a campaign of war and intimidation against the Chickasaws. In 1795, the Spanish signed the Treaty of San Lorenzo and withdrew from American lands on the east bank of the Mississippi River north of 31 degrees latitude.

NATIONAL POLICIES

In 1800, Thomas Jefferson, a Democratic Republican, was designated president by a Federalist-controlled House of Representatives after a tie in the Electoral College vote between him and his running mate, Aaron Burr. Like George Washington, Jefferson had consistently expressed sympathy for Native Americans who had seen their homelands transformed by European settlement. Jefferson's secretary of war, Henry Knox, was also a strong advocate for Native-American rights. Knox contended that by virtue of being "prior occupants," Native Americans retained the "right of the soil," which could not be taken away except by "free consent, or by the right of conquest in case of a just war."

In his second inaugural address, Jefferson officially introduced the notion that the United States could create a buffer zone between settlers and "aboriginal inhabitants" who possessed "an ardent love of liberty and independence" and who had been left "without power to divert or habits to contend" against a "stream of overflowing populations." Although Jefferson attempted to formulate a policy on Indian affairs that could balance American interests with a commitment to treating Native Americans humanely, he failed to provide a framework for preserving tribal lands and cultures. In the end, Jefferson yielded to his vision of what America could be, making westward expansion a major priority. The desire to make America a great nation resulted in the Louisiana Purchase in 1803, paving the way for accelerated western expansion. Over the next several decades, the opening of routes such as the Santa Fe and Oregon Trails made travel safer and accelerated the pace of westward expansion.

Meriwether Lewis and William Clark meeting with a group of Native Americans in the west during their 1804–06 expedition.

Sacagawea

When the Lewis and Clark Expedition reached the American wilderness in the winter of 1804, they were dependent upon Native-American guides. The only female member of the party was Sacagawea, the daughter of a Shoshone chief who had been captured by members of the Hidatsa tribe when she was a child. Later, Sacagawea, which means "bird woman," was sold to Toussaint Charbonneau, a polygamous French-Canadian trapper.

The Shoshone guide Sacagawea was featured on U.S. golden dollar coins after 2000.

Charbonneau signed on with the expedition as a guide and interpreter, but his wife proved to be the greatest asset when the group traveled through her former homeland. She was also adept at finding edible plants to supplement dwindling food supplies.

Sacagawea's first child, Jean Baptiste Charbonneau, whom William Clark fondly dubbed "Pomp," was born in February 1805. On the trip, Sacagawea encountered her brother Cameahwait, also a Shoshone chief, whom she had not seen since her abduction. She discovered that most of her family had died. A daughter, Lisette, was born to Sacagawea in 1812. A few months later, Sacagawea died at Fort Manuel.

Since Toussaint Charbonneau showed little interest in his children, William Clark, who had a well-documented interest in Native Americans and who had been fond of Sacagawea, asked to be made the legal guardian of her children.

In *Journal of a Voyage up the River Missouri Performed in Eighteen Hundred and Eleven*, Henry Brackenridge describes Sacagawea as "a good creature of mild and gentle disposition" and notes that she was "greatly attached to the whites." On December 20, 1812, John Luttig, a clerk for the Missouri Fur Company who had worked at Fort Manuel, noted in his journal that Sacagawea died "of a putrid fever." He remarked that she was "the best woman in the fort, aged about 25 years." Lisette was described as "a fine infant girl." When Fort Manuel was attacked by the Sioux in 1813, Luttig managed to escape with Lisette. He later replaced William Clark as guardian of Sacagawea's children.

Sacagawea's contributions to the settling of the American west have been recognized in a number of ways. A river has been named after her, and she has been memorialized with a U.S. coin and a statue in Washington Park in Portland, Oregon.

In May 1804, the Lewis and Clark Expedition, led by Meriwether Lewis and William Clark, set out for points westward. The team was charged with gathering geographical, geological, botanical, zoological, archaeological, and ethnological knowledge along the way. As the expedition traveled westward, they began traversing the lands of the powerful Nez Perce, a tribe that owned 13.2 million acres of land in what would become the states of Oregon, Idaho, and Washington. The Nez Perce later earned a national reputation for raising Appaloosa horses. While the Nez Perce originally welcomed European settlers, they regretted that action when disease, alcohol, and Christian missionaries began to exact a toll on their lives and culture.

During the War of 1812, large numbers of Native Americans sided with the British in an effort to stem the flow of white settlement. Once it became clear that the United States would win, most tribes reevaluated their position and made peace with the Americans. The Cherokee, Chickasaw, Choctaw, and some Creeks had chosen to fight against U.S. forces during that war.

In the late 18th century, large numbers of Native Americans had left Georgia and Alabama to establish themselves in northern Florida, which was then under Spanish rule. Known for their separatist views, the group had become known as Seminoles. Ostensibly to pursue escaped slaves hiding among the Seminoles, in March 1818, General Andrew Jackson set out with forces composed of 800 regulars, 900 Georgia militiamen, and a group of White Sticks from the Creek Nation. Forewarned of Jackson's advancement, the Seminoles retreated, forcing him to follow them into unfamiliar territory. During that

This cartoon published in Philadelphia condemns the British military's practice of paying Indian allies on the frontier for scalps from their mutual American enemies during the War of 1812.

Seminole Wars, 1816–1858

ATLANTIC OCEAN

Conecuh R.

1817 Fowltown
Ft. Scott

1818

Apalachicola R.

Tallahasee
1818

Suwanee R.

St. Johns R.

St. Augustine
Ft. Peyton
Osceola's Capture 1837

Negro Fort
1816
St. Marks
1818

Pensacola

Ochlockonee R.

Ft. Gadsden

Apalachee Bay

Suwanee
Old Town

Ft. Micanopy
Ft. Drane
1835

Ft. Drane

Gaines's Battle 1836
Withlacoochee R.
Clinch's Battle 1835
Wahoo Swamp 1836
Ft. Armstrong
Ft. Dade

Ft. King
Ft. Mellon
1837

Dade's Battle 1835

Gulf of Mexico

Ft. Brooke (Tampa)

Tampa Bay

Taylor's Battle 1837
Jesup's Battle 1838

Lake Okeechobee

Ft. Jupiter

Big Cypress Swamp 1855–58

Colee Hammock 1842

Ft. Lauderdale
Ft. Dallas

The Everglades

N

▲ Indian villages
● Non-Indian settlements
■ Forts
✳ Battles

Note: Map shown with modern boundaries.

0   400 miles
0   400 km

© Carl Waldman and Infobase Publishing

march, Jackson had two aged Seminole chiefs, two British officers, and a Scottish trader executed for collaboration. After destroying a fort in Pensacola, Jackson declared that western Florida had become a possession of the United States. Spain responded with outrage.

The following year, tensions eased when Secretary of State John Quincy Adams negotiated the Adams-Onis Treaty that gave Florida to the United States in return for an American promise to pay claims of American citizens against Spain up to $5 million. The land west of the Sabine River in Texas; as well as that which makes up modern-day California, New Mexico, Nevada, Utah, and Arizona, and parts of Wyoming and Colorado were ceded to Spain.

CALIFORNIA, NEW MEXICO, AND TEXAS

Western sections of the American colonies remained under Spanish control after inhabitants of the eastern-most states had established themselves as the United States of America. In California, the Spanish had overwhelmed

Native Americans through the joint efforts of the Spanish military and the Roman Catholic Church, adhering to a policy of military conquest, followed by the establishment of missions intent on converting Native Americans to Christianity and teaching them to follow European farming methods and lifestyles. As in the rest of the Americas, Europeans brought diseases; with no resistance to smallpox, influenza, dysentery, malaria, measles, and syphilis, the native population steadily dwindled. By 1848, only a third of the original native population survived.

The Spanish also followed a similar pattern of settlement in New Mexico, where the government subsidized Franciscan missions that were used to teach Pueblo Indians about European lifestyles and beliefs. The Pueblo Revolt in 1680 was quickly stamped out, but it served to make the Spanish more open to the Pueblo's desires to maintain their own language and religion. The 18th century was extremely violent for New Mexico as the Pueblo continued to battle the hostile tribes that surrounded them, and the Spanish resisted the encroachment efforts of other European nations. Because the Spanish were afraid that France would attempt to take over Texas to provide unobstructed access to the rich mining resources of New Mexico, they established missions near French-controlled lands.

Culturally, Native American tribes of California had much in common with those who lived in other sections of the Americas. They generally made their living from fishing and hunting. Villages varying in size from 100 to 1,000 were built along the rivers and lagoons or in the mountains. Those who lived near the water traveled in dugout canoes fashioned from redwood. Weaving was honed to a fine art. Because the fear of natural catastrophes was constant, many tribes held annual ceremonies to pay homage to the forces that controlled nature. The centrally located roundhouse was often the center of tribal social life. The many tribes included the Modoc, the Wappo, and the Serrano.

Traditional Navajo hogan (or diné) home, built from wooden poles, tree bark, and mud.

Although each tribe was independent, they were often connected through marriage ties.

In New Mexico, the Navajo and Apache tribes led nomadic lifestyles of hunting and gathering, in contrast to the Pueblo, who preferred to live in permanent settlements. Pueblo dwellings tended to be made of stone or adobe and were square with thick roofs. To protect from outside invasion, these homes were usually built without doors or windows. The architectural style of Pueblo villages is still evident throughout New Mexico. Descendants of the ancient Anasazi, the Pueblo had been growing corn, beans, squash, and chilies for centuries. Before Europeans came to New Mexico, each Pueblo village was ruled by a chief. Afterward, a governor was elected for a set term. In Texas, where major tribes included the Bidai, the Apache, the Comanche, and the Wichita, Spanish missionaries had little success in convincing Native Americans to adopt European customs. Hunting and weaving were the chief occupations. As a rule, tribes were matrilineal.

ANDREW JACKSON

By 1819, Native-American leaders had ceased to play one nation against another, reluctantly accepting the fact that Americans would never leave the lands they had settled. In the Treaty of Edwardsville, Native Americans ceded ownership of lands in Illinois and Wabash in exchange for territory west of the Mississippi River. The Indian Civilization Fund of 1819 funded $10,000 to be used for helping Native Americans assimilate. The opening of the Erie Canal in 1825 and the discovery of coveted metal deposits in the western United States made both settlers and government officials even more anxious to obtain Native-American lands.

In 1829, Andrew Jackson, a veteran of various Indian wars, entered the White House. Jackson was the first president born west of the Appalachian Mountains and was the first executive not connected to the founding generation in some way. In his first inaugural address, Jackson proposed that Native Americans either voluntarily relocate to lands west of the Mississippi River, or remain and yield their alleged sovereignty to the states in which they resided. Over the next few years, what became known as Jacksonian democracy reshaped the United States both politically and economically. The young country was threatened by powerful forces in England and Spain, and by Native Americans who were willing to work with America's enemies to stymie the flood of encroaching western settlement.

As a veteran of the First Seminole War, Jackson was familiar with the tendency of Native Americans to play one interest against another. Jackson believed that relocation would remove physical threats to frontier settlers while opening up vast tracts of land for development. The War Department had been given responsibility for Indian affairs in 1824, and Jackson's secretary of war, John H. Eaton, actively pursued a removal policy.

The Indian Removal Act

On May 28, 1830, President Andrew Jackson signed the Indian Removal Act, which allowed the federal government to mandate an exchange of historic tribal lands in the east with wilderness lands west of the Mississippi River. Those lands were designated as those that had not already been "included in any state or organized territory, and to which the Indian title has been extinguished."

Approximately 100,000 Native Americans were directly affected by the new law. Jackson was given authority by Congress to divide areas of relocation into districts. The act also pledged that the United States would "forever secure and guaranty" Native Americans "and their heirs or successors the country so exchanged with them." The federal government protected itself by asserting that lands would revert to government ownership "if the Indians become extinct or abandon the same." The president was given authority to bring in appraisers to settle controversies over the value of existing tribal lands.

Jackson charged a three-member commission with overseeing removal of Native Americans. The commission was chaired by Montfort Stokes of North Carolina. Other members included Henry R. Ellsworth of Connecticut and John F. Schermerhorn of New York. The commission was headquartered at Fort Gibson on the Grand River, and a select group of Mounted Rangers was dispatched to the fort to enforce the act and settle any disputes that might arise. Politicians who spoke out for rights for Native Americans were ostracized by their peers. Davy Crockett, a popular folk hero and a representative from Tennessee, was forced out of Congress after he objected to the removal of the highly acclimatized Cherokee tribe. Crockett contended that he "would sooner be honestly damned than hypocritically immortalized."

Jackson elaborated on the implementation of the Indian Removal Act in his second annual message to Congress on December 6, 1830, assuring legislators and distinguished guests that "the benevolent policy" of removal was "approaching to a happy consummation." Although the government set aside $500,000 to provide "such aid and assistance" as was deemed "necessary for support and subsistence for the first year after removal," the aid proved to be woefully inadequate for the needs of relocated Native Americans.

By 1850, virtually all Natives had been relocated to the western United States. As expansion pressed Native Americans even farther west, they began to arrive on lands belonging to the Sioux, the Cheyenne, the Arapaho, the Comanche, and the Kiowa; as well as those of the Hasinai confederacy of Texas, which included members of the Jumano, Lipan Apache, Blackfoot, Crow, Ute, Arikaras, and Shoshoni (or Shoshone) tribes.

REMOVAL

In 1830, Congress passed the Indian Removal Act. Over the next decade, large numbers of Native Americans were ripped from their homes and possessions and relocated to the American west.

The removal plan called for districts to be created within each western territory in areas that had not already been claimed. The policy did not specifically state that all natives should be removed from the eastern United States. Jackson suggested that those of "mixed blood" should have the choice of being removed westward, or opting to register as residents of the United States. Over the course of his presidency, Andrew Jackson oversaw a number of additional laws and treaties designed to rid the eastern United States of Native Americans.

Even before the passage of the Indian Removal Act, some tribes had decided to leave their ancestral lands. By 1827, the Creeks had absented themselves from Georgia. Within two years of the passage of the act, the Choctaw and Chickasaw had exchanged lands in the southeastern United States for areas west of the Mississippi River. Those who remained in other areas of the southeast voted to remain and accept state jurisdiction over their affairs. The federal government disregarded that vote and targeted them for removal.

Under Jackson's registration plan, a third of the Cherokee nation pursued registration. Approval of those applications was at the whim of a designated agent. Records show that of 19,554 applications, only 69 were approved. The Cherokee, who had become acclimatized to a large degree, resorted to legal means to fight removal.

In the Snowbird community in North Carolina, for instance, three sympathetic whites used tribal funds to repurchase 1,200 acres of land and return it to the Cherokee. Approximately 50 other Cherokees relinquished their Indian citizenship to become American citizens, establishing what became the Qualla Reservation in North Carolina.

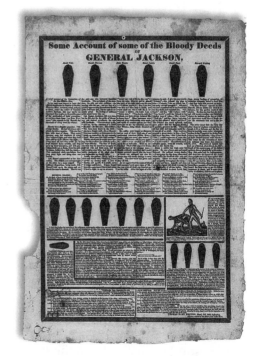

This 1828 broadside accuses Andrew Jackson of atrocities against Native Americans and others. The drawings of coffins represent executions Jackson ordered during his military career.

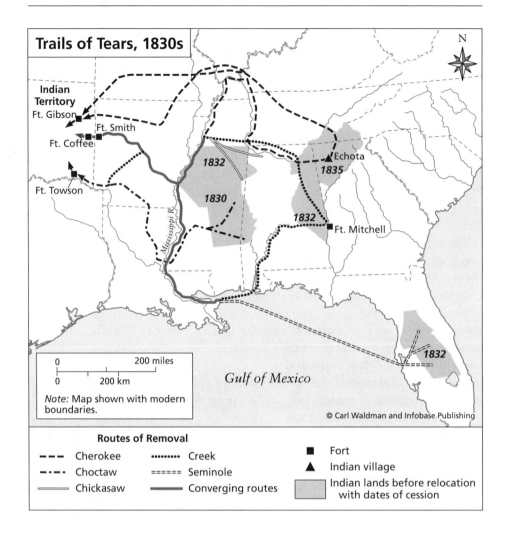

Trails of Tears, 1830s

Routes of Removal

--- Cherokee   •••••••• Creek   ■ Fort
--- Choctaw   ====== Seminole   ▲ Indian village
—— Chickasaw   ▬▬▬ Converging routes   Indian lands before relocation with dates of cession

© Carl Waldman and Infobase Publishing

Ever since gold had been discovered on Cherokee land in Georgia in 1828, state officials had become more determined to remove Native Americans from what they viewed as American lands by right of discovery and conquest. The Georgia legislature passed a series of laws that banned Cherokees from mining activities, restricted their ability to negotiate contracts with whites, and prohibited them from testifying in white courts. After Congress passed the Indian Removal Act, Georgia Cherokees used all legal means at their disposal to fight removal.

Writing for the majority in *Cherokee v. Georgia* (30 U.S. 1, 1831), Chief Justice John Marshall defined the status of Native Americans as "domestic dependent nations" and refused to accept the argument that Native-American tribes were sovereign nations. Nevertheless, the Supreme Court determined the following year in *Worcester v. Georgia* that the Cherokee Nation was not bound by state laws because of existing sovereignty. Thus, the removal law as applied to the Cherokee was invalid. This finding did not protect the Cherokee from removal, partly because President Andrew Jackson refused to protect Native Americans from states that wanted to evict them.

The Choctaws were the first tribe to head westward. It is estimated that 2,500 died on the 500-mile trip from exposure, starvation, illness, and attacks by marauders. When Creeks attempted to negotiate their way out of removal by offering to move to designated reservations in Alabama, whites responded by attacking and harassing them, robbing Creek graves of valuables, and making it illegal for Native Americans to hunt within the state. In 1836, Jackson sent federal troops to Alabama to quell a Creek uprising and forced the tribe to relocate.

Between 1837 and 1838, Native Americans were herded into overcrowded and ill-equipped camps where they were served substandard food. Near-starvation and poor hygiene soon led to deteriorating health. Those who were ill were placed in carts for the trip along with the extremely young and old. Some brought their own horses, but most were expected to travel by foot over poor roads. Because they were only able to bring what they could carry, most of their possessions were left behind. On the trip they slept underneath wagons. Some were lucky enough to sleep in the inadequate tents that had been provided. Many merchants saw the removal as a means of making huge sums fairly quickly. They sold spoiled food and poor-quality products to federal officers in charge of the trip, resulting in a host of diseases and illnesses. In 1837, a major smallpox epidemic devastated the Missouri Valley. Pneumonia was a major problem in the winter, and insects and cholera plagued the summer months. While some federal officers were unsympathetic to the ills that Native Americans suffered on their way west, others were more compassionate. Estimates place the number of Creeks, Choctaws, and Chickasaw who survived the removal at 28,000 to 30,000. Very few of the young or very old survived.

THE TRAIL OF TEARS

Long before the Indian Removal Act was passed in 1830, the Cherokee tribe of Georgia had made great efforts to meet European standards of "civilization." Some owned large plantations, and five to 10 percent owned slaves. Others had opened businesses. Cherokee women wore European-styled clothing. The Cherokee Nation had built its own roads, schools, and churches and had established a form of representative government. Despite this effort to acclimatize, state officials did not create an environment that was

The Cherokee rose has become a popular symbol of the suffering and endurance of the Cherokees.

Tecumseh (1768–1813)

Chief Tecumseh in an illustration from an 1885 history textbook.

Shawnee Chieftain Tecumseh, also known as Shooting Star, is considered one of the most significant Native Americans of all time. Along with his brother Tenskwatawa, a former alcoholic who became known as "The Prophet," Tecumseh became the voice of his people. He fought for their right to retain native lands and cultures in the face of encroaching western settlement. Tenskwatawa told of a vision that informed him that Native Americans should shy away from European habits and products and return to their old ways.

Inclined toward violence to protect Native-American rights, younger Native Americans were willing to follow the lead of the two brothers. Tecumseh promoted the concept of a confederation of all tribes west of the Appalachian Mountains between Canada and the Gulf of Mexico. He contended that since large tracts of land were held in common under the control of the confederation, no single chief or tribe could sign away those lands. Tecumseh promoted the notion that all whites were "evil" beings who had used whiskey to "destroy the bravery of . . . warriors." He argued that the only hope for Native Americans was "a war of extermination against the pale face."

Tecumseh was willing to negotiate when it suited him. A story is told concerning Tecumseh's reactions to a series of meetings with William Henry Harrison, the governor of the Indiana Territory who became the ninth president of the United States. At one point, the two men were sitting on a bench together, and Tecumseh slowly forced Harrison to the end of the bench by moving toward him in stages. When the governor objected, Tecumseh informed him that this was what Americans had been doing to Native Americans for ages. Harrison is credited with persuading, or some say tricking, Native-American chiefs into signing a treaty in 1809 that gave away more than 2.5 million acres to white settlers. Two years later, while Tecumseh was traveling the United States attempting to recruit other Native Americans to his way of thinking, Harrison led an attack on Prophetstown, which the two brothers had established. Tenskwatawa had informed his followers that they would not be harmed by bullets if they fought back. Tenskwatawa was killed in the Battle of Tippecanoe. Despite heavy American losses, Harrison became a hero and was thereafter known as "Old Tippecanoe."

After Tecumseh died fighting for the British in the War of 1812, no other Native-American leader would be able to take his place.

hospitable to Native Americans. In 1780, the Georgia legislature had passed a law making it legal "to put to death or capture" Native Americans who committed "hostilities against the people of this state." In response to government actions and aggressive land-grabbing, other tribes had already begun leaving the state. The Lower Creeks, for instance, had been evicted under a treaty signed in 1825 at Indian Springs near present-day Macon.

Cherokee leaders unsuccessfully turned to the courts for assistance in fighting removal efforts. Despite their best efforts, the Cherokees were herded up in the summer of 1838 by military forces under the command of General Winfield Scott. Old or young, rich or poor, they were all treated the same. One of the soldiers involved in the removal told the story of a frail young widow with three small children who "gathered the children at her feet, prayed an humble prayer in her native tongue, patted the old family dog on the head" and left her home "with [the] baby strapped on her back and [leading] a child with each hand." Before making much progress, "a stroke of heart failure relieved her of her sufferings," and she died "with her baby on her back and her other two children clinging to her hands." The same soldier told of another home where family members were forced to leave the body of a newly dead child behind as they were herded from their home.

The western march toward Oklahoma took place during the fall and winter of 1838 and 1839. The Cherokees were initially housed in makeshift forts. While some were transported by boat, most made the trip on foot under

This 1837 print depicts a scene from the long and costly Second Seminole War, which involved as many as 40,000 troops and militiamen. The Seminoles are shown besieging a fortified blockhouse on the Withlacoochee River in Florida in late 1835 or early 1836.

deplorable conditions. At least a tenth of the group died from dysentery and other diseases. Scott finally responded to repeated requests by Cherokee leader John Ross to allow the Cherokees to oversee their own trip. Broken into smaller groups, individual Cherokees were able to travel more comfortably and forage for their own food. The path the Cherokees traveled to Oklahoma is burned into American history as the Trail of Tears (*Nunna daul Tsuny*, "the Trail Where They Cried") because some 4,000 of the 15,000 who left Georgia died on the trip westward.

According to legend, the mothers of the Cherokees who died were so lost in grief that the chiefs prayed for a sign to give them comfort. The legend says that a white flower with a gold center grew up along the Trail of Tears in all spots marked by a mother's tears. The white rose represents those tears, and the gold center stands for the gold taken from Cherokee tribal lands. The seven leaves of the stem symbolize the seven clans of the Cherokee tribe that made the journey from Georgia to Oklahoma. The Cherokee rose (*Rosa laevigata*), which is now the state flower of Georgia, still grows along the trail.

Several hundred members of the Cherokee tribe hid out in the mountains of North Carolina, managing to escape detection. In 1842, the federal government created a reservation in the Appalachian Mountains, designating it as a permanent home for the remaining Cherokees. Each summer, in an outdoor theater in Cherokee, North Carolina, descendants of the Cherokee Nation perform *Unto These Hills*, a drama commemorating Cherokee history and telling the story of the Cherokees who traveled the Trail of Tears. By the 21st century, only 60,600 Native Americans remained in the states of Georgia, Alabama, Mississippi, North Carolina, Tennessee, and Florida.

In 1819, Spain had ceded Florida to the United States. Most of the Seminoles who remained in the state lived on a reservation in the central part of the state. Whites wanted them cleared out, but the Seminoles actively resisted removal. They engaged in a series of battles that took place between 1833 and 1842. The Seminoles were joined by the remnants of a group of Tecumseh's followers known as Red Sticks. Andrew Jackson had led the attack that wiped out most of the Red Sticks at the Battle of Horseshoe Bend in Alabama in 1814. Survivors had been forced to sign a confession of guilt and agree to cede two-thirds of their land to the federal government. In all, 10,000 U.S. troops and 30,000 citizen soldiers were involved in the Seminole wars. Resistance ended with the forced removal of 3,000 Seminoles. Those who remained were relocated to reservations near the Big Cypress Swamp in the Florida Everglades.

Unlike those tribes who were relocated virtually en masse, the Chickasaw made the trip in small groups over a 10-year period beginning in 1837. Rather than depending on the government for sustenance along the way, the Chickasaw used tribal funds to purchase supplies and paid for transportation by steamboat to the Arkansas River. In this way, they escaped some of the brutal

The Cherokee Constitution

In 1839, members of the Cherokee tribe met in a constitutional convention to proclaim their sovereignty and write a new contract patterned after the U.S. Constitution of 1787. The Cherokee document expanded on an earlier constitution written in 1827, which had established a republican form of government. George Lowrey served as president of the convention, and the draft was written by William Shory Coody. In language similar to that of the Preamble to the U.S. Constitution, the 1839 Cherokee Constitution was designed to "establish justice, ensure tranquility, promote our common welfare, and secure to ourselves and our posterity the blessings of liberty." The Cherokees also pledged "humility and gratitude" to the "sovereign ruler of the Universe."

An 1875 revised edition of the Cherokee Constitution written in the Cherokee syllabary.

Signed on September 6, 1839, Article 1 of the Cherokee Constitution specified existing boundaries of Cherokee land that had been "solemnly guaranteed and reserved forever to the Cherokee Nation by the treaties concluded with the United States." In Section 2, the document acknowledged the right of the Cherokee people to designate common lands while reserving the right of individuals to make improvements. The Cherokee Constitution also set up an executive branch, a bicameral legislative branch, and an independent judiciary. As with the U.S. Constitution, separation of powers was mandated.

Retaining the eight districts already in place, the constitution provided for election of two members from each district to serve two-year terms. The General Council was assigned the authority "to make all laws and regulations, which they shall deem necessary and proper, for the good of the nation, which shall not be contrary to this constitution." The first elections were set for the first Monday in August. Only those who were "free Cherokee male citizen[s]" who had "attained the age of 25" and were "descendants of Cherokee men by all free women (except the African race) whose parents may be or may have been living together as man and wife according to the customs and laws of this nation" were eligible to serve in the General Council. Suffrage was allotted to "all free male citizens (excepting Negroes and descendants of white and Indian men by Negro women who may have been set free) who shall have attained to the age of 18 years." The signatures of August 23, 1939, included those of Aaron Price, Major Pullum, Young Elders, Deer Track, Young Puppy, Turtle Fields, July, the Eagle, and Crying Buffalo.

conditions suffered by other tribes. In Oklahoma, the Chickasaw bought land that had once belonged to the Choctaw.

AFTERMATH

Within a dozen years of the passage of the Indian Removal Act, the Creek, Choctaw, Chickasaw, Cherokee, and Seminole tribes, which had been relocated to the edge of the Great American Desert in Oklahoma, united as the Five Civilized Tribes of the southeast. This group of Native Americans continued to endorse elements of European culture without forsaking their own culture. They embraced European-style agricultural practices and adopted European dress. To celebrate their status as sovereign nations, the Five Civilized Tribes created their own government.

The Cherokees who moved to Oklahoma had a distinct advantage over other native groups because large members of their tribe had already emigrated westward into the Arkansas Territory. Those Cherokees had established a tribal government under the leadership of first, second, and third chiefs. Initially, there was a good deal of friction between the groups of eastern and western Cherokees. Since the eastern Cherokees had the advantage of sheer numbers, they wrested power for their chosen leader, John Ross. Ross's father had been a Scot, and one of his mother's grandparents had been Cherokee. Ross chose to identify himself as Cherokee. He became the leader of the Cherokees at the age of 27 and held that position until his death some 40 years later. Under Ross's guidance, the Cherokees built towns, schools, government buildings, farms, and homes in their new land.

By 1839, Indian removal had been accomplished, except for isolated groups of Native Americans who had fled into the wilderness or into the mountains. In their new homes in the west, Native Americans were allotted lands individually, rather than by tribe. It was suggested that private land ownership would promote capitalism and help natives to become more like Europeans. The plan had the added advantage of providing surplus allotment lands for white settlement.

The Plains tribes found themselves directly in the path of westward expansion, and hunters saw game disappear as settlement increased and modes of transportation became more sophisticated. Along the Oregon Trail, the Sioux responded by forcibly demanding tolls from all who passed through their lands. The federal government solved that problem in 1847 by building forts along the trail to protect settlers. In 1849, the Bureau of Indian Affairs was moved to the Department of the Interior. Two years later, Congress passed the Indians Appropriation Act, earmarking $100,000 for funding the relocation of Native Americans farther westward to free up Indian Territory for white settlement. In 1854, the passage of the Kansas-Nebraska Act formalized opportunities for white settlement in the Indian Territory. The previous year, Jackson had ordered George W. Manypenny, the Commissioner of Indian Affairs, to negotiate a new treaty. Manypenny decried the process by which tribes were "removed, step by step, from mountain to valley, and from river to plain, until they have been pushed halfway across the country. They can go no further."

The 1855 treaty signed by most Native-American tribes granted them control over a 7.5 million-acre reservation. By the following year, the negotiations resulting from 50 separate treaties had shrunk those holdings considerably. Subsequent treaties reduced Native-American lands to only 75,000 acres, and white settlers were still migrating to the west in droves.

ELIZABETH R. PURDY
INDEPENDENT SCHOLAR

Further Reading

Barney, William L., ed. *A Companion to Nineteenth-Century America.* Malden, MA: Blackwell, 2006.

Barrington, Linda, ed. *The Other Side of the Frontier: Economic Explorations into Native American History.* Boulder, CO: Westview Press, 1999.

Brackenridge, Henry Marie. *Journal of a Voyage up the River Missouri Performed in Eighteen Hundred and Eleven.* Baltimore, MD: Coale and Maxwell, 1816.

Cherokee Nation. "Cherokee Constitution." Available online, URL: http://www2.volstate.edu/cbucy/History%202030/Documents/Cherokee%20Constitution-Doc52.htm. Accessed July 2008.

Conn, Steven. *History's Shadow: Native Americans and Historical Consciousness in the Nineteenth Century.* Chicago, IL: University of Chicago Press, 2004.

Crompton, Samuel Willard. *Illustrated Atlas of Native American History.* Edison, NJ: Chartwell Books, 1999.

Edmunds, David R. *Tecumseh and the Quest for Indian Leadership.* Boston, MA: Little, Brown, 1984.

Gibson, Arrell Morgan. *The American Indian: Prehistory to the Present.* Lexington, MA: D.C. Heath, 1980.

Hamby, Alonzo. *Outline of U.S. History.* New York: Nova Science, 2007.

Jefferson, Thomas. "Second Inaugural Address, 4 March 1805." Available online, URL: http://www.bartleby.com/124/pres17.html. Accessed August 2008.

Library of Congress. "Indian Removal Act." Available online. URL: http://memory.loc.gov/cgi-bin/ampage?collId=llsl&fileName=004/llsl004.db&recNum=458. Accessed July 2008.

Luttig, John C. "Journal of a Fur-Trading Expedition on the Upper Missouri, 1812–1813." Available online, URL: http://www.xmission.com/~drudy/mtman/html/Luttig/index.html. Accessed August 2008.

Mancall, Peter C. and James H. Merrell. *American Encounters: Natives and Newcomers from European Contact to Indian Removal, 1500–1850.* New York: Routledge, 2007.

McLynn, Frank. *Wagons West: The Epic Story of America's Overland Trails.* New York: Oxford University Press, 2002.

Nichols, Roger L. *American Indians in United States History.* Norman, OK: University of Oklahoma Press, 2003.

NorthGeorgia.com. "The Trail of Tears." Available online, URL: http://ngeorgia.com/history/nghisttt.html. Accessed July 2008.

Ohio History Central. "Tecumseh." Available online, URL: http://www.ohiohistorycentral.org/entry.php?rec=373. Accessed July 2008.

Page, Jake. *In the Hands of the Great Spirit: The 20,000 Year History of American Indians.* New York: Free Press, 2003.

PBS. "Trail of Tears." Available online, URL: http://www.pbs.org/wgbh/aia/part4/4h1567.html. Accessed July 2008.

People's Path. "1839 Cherokee Constitution." Available online, URL: http://www.thepeoplespaths.net/history/CherConst1839.htm. Accessed July 2008.

U.S. Congress. Northwest Ordinance of 1787. Available online. URL: http://www.yale.edu/lawweb/avalon/nworder.htm. Accessed August 2008.

CHAPTER 4

The Civil War to the Gilded Age: 1859 to 1900

BY THE EVE of the Civil War, most remaining Native Americans had been removed from east of the Mississippi River under the Indian Removal Act of 1830 and various treaties negotiated with the federal government. Many of them had settled in Indian Territory (present-day Oklahoma). The overall aim of U.S. Indian policy was the concentration of Native Americans on reservations in order to open the way for the increasing stream of westward-migrating settlers. The mid-to-late 1800s would only see this trend grow due to federal government policies encouraging emigration such as the Homestead Act of 1862, growth of the cattle industry, discoveries of new deposits along the expanding mining frontier, and construction of railroads and telegraph lines across the country. As a result, many Native-American tribes would endure multiple relocations onto ever-smaller reservations.

American public opinion largely supported the policies of concentration and assimilation, even if it disagreed on the best way to achieve them. Many felt that containment on reservations and, later, assimilation into mainstream society were the only viable solutions to the so-called Indian Question. The federal government pursued both peaceful and military means to enforce these solutions. The years from the Civil War through the Gilded Age were a time of uncertainty, land loss, military warfare, and hardships for Native Americans.

THE IMPACT OF THE CIVIL WAR ON NATIVE-AMERICAN LIFE

Native Americans fought for both the United States of America (Union) and the Confederate States of America (Confederacy) during the Civil War (1861–65), and some tribes were even divided among themselves. Native Americans fought in the Civil War for a variety of reasons, including economic and political survival, conscription laws, treaty obligations and alliances, and the importance of military experience in some tribes' determination of social status. Many felt the war was a crucial chance to stop the process of forced migration and land loss begun centuries earlier and was an ever-present threat. Others were simply drawn into the action as participants or civilians due to the battles and guerrilla warfare that erupted within Indian Territory and along the western frontier. Westward settlement and Indian removal continued during the course of the war even as the federal government began neglecting Indian affairs. Treaty violations, late annuity payments and supplies on western reservations, and a lessened military presence at western forts, coupled with increased westward migration exacerbated preexisting problems.

The so-called Five Civilized Tribes that had been removed from the southeast to Indian Territory under the Indian Removal Act of 1830—the Cherokee, Creek, Choctaw, Seminole, and Chickasaw—signed treaties of alliance with the Confederacy that severed their ties to the Union. These groups had strained relations with the federal government and bitter resentments over their earlier land losses and the Trail of Tears, as well as the Union abandonment of the western forts that provided them some measure of protection from the increasing stream of westward settlers. Some were also slaveholders who felt their interests aligned more closely with those of the Confederacy. Cherokee Stand Watie was a key Confederate leader who became the only Native American to achieve the rank of brigadier general in the Civil War. The Confederacy also signed treaties with a number of other western tribes, including the Comanche, Wichita, Caddo, Osage, Shawnee, Delaware, Seneca, and Quapaw.

While the Chickasaws and Choctaws were completely aligned with the Confederacy, the other three of the Five Civilized Tribes settled in Indian Territory—the Creeks, Seminoles, and Cherokees—were divided. While some of their members were slaveholders who fought for the Confederacy, other factions sought to remain neutral or became loyal to the Union. Chief John Ross led the neutral faction of Cherokees. Creek chief Opothleyaholo established a settlement for a group of neutrals, but a pro-Confederate group destroyed their camp in late 1861 after a series of skirmishes in Indian Territory. The surviving members fled to Kansas as refugees, where a number of the men abandoned their neutral position and joined the First and Second Union Indian Brigades. Other tribes, such as the Sioux, were divided among those who supported the move to reservations and those who wished to fight to retain

Confederate Brigadier General Stand Watie

Stand Watie, a Cherokee, was born in Georgia in 1806. He was educated in a mission school and spoke English from a young age. He became a wealthy slaveholding planter and owned various businesses as an adult. He was a leader of the Cherokee faction that supported removal to Indian Territory under the Indian Removal Act of 1830. He signed the Treaty of New Echota ceding the Cherokees' eastern lands, along with his brother Elias Boudinot, his uncle Major Ridge, and his cousin John Ridge. His actions put him at odds with the majority faction of Cherokee, led by Chief John Ross, who opposed relocation and resented him for the suffering endured along the Trail of Tears to Indian Territory. His brother, uncle, and cousin were killed in retribution, but Watie was saved by a timely warning from a friend.

During the Civil War, Watie led the Cherokee faction that supported the Confederacy. He served as a guerrilla and cavalry leader in Indian Territory, participating in such battles as Pea Ridge and Wilson's Creek and capturing the Cherokee capital of Tahlequah from Ross's followers. He raised the first Cherokee regiment of volunteers, the Cherokee Mounted Rifles, and became the only Native American to rise to the rank of brigadier general. After losing faith in the Confederacy, he still believed that Native Americans could prevail. He stated in Gibson's *The American Indian*, "I believe it is in the power of the Indians unassisted, but united and determined, to hold their country. We cannot expect to do this without serious losses and many trials and privations; but if we possess the spirit of our fathers, and are resolved never to be enslaved by an inferior race, and trodden under the feet of an ignorant and insolent foe, we, the Creeks, Choctaws, Chickasaws, Seminoles, and Cherokees, never can be conquered."

Watie was the last Confederate general to surrender. After the war, he traveled to Washington, D.C., with a Cherokee delegation and resumed his life as a planter until his death in 1871.

their traditional culture off the reservations. Members of eastern tribes also participated in the fighting, including noted Seneca leader and Union General Ely S. Parker.

While some Native-American combatants organized regiments and fought in the main military campaigns of the Civil War, others participated in more informal guerrilla warfare in the west. The internal divisions within the tribes, the incidents sparked by the expansion of the mining frontier, and the growing stream of westward migrants all led to both formal and informal conflicts within Indian Territory during the war. Major engagements in the area ended by 1863, but guerrilla-style skirmishes continued throughout the war's duration, leaving death and destruction in their wake. Native-American combatants suffered the same daily hardships of camp life and warfare as other Civil War soldiers, including high casualty rates, poor sanitation and rampant disease, inadequate medical care, and shortages of food and supplies. Veterans faced the same physical and mental problems, while widows and orphans faced the same struggle for survival.

Both Confederate and Union supporters were the victims of raiders who stole horses and cattle and burned villages. Many lived in terror or had to flee their homes as refugees, leaving their fields untended. Cold and hunger were common companions. Native Americans also faced territory reduction and led raids in the Pacific northwest, the southwest, and the Rocky Mountain regions that often resulted in brutal repression. In the southwest, many Navajo died when they were forced to march hundreds of miles during the "Long Walk" to an internment camp called Bosque Redondo in New Mexico. In Colorado, Colonel John Chivington and his volunteer regiment destroyed Cheyenne leader Black Kettle's village and killed hundreds in what became known as the Sand Creek Massacre of November 29, 1864. In Minnesota, 38 Sioux leaders were hanged after an uprising, while others were forced to flee to Canada and the Dakota Territory. Such engagements left many Native Americans in poverty and more dependent on the federal government for survival by the war's end.

Although many Native Americans had hoped that the Civil War would help them preserve their lands and culture, it often had the opposite effect of helping to accelerate the process of concentration and assimilation. New western settlers, miners, and wagon trains had encroached on Native-American lands while the federal government's attention had been on the war effort. Volunteer recruits training for possible eastern combat practiced their skills in skirmishes with Native Americans. Refugees had been driven from their homes by the fighting. Railroads had begun the process of slaughtering the great herds of buffalo that represented a way of life to the Plains Indians. Confederate Native Americans awaited the consequences of joining the losing side. As historian Laurence Hauptman concluded, "And in the deepest irony of all, many fought because they believed it was their last best hope to halt a genocide that had begun in the East in the early seventeenth century, one that continued throughout the Trail of Tears westward in the 1830s, and exploded again after the California Gold Rush of 1849. Yet the Civil War, rather than the last best hope, proved to be a final nail in the coffin in Indian efforts to stop the tide of American expansion."

POSTWAR RECONSTRUCTION

During the postwar period, the federal government renewed its resolve to subdue the Native Americans, settle them on reservations, and implement a policy of assimilation into mainstream American society and culture,

The "Long Walk" and Bosque Redondo

During the Civil War, General James Carleton set aside a 40-square-mile area in New Mexico for use as a military prison and work camp for Mescalero Apache and Navajo prisoners. Fort Sumner was constructed on its grounds and a constant military guard was present. A group of Mescalero Apache that surrendered were the first to be brought to Bosque Redondo. Carleton and his men next turned their attention to the Navajo in New Mexico and Arizona. Navajo men and women of all ages were forced to march over 400 miles in what became known as the "Long Walk." Those who could not keep up were often shot. Other died due to drowning or exposure to the elements.

This photograph of a Navajo woman with a baby on her back is thought to have been taken for the U.S. Army Signal Corps at Bosque Redondo or Fort Sumner between 1864 and 1868.

Bosque Redondo ultimately held up to 10,000 Native Americans in often-deplorable conditions. They lived in makeshift shelters and spent their days at forced labor under military guard. Thousands died from exposure, starvation, diseases such as dysentery and smallpox, and from drinking contaminated water. In 1868, Navajo leaders signed a peace treaty with the United States that allowed them to leave Bosque Redondo and return to their ancestral homes. Many Navajo families lost loved ones, and the story of Bosque Redondo plays a vital role in their cultural heritage as stories are handed down through the generations. Bosque Redondo was eventually designated a state monument.

whether through peace or warfare. The process began with the negotiation of new treaties with those defeated tribes that had sided with the Confederacy. The Fort Smith Council of September 1865 met to decide terms for Reconstruction treaties for the Five Civilized Tribes that had been loyal to the Confederacy. These peace treaties also abolished slavery, granted the freedmen tribal citizenship, ceded large amounts of Indian Territory land that would be used to relocate other tribes in the path of westward expansion, permitted railroad construction through Indian Territory, and set the stage for the eventual creation of a unified government for all of the tribes. The Little Arkansas Council also met in 1865 to set terms for the Comanche, Kiowa, Cheyenne, Arapaho, and Apache, bringing a temporary peace to the Plains. Ultimately, the federal government at this time sought to contain all Native Americans permanently on reservations under its control.

According to historian Arrell Morgan Gibson, the federal government used the reservation system to instill self-sufficiency rather than tribal identity, isolation from western settlers, education, Christianity, and a system of law. Many tribes felt that further resistance was futile and settled on their allotted reservations, but the process was often not smooth or peaceful. Treaties often offered material goods or other incentives to those who resettled on the reservations, but also included provisions forcing them to adopt new lifestyles. Those who settled on reservations often faced appalling physical conditions, poor soils that made growing food difficult, and shortages of basic necessities, as well as the psychological impact of being forced to abandon their traditional way of life. Those who were used to the freedom of off-reservation life

Many reservations were badly managed by the U.S. government and suffered shortages. This 1875 illustration shows workers at the Red Cloud Indian Agency in Red Cloud, Nebraska, distributing rations to waiting Native Americans.

and extensive travel on buffalo hunts found their drastically altered lifestyle particularly difficult.

The federal Bureau of Indian Affairs, which oversaw the reservations, was noted for its rampant corruption and inefficiency. Meanwhile, the continued push of westward expansion meant that more and more white settlers began settling nearby, leading to inevitable conflicts. Horse thieves raided reservation settlements, railroads and hunters accelerated their wholesale destruction of the buffalo, and corrupt traders fueled a growing alcohol problem on the reservations. Conflicts also arose within the reservations due to the concentration of multiple tribes with different traditions onto the same lands and the fact that some accepted assimilation while others resisted. All of these problems fueled the growing resentment among many Native Americans.

When former Union general Ulysses S. Grant assumed the presidency in 1869, he sought to improve the conditions faced by Native Americans through the implementation of what became known as his "peace policy." Grant gave control of reservations to various Christian denominations in hope of maintaining peace and reducing the fraud characteristic of the Bureau of Indian Affairs. The U.S. Indian Peace Commission had earlier traveled to the reservations to study the troubled relationship between the Native-American tribes and the federal government and to make recommendations for the future. Grant had also appointed a Board of Indian Commissioners to help guide the new federal policy. Missionaries sought to convert the Native-Americans and to stop the practice of their traditional religions. Problems arose, however, due in part to competition among the different religious groups given control over different reservations. Another problem was the conflict between supporters of the peace policy and supporters of a more military approach to enforcing concentration and assimilation, resulting in confusion for many Native Americans.

CONCENTRATION

The federal government pursued a military policy against those Native Americans who refused to surrender their traditional way of life and move to reservations and those who rebelled against the dismal conditions found on many reservations. The new military weapons, tactics, and leaders that emerged from the Civil War were now employed against the Native Americans on the rapidly closing western frontier in order to end their ability to militarily resist concentration. War heroes such as General William Tecumseh Sherman and General Philip Sheridan pursued bands of Native-American raiders and destroyed the camps of any Native Americans not on assigned reservations.

In 1875, the military began exiling captured war chiefs such as Geronimo to military prisons in distant locations like St. Augustine, Florida, in order to break their followers' will. Those who fought the army achieved some stunning military successes, including the Sioux's defeat of General George Custer

"I Will Fight No More Forever"

Nez Perce Chief Joseph was born Hin-mah-too-yah-lat-kekt (Thunder Rolling Down the Mountain) in 1840 in the Wallowa Valley region of northeastern Oregon. His father was a Nez Perce leader, Christian convert, and supporter of peace with the United States who had agreed to settle on a reservation under an 1855 treaty. After a gold rush and federal reduction in the tribe's reservation lands in violation of the old treaty, however, his father renounced his new religion and policy of peace. He refused to sign the new treaty that had reduced their territory by ceding the Wallowa Valley.

The Nez Perce elected Chief Joseph to succeed his father upon his death. In 1877, a group of western settlers trespassed on Nez Perce land, resulting in a skirmish in which a number of the intruders were killed. Chief Joseph and a group of several hundred warriors and their families fled the reservation in anticipation of a military reprisal.

Chief Joseph and his followers traveled over 1,000 miles through Idaho, Wyoming, and Montana, fighting well in a number of major battles and minor skirmishes along the way, despite being greatly outnumbered. Chief Joseph surrendered on October 5, 1877, due to the suffering of the women and children and the futility of further resistance. As he stated in his widely reprinted surrender speech, "I am tired of fighting. Our chiefs are killed. Looking Glass is dead. Toohoolhoolzote is dead. The old men are all dead. It is the young men who say, 'Yes' or 'No.' He who led the young men [Olikut] is dead. It is cold, and we have no blankets. The little children are freezing to death. My people, some of them, have run away to the hills, and have no blankets, no food. No one knows where they are—perhaps freezing to death. I want to have time to look for my children, and see how many of them I can find. Maybe I shall find them among the dead. Hear me. My chiefs! I am tired. My heart is sick and sad. From where the sun now stands I will fight no more forever." Chief Joseph spent his remaining years on various reservations until his death in 1904.

Chief Joseph of the Nez Perce photographed in a war bonnet around 1903.

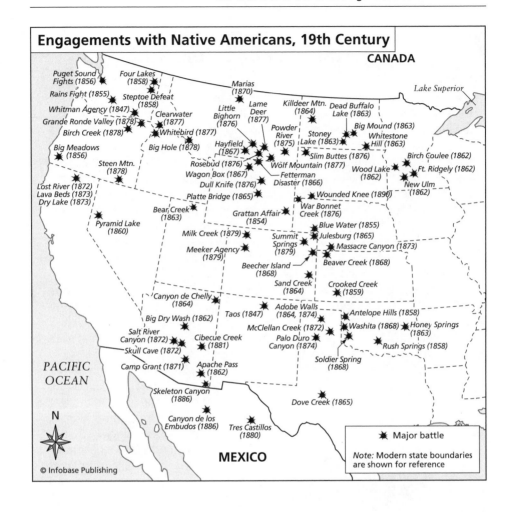

Engagements with Native Americans, 19th Century

CANADA

Puget Sound Fights (1856)
Four Lakes (1858)
Rains Fight (1855)
Steptoe Defeat (1858)
Whitman Agency (1847)
Clearwater (1877)
Grande Ronde Valley (1878)
Birch Creek (1878)
Whitebird (1877)
Big Meadows (1856)
Big Hole (1878)
Steen Mtn. (1878)
Lost River (1872)
Lava Beds (1873)
Dry Lake (1873)
Bear Creek (1863)
Pyramid Lake (1860)
Marias (1870)
Lame Deer (1877)
Little Bighorn (1876)
Killdeer Mtn. (1864)
Dead Buffalo Lake (1863)
Big Mound (1863)
Powder River (1875)
Stoney Lake (1863)
Whitestone Hill (1863)
Hayfield (1867)
Rosebud (1876)
Wagon Box (1867)
Slim Buttes (1876)
Wolf Mountain (1877)
Wood Lake (1862)
Birch Coulee (1862)
Ft. Ridgely (1862)
Dull Knife (1876)
Fetterman Disaster (1866)
New Ulm (1862)
Platte Bridge (1865)
Wounded Knee (1890)
War Bonnet Creek (1876)
Grattan Affair (1854)
Blue Water (1855)
Milk Creek (1879)
Summit Springs (1879)
Julesburg (1865)
Massacre Canyon (1873)
Meeker Agency (1879)
Beecher Island (1868)
Beaver Creek (1868)
Sand Creek (1864)
Crooked Creek (1859)
Canyon de Chelly (1864)
Big Dry Wash (1862)
Taos (1847)
Adobe Walls (1864, 1874)
Antelope Hills (1858)
McClellan Creek (1872)
Washita (1868)
Honey Springs (1863)
Salt River Canyon (1872)
Cibecue Creek (1881)
Palo Duro Canyon (1874)
Rush Springs (1858)
Skull Cave (1872)
Camp Grant (1871)
Apache Pass (1862)
Soldier Spring (1868)
Skeleton Canyon (1886)
Dove Creek (1865)
Canyon de los Embudos (1886)
Tres Castillos (1880)

Lake Superior

PACIFIC OCEAN

N

MEXICO

✳ Major battle

Note: Modern state boundaries are shown for reference

© Infobase Publishing

in 1876. The resisters, however, faced increasingly long odds as the harsh weather and deprivation took their toll. Many realized the futility of further resistance, best exemplified in the immortal words of Chief Joseph. The last of the Indian wars came to an end by the late 1800s, marking the end of the military conquest of Native Americans.

ASSIMILATION POLICIES

In the late 1800s, the federal government and eastern reformers began to increasingly turn to a policy of assimilation to solve the "Indian Question" once and for all. In 1871, Congress declared an end to the treaty system. Instead, Native Americans would be subject to the laws of Congress. Now Native Americans would be treated as wards of the federal government, rather than as separate sovereign nations within the United States, until they were fully Americanized and ready for citizenship. Humanitarian groups known as

Native American Boarding Schools

The curriculum usually included academic subjects such as reading, writing, and arithmetic, Christian religious instruction, citizenship, and vocational training. Males learned agricultural skills, while females learned the domestic arts. Written rules enforced the ban on tribal identity through dress codes and proscriptions against speaking Native languages or practicing Native religions. Most boarding schools were run in a strict, military-style fashion. Common punishments included beatings, solitary confinement, and having one's mouth washed with soap. Students were given American names and rarely allowed to return home for visits. The boarding schools were meant to prepare students for integration into mainstream American society, but graduates often found themselves caught between two worlds and not fully accepted by either their tribes or white society.

Zitkala-Sa (Gertrude Simmons Bonnin), a Sioux from a South Dakota reservation, recorded her experiences at a Quaker missionary school in Indiana in a series of articles that appeared in the *Atlantic Monthly* in 1900. She later attended college, married, and returned to South Dakota to become a Native-American activist. She experienced first hand the trauma of a child's first days at a boarding school and events such as having her hair cut and her style of dress changed. She also encountered the difficulty of reintegration into Native-American society upon her return. As an adult, she understood that supporters of the boarding schools thought they were aiding the children, but she also questioned how well they understood the impact of their actions. She noted that visitors to the schools "walked out of the schoolhouse well satisfied: they were educating the children of the red man! They were paying a liberal fee to the government employees in whose able hands lay the small forest of Indian timber. In this fashion many have passed idly through the Indian schools during the last decade, afterward to boast of their charity to the North American Indian. But few there are who have paused to question whether real life or long-lasting death lies beneath this semblance of civilization."

This March 1884 newspaper illustration depicts a young woman's visit to her family on the Pine Ridge reservation after a stay at an Indian school.

Native Americans lost millions more acres of land with the 1887 Dawes Act. The photo shows horses at a watering hole outside a Lakota camp near Pine Ridge, South Dakota, in 1891.

"Friends of the Indians" emerged to aid the assimilation process. One of the most well known of that era's Indian reformers was Helen Hunt Jackson, an activist whose 1881 book *A Century of Dishonor* achieved national recognition and helped spur efforts to reform U.S. Indian policy. Assimilation furthered the dramatic alteration of Native-American life that had begun under the reservation system.

Many humanitarians and government officials felt that this was the only viable path, as the settling of the frontier left military destruction and extinction as the only other alternative. The policy of assimilation sought to destroy traditional Native-American cultures and lifestyles and replace them with private land ownership, an individual rather than a tribal focus, and a new way of life as farmers and ranchers. The belief in assimilation was tied to a general cultural belief in the idea of the progressive nature of civilization and the responsibility of those further along in the evolutionary progress of society to aid those, such as immigrants and Native Americans, who were not. These reformers viewed assimilation as not only a desirable necessity, but also a humanitarian effort. Assimilation policy often focused on the younger generation of Native Americans through programs designed to separate them from their cultural heritage and immerse them in mainstream American society.

A key component of this separation was education through reservation day and boarding schools, as well as several dozen off-reservation boarding schools that had been founded by various religious and humanitarian groups by 1900. Lieutenant Richard H. Pratt founded the first and most well known of these schools, the Carlisle Indian Industrial School, in 1879, in Carlisle, Pennsylvania. The Carlisle school, with its motto of "Kill the Indian and save the man," became the model for other schools. Children attended these schools from a young age in order to facilitate the separation from their cultural heritage. Many of the schools used military-style discipline, a religious, academic, and vocational curriculum, and strict rules and punishment. Many graduates found themselves caught between two cultures, not fully integrated into mainstream white society, but often shunned by their fellow Native Americans upon their return to the reservations. They also often found that what they had been taught was not applicable to reservation life, as the curriculum focused on preparation for entry into mainstream American society.

Another key component of assimilation policy was the Dawes Severalty (General Allotment) Act of 1887. This act attempted to lessen tribal identity and turn Native Americans into independent farmers or ranchers by introducing the concept of private land ownership onto the reservations as a means of ending the traditional reservation system. Rather than the traditional tribal custody of land—many Native Americans felt that no person could truly "own"

This 1899 chromolithograph poster for Buffalo Bill's Wild West Show depicts a reenactment of an attack on pioneers in covered wagons to promote a performance with Indians from multiple tribes.

Sioux Indians in South Dakota performing the Ghost Dance, which was perceived as threatening, in an engraving published in England in January 1891 in the Illustrated London News.

the land—it would be divided among individual tribal members. Family heads could receive 160 acres of farmland or 320 acres of grazing land, while others would receive lesser amounts. The government would hold the land in trust for 25 years while the process of transformation into individual farmers took effect. The federal government would sell any surplus land to white settlers. Native Americans lost millions of acres of land through the Dawes Act as they became victims of fraud, land sales, and money mismanagement. Despite its failures, the act would remain in effect until the 1930s.

Native Americans exhibited a variety of responses to the confinement on reservations, new patterns of daily life, and attempts at assimilation. Some fully cooperated with missionaries, military officials, and government agents, even finding employment or performing in the popular Wild West shows that toured the country. Others sought to blend new material goods and traditions with their older customs. Many turned to social activities such as racing, gambling, or visiting friends and relatives as ways to relieve the boredom and monotony of reservation life.

Some tribes battled among themselves as assimilation led to tribal fragmentation, and factions developed based on those who accepted assimilation and those who resisted. Many Native Americans experienced feelings of uncertainty, alienation, and dejection, leading to widespread problems such as alcoholism. Most Americans would remain unaware of these problems, however, as public attention turned elsewhere by the beginning of the 20th century.

Some openly resisted despite the threat of brutal repressions, while others chose more passive forms of resistance, such as hiding children so they could not be sent to boarding schools and secretly practicing old customs. The centrality of religion to most Native Americans' daily lives led many to

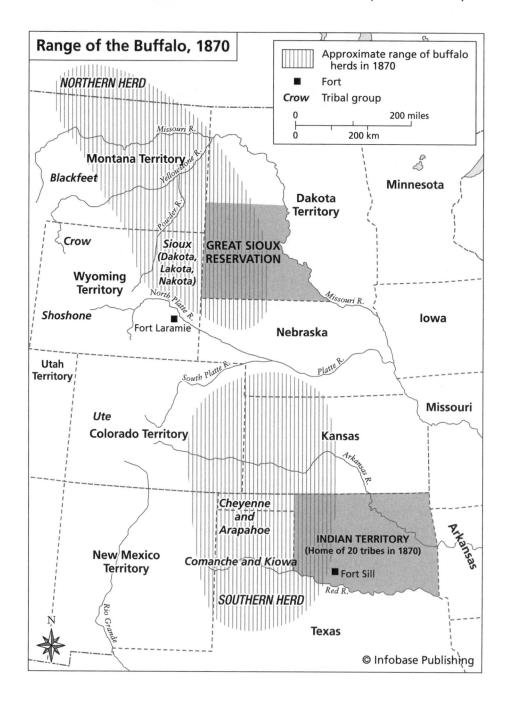

Range of the Buffalo, 1870

Approximate range of buffalo herds in 1870

■ Fort

Crow Tribal group

0   200 miles

0   200 km

seek comfort in prophets who spoke of a future return to the old homelands and way of life. The most well-known example was the Ghost Dance religion introduced by the Paiute prophet Wovoka, whose popularity and promise of an Indian reclamation of the land so frightened government officials that it was banned on some reservations. When the Sioux of South Dakota continued its practice, the military was sent in, leading to the killing of renowned leader Sitting Bull, the escape of Big Foot and his followers, and the massacre of Sioux men, women, and children during the 1890 Battle of Wounded Knee, the last major incident of the period.

MARCELLA BUSH TREVINO
BARRY UNIVERSITY

Further Reading

Adams, David Wallace. *Education for Extinction: American Indians and the Boarding-School Experience, 1875–1928*. Lawrence, KS: University Press of Kansas, 1995.

Armstrong, William H. *Warrior in Two Camps: Ely S. Parker, Union General and Seneca Chief*. Syracuse, NY: Syracuse University Press, 1990.

Bonnin, Gertrude Simmons (Zitkala-Sa). "The School Days of an Indian Girl." *Atlantic Monthly* (v.89, 1900).

Churchill, Ward. *Kill the Indian, Save the Man: The Genocidal Impact of American Indian Residential Schools*. San Francisco, CA: City Lights, 2004.

Coleman, Michael C. *American Indian Children at School, 1850–1930*. Jackson, MI: University of Mississippi Press, 1993.

Colton, Ray C. *The Civil War in the Western Territories: Arizona, Colorado, New Mexico, and Utah*. Norman, OK: University of Oklahoma Press, 1984.

Cottrell, Steve. *Civil War in Indian Territory*. Gretna, LA: Pelican Publishing Company, 1995.

Gibson, Arrell Morgan. *The American Indian: Prehistory to the Present*. Lexington, MA: D.C. Heath, 1980.

Grayson, George W. *A Creek Warrior for the Confederacy: The Autobiography of Chief G. W. Grayson*. Civilization of the American Indian Series. Norman, OK: University of Oklahoma Press, 1991.

Hatch, Thom. *The Blue, the Gray, and the Red: Indian Campaigns of the Civil War*. Mechanicsburg, PA: Stackpole Books, 2003.

Hauptman, Laurence M. *Between Two Fires: American Indians in the Civil War*. New York: Free Press, 1995.

Martinez, David and Elan Penn. *The Legends and Lands of Native Americans*. New York: Sterling, 2003.

Moulton, Candy. *Everyday Life among the American Indians*. Cincinnati, OH: Writer's Digest Books, 2001.

O'Neill, Terry. *The Indian Reservation System*. San Diego, CA: Greenhaven Press, 2002.

Prucha, Francis Paul. *American Indian Policy in Crisis: Christian Reformers and the Indian, 1865–1900*. Norman, OK: University of Oklahoma Press, 1976.

———. *Americanizing the American Indians*. Cambridge, MA: Harvard University Press, 1973.

———. *The Churches and the Indian School, 1888–1912*. Lincoln, NE: University of Nebraska Press, 1979.

Sides, Hampton. *Blood and Thunder: An Epic of the American West*. New York: Anchor Books, 2006.

Tebbel, John and Keith Jennison. *The American Indian Wars*. London: Phoenix, 2001.

Trafzer, Clifford E., Jean A. Keller, and Lorene Sisquoc. *Boarding School Blues: Revisiting American Indian Educational Experiences*. Lincoln, NE: University of Nebraska Press, 2006.

Weeks, Philip. *Farewell, My Nation: The American Indian and the United States 1820–1890*. American History Series. Arlington Heights, IL: Harlan Davidson, 1990.

White, Richard. *"It's Your Misfortune and None of my Own": A History of the American West*. Norman, OK: University of Oklahoma Press, 1991.

Witmer, Linda F. *The Indian Industrial School, Carlisle, Pennsylvania, 1879–1918*. Carlisle, PA: Cumberland County Historical Society, 1993.

CHAPTER 5

The Progressive Era and World War I: 1900 to 1920

THE PROGRESSIVE ERA for Native Americans (1900–17) was a time of change, innovation, and adaptation in the face of enormous hardships. In many ways World War I accelerated these processes, and Native American contributions to the Allied war effort were so laudable that the federal government necessarily reconsidered its discriminatory policies. Still, Native Americans of both eras confronted economic and educational plans designed to assimilate them into the greater American mainstream. These policies left them impoverished, disconnected from traditional life, and undereducated for the demands of a modernizing nation. However, they survived these challenges, and constructed new social and cultural mechanisms to assure the continued existence of unique Indian cultures. Many chose new paths that combined the best of the traditional and modern worlds.

Despite indigenous efforts, the Progressive agenda was distinctly hostile to Native Americans, who were viewed as a "problem." Middle-class reformers dominated the movement, and they insisted that issues of poverty and crime had their root causes among peoples—Native Americans, immigrants, and African Americans—that did not conform to the norms of Anglo-Saxon America. The call to "reform" Native societies was perhaps best voiced by U.S. Supreme Court Justice Edward Douglas White who, in *Lone Wolf v. Hitchcock* (1903), opined that white, mainstream America represented "Christian people" and

Indians were "an ignorant and dependent race." Consequently, the best option for indigenous peoples was to adopt American economic, social, and political structures and leave their old communal worldviews behind. Native peoples were not consulted about these goals, but their survival as distinct peoples was proof of their resolve to adapt to modern America, rather than assimilate.

NATIVE-AMERICAN DEMOGRAPHY

Indians, when considered as a single ethnic group, reached the nadir of their population during the Progressive Era. Their numbers were depleted by decades of warfare, followed by despair, disease, and alcoholism during the early reservation years. Population loss was so extreme that mainstream observers assumed Native Americans were a dying race.

Being counted as "Indian" was not generally a matter of self-identification during this era. Instead, place of residence and appearance were central to the issue. Native Americans in the first column of figures were defined as people living in tribal units that were recognized as part of that body by federal agents. (See Table 1.) Enrollment in the Omaha Nation prior to 1934, for example, required direct lineage to an individual who removed to their reservation in northeastern Nebraska in 1854. It was the responsibility of employees of the Office of Indian Affairs (today's BIA) to maintain, tribal rolls, and, as over 90 percent of Native Americans lived on reservations prior to 1920, estimates of the total population where fairly simple to produce.

The other columns' figures were gathered by the U.S. Census Bureau, which elicited a great deal of information in 1910 using "Indian Schedule Form 8" as their guide. In 1915, it published a 285-page report of the Indian and Native Alaskan populations. Numbers were slightly lower than those compiled by the Indian Office, but the census officials suggested this was partly due to the careless work of their enumerators in remote areas. It was also likely that some Native Americans avoided these federal employees.

Table 1: Native American Population, 1900–20

Year	Commissioner of Indian Affairs Estimates	U.S. Census Returns	Alaska Native Estimates (not included in other totals)
1900	250,000	237,000	30,000
1910	279,000	266,000	25,000
1920	NA	244,000	NA

Those included as Indians in these counts looked like Native Americans physically, although it was well understood that indigenous peoples and other races were intermingling. About 57 percent of the total Native-American populations in the contiguous states were identified as "full-blood Indians." In Alaska, 85 percent were distinguished in this manner. Most of the others were "less than half white," and a small percentage had African-American heritages.

In general, Indian populations were quite young, and most resided in the American west. The average age of Native Americans in 1920 was only 19, a figure three to six years younger than any other ethnic group. Although Indians lived in all states, Delaware and a number of others had less than 50 Native Americans. With the exception of Wisconsin, New York, Michigan, and North Carolina, all sizable populations of Indians were in states west of the Mississippi River. In fact, over 70 percent of the Indian population lived in just eight states: Oklahoma, Arizona, New Mexico, South Dakota, California, Washington, Montana, and Minnesota. Scholars suspect that Indian numbers were undercounted, and great population swings in some places suggest some error in the figures.

As Americans were deeply concerned about race in the Progressive years, the Census Bureau paid a great deal of attention to ethnic stock and language family of the remaining Native Americans. It recorded 280 tribes, although only 77 had more than 500 members. Alaska Natives had 66 tribes of various sizes. It also suggested that full blood populations were in decline, and any increase in Native numbers in the future would be due to further intermingling.

ASSIMILATORY PRESSURES: LAND LOSS

The disappearance of Native American cultures was expected to be a gradual, but sure process. To ease their passage, Progressives promoted a series of programs designed to end federal oversight of all Native Americans and close all reservations. This agenda was to be accomplished through education and land allotment; both these mechanisms of assimilation were implemented during the Gilded Age and eagerly expanded after 1900. The theory was that if Native Americans accepted the responsibilities of private land ownership and competitive economic structures, they would abandon their cultures.

A young Yakima Indian woman photographed in Seattle, Washington, in 1899.

An Indian woman, probably from the Ute tribe, encamped with a teepee, her two dogs, and a horse around 1915. In the early 20th century, the Dawes Act continued to try to force Indians to farm small parcels of allotted land, rather than live in traditional ways.

Allotment began in earnest in 1887 with the Dawes Severalty Act (General Allotment Act) and continued as federal official policy through 1934. Small parcels of reservation lands—generally 40 to 160 acres—originally owned by entire tribes were assigned to individual Native Americans. They were expected to farm the land in the mainstream tradition and live on their homesteads rather than in villages. Native Americans who accepted allotments were promised U.S. citizenship, federal trust protection of their land for 25 years, and vocational training. The ultimate goal was full participation in American society, including voting rights and being placed on local tax rolls. The program was so extensive that 194,000 Native Americans were subject to local taxation by 1910.

Allotment, however, was also meant to satisfy an intense American land lust. By 1920, most good Native American lands passed to white ownership or were placed under long-term lease agreements. The Dawes Act allowed "excess" reservation lands—territory left in tribal possession after all members were assigned parcels—to be sold on the open market. Congressional action and Supreme Court rulings during the 1900s, made the loss of allotted parcels possible. The Indian Appropriations Act of 1902 gave heirs of allotted Native Americans the ability to sell lands before the 25-year trust period ended. These land sales were challenged as violations of treaty rights, but the U.S. Supreme Court dismissed Native claims in *Lone Wolf v. Hitchcock* (1903). The Court insisted that Native Americans had a "relation of dependency" with the

"The Last to Know"

By 1909, many members of the Omaha nation were deemed competent enough to manage their own affairs, and in 1910, their lands were placed on local tax rolls. Only two years later, 90 percent of the lands owned by this group of Indians were in the hands of mainstream Americans through tax foreclosure or outright fraud. The following is excerpted from a speech by Thomas L. Sloan (Omaha) at the First Annual Conference of the Society of American Indians in 1912, in which he argues that the Indians were "treated as arbitrarily as the subjects of the Czar of Russia."

The local communities about the reservation always desire something to be done with it. The representatives of the business people of the town adjoining a reservation desire that the land be obtained in fee, sold or otherwise disposed of, not for the welfare of the Indian, but to enable them to develop business or trade. Business men, politicians, farmers, railroad men, grafters and sharks in the vicinity of a reservation wish it open, not for the benefit of the Indian, but for a larger opportunity for each in his own line. Such influences reach the executive branches of the government as well as Congress more readily than the Indian, and when something is to be done with the Indian land or property under the general guise of some good for him, he is the last person to know about it, through some action taken that affects his property or his income. Among the Omaha Indians, admittedly among the most advanced, there was a new scheme about leasing their allotments. It was discussed at Washington by the commissioner and the delegates from the towns around the reservation, and with the superintendent in charge and the leading citizens about the reservation, but not with the Indians. The last to know anything about it were the Indians. Yet it was their property; they were affected most by any change as to their income or manner which they should get it, but they were the last to learn anything about it and were not consulted as to what might be best in reference to their land. Those people who were consulted were those who had interests adverse to the Indian. They, because of their position or political influence or the two combined, were the first who were given consideration, and those who were most affected, whose rights were being considered, were the last to be notified, not consulted, simply notified."

federal government. Consequently, Congress's "guardianship over their interests" was so necessary that past treaty negotiations could be ignored because Indian agendas might be detrimental to their own well-being. The Burke Act of 1906—described by Charles Eastman (Dakota) as a bill "for the grafters"—allowed reservation officials the option of issuing Native Americans certificates of competency as a means to end the trust period early.

Even Indian Territory was eliminated during the early Progressive years. Members of the "five civilized tribes"—the Choctaws, Chickasaws, Creeks, Cherokees, and Seminoles—and their neighbors were relocated west of the Mississippi River during the Indian removal era of the 1830s and 1840s. As mainstream pressures to make land available became increasingly intense, Native Americans attempted to protect their interests by founding the all-Indian state of Sequoyah in 1902 and then again in 1905. Despite these efforts, a single mainstream-dominated Oklahoma joined the United States in 1907, and allotment of Native American lands began. Uprisings of Creeks and others to resist the process were put down by force by the Oklahoma National Guard.

ASSIMILATORY PRESSURES: EDUCATION

Native children were often forcibly removed from their homes to be schooled in manners foreign to their cultures. Declaring Native peoples "educable," students were systematically isolated from their homes and families, and they were encouraged to assimilate into mainstream society. A collection of institutions was cobbled together that, by 1913, taught approximately 82,000 Native American children—roughly 80 percent of school-age individuals. Mission schools were the pioneers in assimilatory education, and a few remained viable through 1920. Additionally, a system of 25 off-reservation industrial-boarding schools scattered around the United States was founded between 1879 and 1900, and all of the schools remained open through World War I. Day schools for Native Americans on reservations became more common after 1900. Finally, some children of allotted Native Americans were sent to the local public schools founded for mainstream-American children in the districts where excess land was transferred to non-Indians.

All of these schools turned Native-American education upside down. In Native American cultures, the entire community shared responsibility for passing on beliefs, customs, folklore, and material skills from one generation to the next. Mostly, this was done on a one-on-one basis. These methods of instruction were largely foreign to European Americans, who increasingly relied on professional teachers and standard curricula to train their children. Because the cultural context of the curriculum was inappropriate for most Native Americans, students were often given remedial placements. Children old enough to be in fourth grade, for instance, were put in second or even first grade.

While educational settings and facilities varied widely, instructional practice was fairly uniform; Native American students were required to cut their hair, speak English, wear uniforms, and exchange their given names for American names assigned by their teachers. They were taught that being Indian was bad. Discipline was rigorous, and speaking Native American languages was cause for corporal punishment. Finally, they were trained for occupations that were either not available on their reservations, or were already vanishing in the modern industrial society.

These uniformed Indian boys and girls lined up for a photograph at an Indian school in Cantonment, Oklahoma, in 1909.

"Eighth Grade and No More"

Many educated Indians, including anthropologist Arthur C. Parker (Seneca) and Carlos Montezuma, M.D. (Yavapai), criticized the policies of government schools. Parker accused them of being intentionally "low grade" and suggested the educations they offered would not allow Indians to compete in the modern world. He encouraged Native Americans to get university educations whenever possible and then work to advance their peoples. Montezuma concurred with his colleague's assessment. In a 1915 address to the Society of American Indians, Montezuma said:

[I]t should be no longer possible to evade the issue; the responsibility rests with us to be message runners to every camp and to let every Indian know that it remains with every individual Indian to be free.

It is appalling and inexplicable that the palefaces have taken all of the Indian's property—the continent of America—which was all he had in the world. The Indian asks for public school, college, and university education for his children. To refuse such a noble request would be as cruel as to give a stone when he asks for bread. Will the department defray the expenses of any college or university Indian students? The Indian Bureau's motto seems to be, "Eighth grade and no more." And therefore we may assume that the Indian Department does not want the Indian to be educated. It may be wise, and is afraid that they will make too many lawyers who will fight to a finish. It may be that the Indian Bureau fears something may happen from the Indian's knowledge of doing something.

These young Indian women at the Carlisle Indian School in Carlisle, Pennsylvania, were learning how to cook breakfast in a home economics class around 1901.

Girls and young women were especially important in the assimilation process as they were supposed to teach "civilization" to their future husbands and children. Mainstream reformers also believed schooling could liberate Native American women from the excessive labor demanded by their men folk. Women trained at these schools, however, were generally disadvantaged. Reformers failed to recognize that Native gender norms provided Native American women rights and privileges that mainstream women could only dream of at the time. If students lost touch with these gender traditions, they were often ostracized when and if they returned home to their reservations.

Like their brothers, women's educations tended to focus on manual labor, and higher education was discouraged after 1900. Most girls were trained in "domestic science"—an eight-year course. Completion was uncommon, however, and after three years students generally entered the "outing system" where they worked as domestic help for wealthy white matrons. Unfortunately, little work in mainstream communities was available after they finished their low-wage apprenticeships. Consequently, the Indian Office became the largest employer of these young women, and they served as cooks and washerwomen in the school system. Most teachers, matrons, and administrators at these institutions were non-Indians.

ADAPTATION: RESERVATION LIFE

Although assimilation was the policy of the era, most Native Americans preferred to reside on their reservations and generally thought of them as home. In this manner, Native Americans were able to live among their own people and maintain some aspects of their traditional cultures. Still, it was always a difficult proposition. Social and political divisions were common, employment was hard to come by, poverty was endemic, and public health was uniformly unsatisfactory.

Political conflict was common on many reservations during the first several decades of the 20th century. In some cases, very different peoples were confined in the same geographic space by federal agents who saw "Indian" as a single ethnic category. Split-nation reservations included Wind River in Wyoming, which housed Northern Arapahos—an Algonkian people—and Eastern Shoshones—a tribe of Uto-Aztecan extraction. Similarly, Ft. Belknap in Montana was home to Gros Ventres—another Algonkian people—and Assiniboines—a Siouan nation. These groups remained physically and socially separate throughout the era. Even reservations that contained a single cultural identity were divided by centuries of tradition. The Anishinaabe (also called Ojibwe and Chippewa) reservation in northern Minnesota became a magnet for related bands that formerly occupied a vast swath of the northern woods of several states. They were joined by Metis relatives—mixed peoples of European and Native descents. The various bands arrived separately and settled in insular communities.

Making a living on reservations was challenging. Some Native Americans attempted to maintain parts of their traditional economies. Yakimas around Walla Walla, Washington, for example, continued fishing and gathering off-reservation along the Columbia River as allowed in an 1855 treaty. Sixty years later, Meninock, a tribal leader, returned to the shoals of the river with his followers, but was arrested for violating fish and game laws. His argument in protest was simple, but eloquent: "I do not go into the white man's field or destroy his things. I keep out, but the salmon does not belong to him. It is sent free from the ocean by God for my use." The state courts in Washington insisted Native Americans had no right to fish off the reservation, however, and caused the activity to cease, despite the treaty.

An Ute leader known as Buckskin Charlie around the turn of the century.

These Indians were photographed peddling handcrafted baskets and a pair of snowshoes on a roadside on Mackinac Island in Michigan in 1905.

Most tribes, though, had little opportunity to engage in their old economies; consequently, new forms of employment were pursued. Many Native American men sought wage labor on farms and ranches surrounding their reservations. This was preferred work, as it corresponded to familiar migratory habits. Others worked for the Indian Office directly as teamsters and laborers. Women, when possible, continued gathering vegetable foods. They also sold bead work and other arts when there were markets.

Despite these activities, extreme poverty was the norm on most reservations, and the number of very poor Native Americans only increased with the land loss that accompanied allotment. The Census Bureau suggested in both 1900 and 1910 that only about 27 percent of Native individuals age 10 and above were "engaged in gainful occupations." Although federal wards, health care for Native Americans was very poor, and tuberculosis, trachoma, malnourishment, and alcoholism rates were all extremely high. Government reports made this clear in 1903, but adequate funding lagged until 1912. Conditions only improved moderately, even after health care facilities were constructed. Involvement in World War I reduced spending on Indian reservations across the country as the money was diverted to war efforts.

Still, ancient cultural traditions merged with new economic realities on many reservations. Despite the efforts of Progressive reformers, communal values and respect for age-old generosity requirements often superseded mainstream materialism. William Wash, for instance, was a Ute rancher who emerged as a leader on the Uintah-Ouray Reservation. Indian Office employees saw their contact with him as successful because he accepted allotment and by 1903 was farming fodder crops, wheat, and potatoes. By 1912, he and his followers were raising cattle and sheep as the federal agency had encouraged. Wash, however, remained unassimilated to mainstream values. In addition to cattle and sheep, he maintained large horse herds that were not particularly valuable on the market. They were, however, a traditional source of wealth and prestige among Utes. Additionally, most of his food crops were never sold, rather they were given away to feed hungry members of his tribe. Wash's status among his people was enhanced more through traditional generosity than any measure of monetary success, and he acted accordingly.

ADAPTATION: NATIVE RELIGIONS

Native peoples also modified their religious structures on the reservations. Indians in general recognized little or no separation of church and state; and social structures, individual lives, and governments tended to be based on religious activities. These worldviews and practices faced enormous challenges at the turn of the 20th century. Some groups were simply unable to continue traditional practices. Once bison were gone, for instance, Plains tribes that had made the animal central to their rites needed to make significant changes. Most surviving ceremonies were officially banned by 1900 for fear of widespread Ghost Dancing. In response, Indian peoples moved ceremonies underground when possible, adopted practices from other tribes when deemed appropriate, and created distinctly Indian forms of Christianity.

Uintah-Ouray Utes, like many nations, took a number of approaches. They maintained their traditional Bear Dance, but its original meanings were associated with pre-reservation economic activity, and its vitality appears to have faded. They

A 1914 photograph of a bear dancer of the Kwakiutl people, who inhabited parts of the Pacific Northwest and British Columbia.

also adopted the Sun Dance practiced by Lakotas, Cheyennes, and Arapahos. This ceremony called on tribal members to make sacrifices for the good of the entire community. While originally foreign to Utes, its meanings fit their new circumstances. Concern about immorality by Indian agents led to its prohibition in 1913, but Utes continued to dance in remote corners of the reservation. By 1916, the Sun Dance seemed benign to agents who were facing widespread acceptance of peyote rituals on the reservation.

Omahas necessarily abandoned their most sacred rituals because they were performed while the tribe was buffalo hunting. In the early reservation years, many turned to the religions of Mormon, Dutch Reformed, Methodist, and Presbyterian missionaries. By the Progressive Era, however, the most influential denomination became the Native American Church (NAC). Omahas started following the Peyote Road in winter from 1906 to 1907 when Otoes returning from Oklahoma gave them the religion as a gift. The new faith spread rapidly, and, by 1911, about 50 percent of the tribe had converted.

Cofounded in 1906 by Quannah Parker (Comanche), the NAC tailored Christian doctrine to fit Plains religious styles. The church employed familiar ceremonial items such as sage, cedar, and eagle feathers, but worship centered on ingesting peyote—a mild hallucinogen—as a sacrament. Road Men taught that peyote was a conduit to gain access to the spiritual world. They insisted followers reject alcohol, practice monogamy in marriage, and work to financially support their people. Although some states, including Nebraska, permitted the religion, the use of peyote was threatening, and many states and reservations outlawed the practice.

EARLY PAN-INDIANISM

Assimilation efforts also created a whole new class of young Native leaders who were educated in boarding schools and universities. Their ranks included Laura Cornelius (Oneida), Charles E. Dagenett (Peoria), Charles Eastman (Dakota), Francis La Flesche (Omaha), Carlos Montezuma (Yavapai), Arthur C. Parker (Seneca), Thomas L. Sloan (Omaha), and Zitkala-Ša (Yankton Nakota). Errantly labeled Red Progressives or placed in a "traditional" versus "progressive" dichotomy, these individuals were intent on mixing the best aspects of new and old cultures. In many respects these new Indian leaders were showing the beginnings of Pan-Indian consciousness. They were also dedicated to educating mainstream America about the cultural values and intellectual abilities of Native peoples.

Carlos Montezuma was born in Arizona sometime in the 1860s. He was disconnected from his tribe and family as a boy, and would not return to the Yavapai people until well into adulthood. Trained by an adoptive white parent and missionaries, he eventually earned a university degree in Illinois and went on to become a medical doctor in 1889. He used his education to help Native peoples, as a reservation physician and an advocate. He came

Charles A. Eastman

Charles A. Eastman (1858–1939) was born Hakadah and renamed Ohiyesa as a boy, and was raised in a traditional Dakota household in Minnesota. As his maternal grandfather was a U.S. military officer, Eastman grew up in a multicultural environment. He attended Santee Normal School in Nebraska, Beloit College in Wisconsin, Dartmouth University, and medical school at Boston University. Like Carlos Montezuma, he joined the Indian Office and brought healthcare to reservations.

Eastman's familiarity with the dire conditions in Indian Country caused him to become an early proponent of allotment as a means to move Indian people forward. He was still a proponent of Indian rights, however, and he argued the Office of Indian Affairs needed to be replaced by a commission with a membership that was at least half Indian. He encouraged the federal government to respect the terms of all Indian treaties appeared before both houses of Congress, and met with four presidents on the subject.

Like many of his generation, Eastman forwarded the best-of-both-worlds approach, at least early in his life. After listening to his elders, he came to believe mainstream society lacked spiritual depth and long-term economic sustainability. He eventually retired from medicine and returned to Indian traditional life, the best he could reconstruct it. He penned an autobiography, *From the Deep Woods to Civilization*, as a critique of his life experiences, excerpted below:

I traveled over a large part of the western states and in Canada, visiting the mission stations among Indians of all tribes and organizing young men's associations [YMCAs] wherever conditions permitted. I think I organized some forty-three associations. . . .

I was constantly meeting with groups of young men of the Sioux, Cheyennes, Crees, Ojibways, and others, in log cabins or little frame chapels, and trying to set before them in simple language the life and character of the Man Jesus. I was cordially received everywhere, and always listened to with the closest attention. Curiously enough, even among these men who were seeking light on the white man's ideals the racial philosophy emerged from time to time.

I remember one old battle-scarred warrior who sat among the young men got up and said, in substance: "Why, we have followed this law you speak of for untold ages! We owned nothing, because everything was from Him. Food was free, land free as sunshine and rain. Who changed all this? The white man; and yet he says he is a believer in God! He does not seem to inherit any of the traits of his Father, nor does he follow the example set by his brother Christ."

Carlos Montezuma in 1890, the year after he obtained his medical degree.

to understand the challenges of reservation life by working for the Office of Indian Affairs at Fort Stevenson in North Dakota, with the Shoshones in Nevada, and among the Colville Confederated Tribes in Washington State. After a stint at Carlisle Indian School in Pennsylvania, he returned to the southwest to find his Yavapai roots. Aggressive in his political demands and sure of his intentions, from 1901 on, he spent the majority of his time lobbying for Native-American rights. He spoke out against attempts to move Yavapais onto a reservation already occupied by Pimas and Maricopas, as the groups were traditionally enemies. Accepting a broader agenda, he also insisted these peoples were now his friends and championed their rights.

Arthur C. Parker (1881–1955) was born on the Seneca Reservation in upstate New York. His grandfather was likely "full blood," but married a woman of European descent as did his father. Consequently, Parker had no standing in the Seneca's matrilineal government. As a person with feet in two cultures, he grew up both on and off the reservation, but his education was largely in mainstream schools. Although not formally trained in the field, Parker was both an anthropologist and ethnographer, who spent most of his energy studying and writing about Iroquois cultural traditions. He championed integration of Native individuals into mainstream society as Native Americans, rather than assimilated peoples. To further this agenda, he criticized Progressive Era racial constructions. He suggested race was an arbitrary, intellectual construction, and argued that white superiority had absolutely no scientific basis.

Zitkala-Ša (1876–1931) was born to a European-American father and Native-American mother. Like many of her generation, she was educated at missionary and boarding schools where she was known as Gertrude Simmons. After she married Ray Bonnin (Lakota), she took his last name. She was an educator—both at boarding schools and reservation schools—and an activist for Native American rights. Perhaps most importantly, she gracefully bridged two very divergent cultures and was famous for recording the stories and traditions of her Nakota people for a broad audience. She took on the pen name Zitkala-Ša—"blackbird"—in 1901, the year she published *Ikotomi and the Ducks and Other Sioux Stories.* These tales were originally told to Nakota children as a form of entertainment and a means to teach acceptable values and behaviors.

By writing them down in English, mainstream audiences were exposed to Native values as the Native Americans learned them. Zitkala-Ša proposed that these stories belonged to all American children, and she employed them as tools to promote respect for America's indigenous peoples.

To further their collective political agendas, these individuals helped found the Society of American Indians (SAI) on Columbus Day 1911. The goals of the organization were to change the way mainstream Americans perceived Native Americans, and to forward legal compensation for treaty violations and land loss. Their program was supported by an official organ originally called *Quarterly Journal* (1913–15) but renamed the *American Indian Magazine* (1915–20). SAI was the first national organization to house all interested Native peoples under a single roof. Their efforts spawned regional rights organizations including the Alaska Native Brotherhood and Alaska Native Sisterhood, founded in 1912; the Northwest Federation of American Indians, started in 1914; and the All-Pueblo Council League, which emerged in 1922.

WORLD WAR I

Some of SAI's demands were achieved through political work, but the collective actions of Native peoples during World War I also proved to be catalysts for many changes. Young men found ready employment in the military and the chance to reinvigorate an important warrior tradition, which, in turn, allowed some to claim positions of leadership among their people. Other members of reservation communities demonstrated their patriotism to the United States through financial contributions and by moving to cities to work in war industries. The ultimate result was blanket citizenship for all Native Americans.

However, Native-American soldiers still needed to overcome mainstream prejudices. Some politicians and military officers considered all-Indian units at the outset of the war. While African Americans were subject to this sort of segregation, Native soldiers served in integrated units, but they were often assigned or accepted dangerous combat duties. Native Americans were recruited to serve as scouts—a job that required frequent entry into the notorious "No-Man's Land." Consequently, about five percent of Native Americans soldiers died in combat, compared to one percent among American troops in general. Scholars argue that the persistent stereotype of Native Americans as innate warriors led to a disproportionate number of Native Americans assigned to such tasks.

Despite the risks, Native Americans had their own reasons for being scouts. Some chose this course as a means to gain entrance into warrior societies or into positions of tribal leadership. Crows, for instance, needed to perform four specific duties to become chiefs: lead a successful raid, steal enemy horses, count coup by touching an opponent, and take an enemy's weapon. Such feats were not possible on reservations, so the war offered immense opportunity for social advancement.

Whatever their motivations, Native Americans answered the call to arms in 1917 in large numbers. Between 20 to 30 percent of military-aged men served as sailors, soldiers, and aviators in all major military campaigns in the decisive summer and fall campaigns of 1918. These Indian Doughboys set many service precedents. The Choctaw Telephone Squad, for instance, contributed as "code talkers"—a practice that became even more important in World War II. These soldiers—along with some Comanches, Osages, Cheyennes, and Lakotas—communicated in their Native dialects as a means of broadcasting messages that enemies could not decipher. Plains Indians serving as rangers also employed their regional sign language to speak silently among themselves while on maneuvers

Although service records were exemplary, confusion still clouds some details of the military experience. Estimates of the total number of Native American soldiers in uniform, for instance, vary from 10,000 to 17,000 individuals, and it is still unclear how many were drafted and how many enlisted. Additionally, fully one-third of the Native population had yet to gain American citizenship in 1917. Consequently, there was often great uncertainty on reservations about who needed to register for Selective Service, and even who was eligible to serve in the armed forces. Despite these issues, those who opted to fight generally did their best.

This Cherokee soldier serving with U.S. forces in World War I was recuperating from wounds at U.S. Army Base Hospital Number 41 in Paris, France, in 1917 or 1918.

Similarly, on the home front, Native American families purchased war bonds and contributed to the Red Cross. On average, each man, woman, and child purchased $75 in bonds—nearly $25 million in total. Considering their meager incomes, this was an enormous contribution. Others migrated—at least temporarily—to cities to work in defense industries. Despite aversions to farming felt by many Indian men, more reservation lands were brought under cultivation to support the war effort. Following the war, veterans and industrial workers alike tended to return to their reservations where they commemorated the war in a variety of ways. Veterans' organizations became prominent. These included the American Legion and a new organization called American Indians of the World War that was founded in 1920. Additionally, traditional military ceremonies and dances were held throughout Indian Country. Lakota victory dances had not been held since 1876 when they celebrated the Battle of Greasy Grass (Little Big Horn). Other practices appeared to be a mixture of traditional and mainstream influences. The Omaha flag song, for instance, was presented to World War I veterans for meritorious service in 1918. At that time, the colors of the American flag were reinterpreted to fit into an Omaha worldview. Red represented "Indians," white stood for the color of the "ghost of the NAC (Native American Church)," and blue signified the "world of darkness." In the mainstream cosmos, red represented hardiness and valor, white was indicative of purity, and blue stood for vigilance, perseverance, and justice.

CONCLUSION

The Progressive Era in Indian Country was about survival and adaptation. Despite efforts to assimilate Native peoples into the mainstream, most individuals remained connected to distinct tribal groups. Even with deplorable conditions on reservations, populations remained stable. Although dances and rituals were frequently forced out of public view, they continued to be performed so long as they remained vital. Traditional Native American social values, such as generosity and bravery in times of war, were maintained, often at great personal expense. Native peoples between 1900 and 1920 employed a myriad of ways to adapt to their ever-changing circumstances. New religions emerged to address spiritual needs left unfulfilled by economic and environmental degradation. New leaders appeared—some through mainstream educational programs, and others through valorous acts performed during World War I. New ideas about what leadership meant also grew. Some employed new economic methods to fulfill ancient expectations. Others formed Pan-Indian alliances and began to work for Native-American social and political rights. Most remained deeply committed to raising the next generation of Indians and preparing the mainstream to accept their presence.

KURT E. KINBACHER
SPOKANE FALLS COMMUNITY COLLEGE

Further Reading

Awakuni-Swetland, Mark. *Dance Lodges of the Omaha People: Building from Memory*. Lincoln, NE: University of Nebraska Press, 2001.

Britten, Thomas A. *Indians in World War I: At War and at Home*. Albuquerque, NM: University of New Mexico Press, 1997.

Eastman, Charles A. (Ohiyesa). *From the Deep Woods to Civilization: Chapters in the Autobiography of an Indian*. Lincoln, NE: University of Nebraska Press, [1916] 1977.

Hoxie, Frederick E., ed. *Talking Back to Civilization: Indian Voices from the Progressive Era*. Boston, MA: Bedford/St. Martin's, 2001.

Hurtado, Albert L. and Peter Iverson, ed. *Major Problems in American Indian History*. Lexington, MA: D.C. Heath, 1994.

Iverson, Peter, ed. *The Plains Indians of the Twentieth Century*. Norman, OK: University of Oklahoma Press, 1985.

La Barre, Weston. *The Peyote Cult,* 5th ed. Norman, OK: University of Oklahoma Press, 1989.

Moquin, Wayne and Charles Van Doren. *Great Documents in American Indian History*. New York: Praeger Publishers, 1973.

Thornton, Russell. *American Indian Holocaust and Survival: A Population History Since 1492*. Norman, OK: University of Oklahoma Press, 1987.

U.S. Census Bureau. *Thirteenth Census of the United States—1910: Indian Population in the United States and Alaska*. Available online, URL: http://www.census.gov/prod/www/abs/decennial/1910.htm. Accessed February 2010.

U.S. Senate. "Condition of Indian Affairs in Wisconsin: Hearings before the Committee on Indian Affairs." *Turning Points in Wisconsin History*. Available online, URL: http://content.wisconsinhistory.org/cdm4/document.php?CISOROOT=/tp&CISOPTR=6119. Accessed February 2010.

Wunder, John R. *"Retained by The People": A History of American Indians and the Bill of Rights*. New York: Oxford University Press, 1994.

Zitkala-Ša. *Ikotomi and the Ducks and Other Sioux Stories*. Lincoln, NE: Bison Books, 2004.

CHAPTER 6

The Roaring Twenties and the Great Depression: 1920 to 1939

IF THERE WAS one period that signaled a transformation in the ways that American Indian nations and the federal government related to each another, it was the 1920s through the 1930s. During this period, the entire premise of the Indian–federal government relationship changed. The explicit campaign to eliminate Native cultures and languages ended, and a new federal commitment to saving Native cultures and helping them to survive in the modern world emerged. The campaign to deprive Indian nations of their reservations ended, and new mechanisms to allow Indian nations to preserve their lands emerged. The campaign to end any remaining sovereignty left to Indian nations from the seminal Supreme Court decisions of the 1820s ended, and a new commitment to viable Indian governments emerged. Though there is ample evidence that none of these transformations resulted in the large-scale practical changes that their engineers envisioned, the legacy of the changes set the stage, in both positive and negative ways, for the rest of the 20th century.

Non-Indian ideas about Indians during the 1920s bore little resemblance to the daily situation with which most Native Americans dealt. Media attention largely focused on those who had struck it rich during the Oklahoma oil boom, such as Creek Indian Jackson Barnett, who became a local celebrity in his adopted home of Beverly Hills, due to both his Indianness and his eccentricities. However celebrated the rich "oil Indians" were, they numbered between only 2,000 and 3,000, and, like the casino tribes of the late 20th and early 21st centuries, the stories of their wealth were often wildly exaggerated. More often, unscrupulous whites deprived them of their wealth, either through fraud or by having the Native Americans declared legally incompetent, then having themselves appointed as guardians of the Natives' fortunes for as long as the money lasted. For the vast majority of Native Americans not fortunate enough to have oil on their lands, the reality was much harder. The legacy of the allotment era of the late 19th century had taken away approximately two-thirds of tribal lands in less than 50 years. Those lands that were left to Indians were relatively barren and difficult, if not impossible, to farm effectively. However, poverty was only one of the many problems.

THE IMPACT OF FEDERAL POLICY IN THE 1920s

For most of the 1920s, federal Indian policy continued as it had since the Civil War: the forced conversion, relocation, and assimilation of Native Americans, as well as the acquisition of their lands. However, events began to occur during the 1920s that would be the beginning of massive changes in the ways Indians were viewed by the American government. One group of so-called reformers was comprised of those who wanted businesses to have unhindered access to mineral and petroleum resources on Native lands and reservations. These people sought to force Indians to assimilate into white American society and to break up the reservation system. To this end, during the early 1920s, Secretary of the Interior Albert B. Fall continued to issue orders forbidding Indians to perform dances and ceremonials and issued an order opening 22 million acres of Indian land to oil drillers. His successor, Hubert Work, continued these policies through most of the rest of the decade.

While the goal of some American businessmen was to deprive Indians of their resources, the goal of the federal government, as implemented by the Bureau of Indian Affairs (BIA) and its commissioner, Charles H. Burke, was to deprive Indians of their cultures through the elimination of their religions and traditional dances. Christian missionaries, who were active in so-called reform groups like the Indian Rights Association, heavily influenced the attitudes of federal officials toward Native Americans. Ever since President Ulysses S. Grant implemented his "peace policy" in the 1870s, missionaries of various Protestant denominations had come to exercise immense influence over the treatment of Native Americans. Although many sought to curb the worst abuses of Indians in the aftermath of the Indian wars of the 1860s–1880s, their reforms almost uniformly lacked any regard for Native American cultures and lifestyles. Assimilation was considered the only hope for the Indians' survival, and this was thought best accomplished through the forced relocation of Indian youth to boarding schools, where they would be indoctrinated with the idea of the superiority of white culture and the imperative need to incorporate into the American body politic.

However, during the 1920s, there were some new reform voices called the Red Progressives. Led by a New York social worker named John Collier, they advocated the improvement of the Indian living conditions and appreciation of the different cultures. During the early 1920s, Collier became involved in Native-American cultures, an involvement that would dominate the rest of his life. The courts of New Mexico were often very prejudiced against the Pueblos, and allowed white squatters to claim lands that were part of the Indian grants. At the same time, however, the federal government wanted to control the liquor trade among the Pueblos, and thus, the Supreme Court ruled that although the Pueblos had the land grants, they were still under the direct control of Congress. As a result of this ruling, white land claims on Pueblo lands had to be reviewed by Congress.

This ruling infuriated white New Mexicans and they spurred their U.S. senator, Holm O. Bursum, to introduce a bill that would validate white land claims on Pueblo lands. On May 31, 1921, the first Bursum Bill would have confirmed any non-Indian claims of title to Pueblo land, either with or without color of title, as long as they had been held at least 10 years prior to 1912. Due to the numbers of such claimants, such a sweeping bill would have virtually destroyed the Pueblos' land base, and the Indian Rights Association protested the legislation directly with Secretary of the Interior Fall. Fall was able to convince Bursum to rework the bill to be, at least theoretically, more fair to the Pueblos. After meeting with both Fall and Commissioner of Indian Affairs Burke, Bursum introduced his revised bill to Congress on July 20, 1922. It had passed the Senate, and was being discussed in the House when the Pueblos realized what was at stake.

Although Collier, as a social worker who was working under the auspices of the U.S. Federation of Women's Clubs, was already well aware of the issue; by September the Bursum Bill had caught the attention of numerous national and local groups working for reform in Indian affairs. But the issue received even wider publicity within New

U.S. Indian Commissioner John Collier at a Senate Indian Affairs Committee meeting in Washington, D.C., on June 10, 1940.

Passing the Indian Reorganization Act

The centerpiece of Bureau of Indian Affairs Commissioner John Collier's reform platform was the Wheeler-Howard Act, more popularly known as the Indian Reorganization Act. Collier and other advocates had to fight against the direction that Indian policy had taken during the preceding 100 years. Although not all Indians supported the act, Collier traveled across the country in his efforts to convince tribes to support him. Some accused him of using less-than-scrupulous tactics, but many tribes supported the act. The following is from the testimony of Menominee Indian Ralph Fredenberg before the U.S. Senate Committee on Indian Affairs.

Mr. Fredenberg: The self-government title, I understand, will give us the authority to organize and to submit a charter.

I recollect very distinctly that when the last administration came in there were a number of letters written to the chairman of the committee here setting forth the need of allowing Indians to organize, and we felt that something would be done under that administration, some proposal would be offered that would answer this thing that everybody recognizes is a need of the Indians—the right to govern their own lives and work out their own destiny. But while we got some very encouraging letters, and the attitude of everybody seemed to be to give the Indian that thing, nothing has been done. This is the first move I know of of any significance and that at least is working toward some method by which the Indian could get the thing he desired.

Senator Thompson: Can you give me an idea of how you operate, as to your schools and so forth, and how you live; whether you live in tribal relations or whether you live in separate families?

Mr. Fredenberg: We live very much as any other community does. We have our own schools. We operate everything on our reservation out of our own funds, and we have about $1,600,000 in the treasury. We have never cost this Government any money. We maintain our entire life out of our own tribal funds. We have our own milling industry, and we hope to be able to do that continuously. Some of our people are in the lumbering industry and some of them log; others work in the mill, and a large portion of them follow agriculture. They have farms, dairy herds, and modern machinery; not all of them, but a great number of them.

Mexico when it was given prominent space in the *Santa Fe New Mexican*. The entire text of the legislation was presented in the November 20, 1922, issue, and only five days later, Collier's response to and criticisms of the bill appeared. At this point, Collier made it his mission both to inform the American

These men were part of a delegation of Pueblo Indians who appeared before the Senate Lands Committee on January 15, 1923, to protest the Bursum Bill. In the photograph, Santiago Naranjo, Waihusing, James Miller, and Jesus Baca (l. to r.) display canes given to them by Abraham Lincoln as a symbol of his promise that the Pueblos could keep their lands in perpetuity.

public of this injustice and to help organize the Pueblos to fight the bill. Organized by Collier and numerous Pueblo leaders in response to the threat posed by the Bursum Bill to Pueblo Indian lands, water, and by extension, their entire way of life, a meeting took place on November 5, 1922, at Santo Domingo Pueblo of over 100 representatives from all the Pueblos of New Mexico. The meeting was momentous in that it saw the creation of a Pueblo-wide lobbying and political action group, to become known as the All Indian Pueblo Council (AIPC), that would help coordinate Pueblo efforts in land, water, educational, religious, and cultural issues for years to come. What set this new council apart from the traditional council that had met periodically to deal with issues affecting all of the Pueblos was the idea that they could organize to directly impact the federal government's legislative and judicial decisions that affected them, and this was largely thanks to Collier.

The initial passage of the Bursum Bill seemed to many Pueblo leaders to constitute another in a long line of attempts to deprive the Pueblos of their land. Collier's influence on the Pueblos and his insistence that only through organization could the Pueblos overcome this assault on their rights cannot be discounted. Although the Pueblos saw the need to organize to fight the Bursum Bill, Collier helped direct many of the early activities of the council, and was very instrumental in orchestrating the campaign against the Bursum Bill. According to Pueblo council chairman Martin Vigil, it was Collier who organized trips all over the west to raise funds, as well as trips to Washington, D.C., to fight the bill directly. These activities of Collier and the AIPC during the 1920s and 1930s formed the origins of Pueblo activism in the 20th century. From this beginning, Collier formed his ideas regarding the restoration of Native American tribes.

CONDITIONS IN INDIAN COUNTRY: THE MERIAM REPORT

Rather than seeking assimilation of Indians into American society, Collier and other reformers sought an end to the policy of land allotment that had deprived Indian nations of so much of their land base, full U.S. citizenship, improved health and educational facilities on reservations, establishment of sovereign tribal governments with a limited amount of self-determination, and the preservation of Native religions and cultural ceremonies. Their voices may have fallen on Interior Secretary Fall's deaf ears, but, fortunately for them, he resigned his office in disgrace in 1923, the first cabinet official ever to be convicted of a felony due to his complicity in the Teapot Dome scandal.

The photographer Dorothea Lange documented the conditions at this seasonal Yakima Indian salmon fishing village along the Columbia River at Celilo in Wasco County, Oregon, in October 1939.

Living Conditions

During the 1920s, day-to-day life for most Native Americans consisted of effort with little opportunity for success and little hope for the future. This came to the attention of the American public with the publication of the 1928 report "The Problem of Indian Administration" (also known as the Meriam Report). The report, which is excerpted below, detailed the ways in which the U.S. government had failed to live up to the obligations that it had agreed to in treaties with many Indian tribes, and gave evidence to support the assertion, which was still true at the beginning of the 21st century, that Native Americans were the most impoverished ethnic group in the United States.

The prevailing living conditions among the great majority of the Indians are conducive to the development and spread of disease. With comparatively few exceptions, the diet of the Indians is bad. It is generally insufficient in quantity, lacking in variety, and poorly prepared. The two great preventive elements in diet, milk, and fruits and green vegetables, are notably absent. Most tribes use fruits and vegetables in season, but even then the supply is ordinarily insufficient. The use of milk is rare, and it is generally not available even for infants. Babies, when weaned, are ordinarily put on substantially the same diet as older children and adults, a diet consisting mainly of meats and starches.

The housing conditions are likewise conducive to bad health. Both in the primitive dwellings and in the majority of more or less permanent homes which in some cases have replaced them, there is great overcrowding, so that all members of the family are exposed to any disease that develops, and it is virtually impossible in any way even partially to isolate a person suffering from a communicable disease. . . .

Sanitary facilities are generally lacking. Except among the relatively few well-to-do Indians, the houses seldom have a private water supply or any toilet facilities whatever. Even privies are exceptional. Water is ordinarily carried considerable distances from natural springs or streams, or occasionally from wells. In many sections the supply is inadequate, although in some jurisdictions, notably in the desert country of the Southwest, the government has materially improved the situation, an activity that is appreciated by the Indians.

Fall's successor, Hubert Work, was at least honest, and established a commission to investigate the reports that had been flooding into his office about the alarmingly poor conditions on Indian reservations. On June 12, 1926, Work asked the Institute for Government Research to conduct a survey and provide him a report on what conditions were truly like on the reservations and what could be done about them. The chair of the new commission, Lewis Meriam, gathered a staff to travel to Indian reservations across the United

States during 1926 and 1927 to discuss conditions with Indian leaders, BIA officials, and other local residents. The impact of Collier and the other Red Progressives can be seen in the commission's 1928 report titled "The Problem of Indian Administration," which outlined the direction federal Indian policy was to take in the next decade.

Often referred to as the Meriam Report, it highlighted the poverty experienced by Indians nationwide, and the failure of the policy of allotment to give Native Americans a viable economic life. The BIA, which was supposed to fill the gap until Native Americans were properly assimilated, was the main target of the report, and its efforts in healthcare and education were characterized as completely inadequate. In education, the report accused the BIA of exhibiting "the absence of any well considered, broad educational program for the Service as a whole." In healthcare, the report said that BIA facilities were "generally characterized as lacking in personnel, equipment, management, and design" and that doctors and other medical staff had been, on the whole, neglectful of keeping accurate patient records, which is the most basic task necessary for an effective healthcare system. When speaking of Native-American cultures, the report noted, "The tendency has been rather toward weakening Indian family life and community activities than toward strengthening them. The long continued policy of removing Indian children from the home and placing them for years in boarding school largely disintegrates the family and interferes with developing normal family life. The belief has apparently been that the shortest road to civilization is to take children away from their parents and insofar as possible to stamp out the old Indian life."

Although the Meriam Report did much to alert people to the conditions in Indian Country, Collier argued that its recommendations did not go far enough to solve the problems. However, it did begin the process of mitigating the worst of the circumstances on Indian reservations. Even though it would be another five years before the reformers were appointed to positions of power over Indian Country, the report did spur the administration of President Herbert Hoover to appoint a new commissioner of Indian affairs, Charles J. Rhoads, who undertook the first steps to reform the BIA and to curb the worst examples of deficiencies in the ways that the federal government dealt with Native Americans. The reforms might have ended there, but greater forces intervened in 1929 with the onset of the Great Depression, which three years later led to the election of Franklin D. Roosevelt to the presidency. He appointed a new commissioner of Indian affairs, who would push the reforms to what many at the time considered radical extremes.

THE INDIAN NEW DEAL

Although most New Deal programs did not affect Native American tribes much, Roosevelt's new commissioner of the Bureau of Indian Affairs, John Collier, proposed a thorough reform of federal Indian policy, ending allotment,

The Goals of the Reforms of the 1930s

The commissioner of Indian affairs under President Franklin D. Roosevelt was John Collier, who by 1933 had already earned a reputation as a reformer and Indian advocate based on a decade of activity on behalf of the tribes. The centerpiece of his reform effort was the Wheeler-Howard Act, or Indian Reorganization Act (IRA). This act sought to do more to positively change life on Indian reservations than any previous action undertaken by the federal government, largely because it sought to put at least some of the power of self-determination back into the hands of Native Americans. The following is how Collier described the aim of the IRA:

The Wheeler-Howard Act, the most important piece of Indian legislation since the eighties, not only ends the long, painful, futile effort to speed up the normal rate of Indian assimilation by individualizing tribal land and other capital assets, but it also endeavors to provide the means, statutory and financial, to repair as far as possible, the incalculable damage done by the allotment policy and its corollaries. . . .

The repair work authorized by Congress under the terms of the act aims at both the economic and spiritual rehabilitation of the Indian race. Congress and the President recognized that the cumulative loss of land brought about by the allotment system, a loss reaching 90,000,000 acres—two-thirds of the land heritage of the Indian race in 1887—has robbed the Indians in large part of the necessary basis for self-support. They clearly saw that this loss and the companion effort to break up all Indian tribal relations had condemned large numbers of Indians to become chronic recipients of charity; that the system of leasing individualized holdings had created many thousands of petty landlords unfitted to support themselves when their rental income vanished; that a major proportion of the red race was, therefore, ruined economically and pauperized spiritually. . . .

Through 50 years of "individualization," coupled with an ever-increasing supervision over the affairs of individuals and tribes so long as these individuals and tribes had any assets left, the Indians have been robbed of initiative, their spirit has been broken, their health undermined, and their native pride ground into the dust. The efforts at economic rehabilitation cannot and will not be more than partially successful unless they are accompanied by a determined simultaneous effort to rebuild the shattered morale of a subjugated people that has been taught to believe in its racial inferiority.

The Wheeler-Howard Act provides the means of destroying this inferiority complex, through those features which authorize and legalize tribal organization and incorporation, which give these tribal organizations and corporations limited but real power, and authority over their own affairs, which broaden the educational opportunities for Indians, and which give Indians a better chance to enter the Indian Service.

The Navajo, who have the largest reservation within the United States, were one of 77 tribes to reject the Indian Reorganization Act. Above, a field of corn planted by Navajo Indians grows in the Canyon del Muerto in Arizona in the early 20th century.

consolidating Indian land holdings, creating tribal governments, and instituting Indian courts. Collier believed in cultural pluralism, rather than assimilation, and spent much of the first year of his tenure working to lobby the Indian Reorganization Act (IRA) through Congress.

However, opposition to Collier's proposals was swift, vocal, and aggressive. Conservative white assimilationists said that the only future for the Indians was "Christian assimilation into American life." Business interests that had

Livestock Reduction

One of the centerpieces of President Franklin D. Roosevelt's New Deal was the Agricultural Adjustment Act (AAA). The goal of the act was to raise depressed crop prices by limiting production, and to reduce supply of excess grain and meat that were driving down prices. It paid farmers to keep a portion of their land out of production and ranchers to reduce the size of herds. The government bought excess grain and cattle (which it then slaughtered) to keep prices artificially high. Many non-Native American farmers did not accept the basic premise of the AAA because the idea of being paid to grow less went against their work ethic, but the disagreement of some Native Americans with the AAA was on a much more fundamental, cultural level. Tribes like the Navajo and Tohono O'odham (Papago) viewed livestock as more than just a source of meat and money. Peter Blaine, Sr., a Tohono O'odham, explains:

Before the white man moved the Papago Agency from San Xavier to Sells, there was plenty of cattle, plenty of grass, and plenty of rain. . . . The government tried to tell the Papago cattlemen that cattle died on our ranges because of too many mesquite trees and too many rodents. Mesquite clearing had started before I came out to Sells. The CCC [Civilian Conservation Corps] started this around Crowhang village. The government claimed that the pasture grass would be better if mesquite trees were cleared off. But the people didn't like this because the cattle ate the beans of the mesquite trees and, more importantly, the mesquite beans were a native food for the Papagos. . . . Then the government came up with some thought that rodents were eating grass and grass seeds. We ran a little experiment in the Forest Service, just to see if rodents were causing the grass to go away. There were little plots of land where grass was planted to see if it could grow. We put a little fence around each plot to keep any rodents out. Soon after the experiment started we had some big rains. I took Mr. Holst out to the Baboquivari Valley to show him all the grass that had grown after the rains. After all good rains there was grass over all the country. The grass around those plots had grown so high that we couldn't see the fences marking the protected areas. It wasn't rodents at all that hurt our grass. It was just the drought. . . .

I say that we never overgrazed! The thing that cut down our cattle was drought. If drought hits, grass dies. We leave it up to the drought, he'll cut down on cattle. We didn't get rid of our cattle just because someone told us to. The Indians knew that it wasn't rodents or too many mesquite trees that caused the lack of grass. It was the lack of rain. We didn't see any sense in cutting our cattle down; we took our chances with the rain. If it rains, good. If not, then we are hurt. If the cattle are going to die, let them die. But they will die right here on their reservation. Right here in their home country. That was the answer that we gave the white man and his Agency. I fought my boss all the way on this cutting down of Papago cattle on the reservation. The white man never understood our way on this.

leasing rights on the reservations opposed the land consolidation provisions. Even some Indians saw the tribal council system of government espoused by the IRA as another imposition from Washington that would displace traditional leaders and give an advantage to English-speaking Christian Indians. Others considered Collier's concepts of cultural pluralism naive and elitist. Unfortunately for Collier, the legislation that eventually passed, called the Wheeler-Howard Act, was not the bill originally drafted.

What eventually did pass into law in 1934, which became known as the Indian New Deal, did not fundamentally change the relationship between Native Americans and the larger American society, although it did curb some of the worst abuses. It also signaled a fundamental shift in the direction of American Indian policy that would dominate the BIA throughout Collier's tenure. Although the late 1940s through the 1950s would see a hiatus in the reforms and a return to an assimilationist ideal, the wheels were set in motion for the 1960s–1970s move toward self-determination. Perhaps the IRA's greatest impact was the creation of Indian tribal governments with rights and responsibilities like the federal government. The act gave tribes one year to hold a vote to decide if they wanted to adopt a constitution and to set up tribal councils.

After the passage of the act, Collier and his team embarked on a whirlwind tour of Indian reservations across the nation, concentrating on getting key reservations to approve the act and create a bandwagon effect. By 1935, 181 tribes accepted the IRA and set up tribal councils (including the Sioux tribes), and 77 tribes rejected it, most notably the Navajo, who had (and still have) the

A Hopi house in Arizona in 1920. Different groups of Hopis lived under separate leadership in 12 villages, but were treated as one monolithic group by the U.S. government.

A Navajo silversmith at work shaping silver wares by a fire in the early 20th century. The Bureau of Indian Affairs encouraged Indian craftspeople to market their work as a way to alleviate poverty.

largest reservation in the country. Some tribes, like the Hopi, divided into factions over IRA reforms. Like the Pueblos of New Mexico, the 12 separate Hopi villages each functioned as independent cities, with their own leaders and clans. The idea of one Hopi tribe existed only in Washington. Those villages that did go along with the IRA were led largely by English-speaking Christian or Mormon Indians, whereas many traditionalists opposed the IRA. This struggle has continued within Hopi communities into the 21st century.

In the long term, the Indian Reorganization Act had relatively positive effects—restoring lands that tribes had lost in the 1920s, giving the tribes greater autonomy and authority, and ending assimilationist policies in place since the 1890s. But it did not end the poverty many tribes experienced as part of reservation life. The role of the Bureau of Indian Affairs under John Collier changed: it now tried to help Native Americans retain their culture, and even commercialized it so that they could earn money from jewelry, art, blankets, and the like.

The impact of other New Deal programs on Indian Country was less positive. The Agricultural Adjustment Act's ideal of increasing market prices for foodstuffs by limiting supply resulted in forced reduction in livestock herds. This created social problems for tribes like the Navajo, where the value of livestock had much more to do with social standing than individual wealth. However, other tribes welcomed more freedom to direct their own affairs, rather than have the BIA force them to be farmers. Also, the Indian Emergency Conservation Work Program was started in 1933 as an Indian version of the Civilian Conservation Corps. It received $6 million for emergency projects on 33 reservations. This created some tension with the BIA, however, which previously had handled all reservation work projects and now had to share the power to oversee such programs.

CONCLUSION

Although it has been debated just how much impact federal directives like the IRA had on Native Americans on the reservations, and although the next two decades witnessed a return to assimilation as the end goal of federal Indian policy, the 1920s–1930s were certainly a turning point in the ways that Native American leaders and peoples saw themselves and their relationships with non-Indian governments and peoples. The empowerment of tribal councils to at least a modicum of the reservations' affairs was one of the first steps toward the basic right of self-government, which had almost never been granted to Indian peoples.

However, looking at the impact of the changes that took place during 1920s–1930s from a purely financial standpoint, the results were less than impressive. Although the Indian land base ended its century-long downward slide, and some tribes were able to actually acquire new lands, the lives of Indians on the reservations did not improve perceptibly. The funds that were available during the 1930s dried up during World War II, not to return until the late 1960s and 1970s.

Native Americans were, and still are, the most impoverished ethnic group in the United States. Poverty was a basic fact of life on many reservations, framing the choices that Native Americans had to make in their lives. This, perhaps, explains the great movement to America's cities that took place during the 1950s. The failure of the reforms of the 1920s and 1930s to deal with that most fundamental determinant is the most trenchant criticism that can be leveled against John Collier and his reforms.

Steven L. Danver
National University

Further Reading

Blaine, Peter, Sr. *Papagos and Politics*. Tucson, AZ: Arizona Historical Society, 1981.

Collier, John. *From Every Zenith*. Denver, CO: Sage Books, 1963.

Critchlow, Donald T. "Lewis Meriam, Expertise, and Indian Reform." *The Historian*, v.47 (1981).

Deloria, Vine, Jr., ed. *American Indian Policy in the Twentieth Century*. Norman, OK: University of Oklahoma Press, 1985.

Deloria, Vine, Jr. and Clifford M. Lytle. *American Indians, American Justice*. Austin, TX: University of Texas Press, 1983.

————. *The Nations Within: The Past and Future of American Indian Sovereignty*. Austin, TX: University of Texas Press, 1984.

Fixico, Donald L. *The Invasion of Indian Country in the Twentieth Century: American Capitalism and Tribal Natural Resources*. Niwot, CO: University Press of Colorado, 1998.

Hauptman, Laurence M. "The Indian Reorganization Act." In *The Aggressions of Civilization: Federal Indian Policy Since the 1880s*. Ed. by Sandra L. Cadwalader and Vine Deloria, Jr. Philadelphia, PA: Temple University Press, 1984.

Iverson, Peter. *"We Are Still Here": American Indians in the Twentieth Century*. Wheeling, IL: Harlan Davidson, 1998.

Josephy, Alvin M., Jr. "Modern America and the Indian." In *Indians in American History: An Introduction*, 2nd ed. Ed. by Frederick E. Hoxie and Peter Iverson. Wheeling, IL: Harlan Davidson, 1998.

Kelly, Lawrence C. *The Assault on Assimilation: John Collier and the Origins of Indian Policy Reform*. Albuquerque, NM: University of New Mexico Press, 1983.

————. "The Indian Reorganization Act: The Dream and the Reality." *Pacific Historical Review*, v.44 (August 1975).

Lame Deer, John Fire, and Richard Erdoes. *Lame Deer: Seeker of Visions*. New York: Simon & Schuster, 1972.

McNickle, D'Arcy. "The Indian New Deal as Mirror of the Future." In *Political Organization of Native North Americans*. Ed. by Ernest Schusky. Lanham, MD: University Press of America, 1980.

Meriam, Lewis, et al. *The Problem of Indian Administration*. Baltimore, MD: Johns Hopkins University Press, 1928.

Parman, Donald. "Twentieth-Century Indian History: Achievements, Needs, and Problems." *OAH Magazine of History*, v.9 (Fall 1994).

Philp, Kenneth R. *John Collier's Crusade for Indian Reform 1920–1945*. Tucson, AZ: University of Arizona Press, 1977.

————, ed. *Indian Self-Rule: First-Hand Accounts of Indian-White Relations from Roosevelt to Reagan*. Logan, UT: Utah State University Press, 1995.

Prucha, Francis Paul. *The Great Father: The United States Government and the American Indians*. Lincoln, NE: University of Nebraska Press, 1984.

Taylor, Graham D. *The New Deal and the American Indian Tribalism*. Lincoln, NE: University of Nebraska Press, 1981.

Thorne, Tanis C. "The Indian Beverly Hillbillies: Displacement, Rituals of Place and the First Wave of Urbanization in the 1920s." *Journal of the West*, v.46/2 (2007).

U.S. Senate, *Hearings before the Committee on Indian Affairs, United States Senate, 73d Congress, 2d session*. On S. 2755 and S. 3645, Part 2, pp. 110–113.

CHAPTER 7

World War II and the Forties: 1939 to 1949

BY 1939, THE Indian Reorganization Act and other parts of the Roosevelt administration's New Deal, intended to relieve the economic suffering of the Great Depression, had produced a profound effect on life in some parts of Indian Country. However, the effects of the Indian New Deal were uneven. The Indian New Deal had three main goals: economic development on reservation land, Indian self-government, and the protection of Indian civil rights and cultural forms. In terms of land, the program was quite successful. Significantly, it ended the disastrous policy of allotment, which had devastated Native-American landholdings. It also allowed the federal government to purchase lands next to reservations and to turn those lands over to the tribes, or to turn over federal lands through other processes. As a result, millions of acres reverted to Native-American control. Stock reduction programs, though highly controversial, especially in Navajo country, had made ranching more profitable by 1939. Reservations had more paved roads, improved health services, and more water.

Life in Native America was also improving by other measures In terms of population, Native-American prospects were bright. From an all-time low of 237,196 in 1900, the population had risen to 345,252 in 1940. John Collier's New Deal for Indians had provided employment and training for 80,000 Native-American men. Culturally, Native Americans were more visible culturally

INDIANS
AT WORK
JULY 1940

The July 1940 cover of Indians at Work, *a New Deal–era magazine created by the U.S. Indian Service and the Office of Indian Affairs.*

to non-Natives than they had been previously. By 1939, Native Americans were no longer a "vanishing race," as previous generations of white people claimed.

The New Deal did not fix every problem in Native America. Native Americans remained poor and in poor health compared to the American population as a whole. The Indian Reorganization Act had more dramatic effects on larger tribes and in the west than it did on other Indian communities. Some tribes rejected it altogether, fearing new layers of governmental control over their lives and preferring to live under the treaty system. It is impossible to predict how the Indian New Deal would have continued to affect life for Native Americans, had World War II not broken out. War in Europe and in Asia had already begun to influence domestic affairs in the United States, as heavy industry stepped up production of vehicles and weapons. When the first-ever peacetime draft in the United States began in late 1940, thousands of young Native-American men registered.

THE DRAFT

Since most Native Americans were not citizens of the United States during the draft that accompanied World War I, the draft caused some confusion in Indian Country. It also sparked protests and resistance in some quarters. Still, the majority of Native Americans eligible to register did so in relatively short order.

One of the goals of the Indian New Deal was to preserve tribal identity, yet the Selective Service Act made no special provisions for Native Americans in the armed forces (as it did for African Americans, who were segregated from their white counterparts from the outset). Arguments for separate Native units came from two different ideological perspectives. The assimilationist Navajo leader, J.C. Morgan, argued that separate units would allow Navajos to learn English with the eventual goal of assimilating into American society. Collier argued that separate Indian units might foster the preservation of distinct Indian ways of life and reinforce tribes' special status. Though national-level policy made little accommodation for Native Americans' tribal status, the Bureau of Indian Affairs (BIA) oversaw registration on larger reservations. Smaller Native-American communities and

Native Americans Declare War on the Axis

As the United States entered the global fight against fascism, the federal government was not alone in declaring war on the Axis powers. Native-American governments also issued declarations of support, and even declarations of war, against Germany, Japan, and Italy. Jemex Pueblo Indians from New Mexico, Iroquois from New York, and Chippewas from Michigan were among the groups that declared war on the Axis. Doing so highlighted their opposition to the Axis, but also served to show that Native Americans maintained separate, viable, and valuable governments of their own, apart from their recent status as citizens of the United States. Declaring war is an action generally performed by nations against other nations, so Native Americans could also use the show of support to claim their national status within the United States. The following article is from the June 13, 1942, edition of the *New York Times*.

Syracuse, N.Y., June 12—The New World's oldest democracy today moved nearer a formal state of war with the Axis, as Indian chiefs of the Iroquois Confederacy voted to join the United Nations in battle.

A council of chiefs signed a resolution urging a tribal declaration of war by the Confederacy's Six Nations against Germany, Italy, and Japan and their allies with whom the United States is at war. The actual declaration awaits approval of all tribal chiefs of the nations—Onondaga, Mohawk, Cayuga, Seneca, Tuscarora, and Oneida—at a conference July 18.

Meanwhile, the six chiefs who signed the document left for Washington, where on Monday they expect to present their resolution for President Roosevelt's approval, and appear before the House of Representatives.

A number of braves are already in the nation's armed forces. The confederacy embraces about 10,000 members. The Six Nations declared war against Germany in 1917.

The resolution condemned "the atrocities of the Axis nations" and "this merciless slaughter of mankind upon the part of these enemies of free peoples," and added that:

"It is the sentiment of this council that the Six Nations of Indians declare that a state of war exists between our Confederacy of Six Nations on the one part and Germany, Italy, Japan and their allies against whom the United States has declared war, on the other part.

"It is further resolved that the committee shall present this resolution to the conference of the Six Nations to be held on July 18, 1942, at which time the conference of the Six United Indian Nations will be requested to make a formal and solemn declaration of war."

The signers represented the Mohawk, Onondaga, Cayuga, and Oneida Nations. Chiefs of the Senecas and Tuscaroras are expected to affix their signatures later.

individual Native Americans usually registered at their local county clerk's office. The BIA also bent rules to accommodate Native registration by expanding the time period for registration from one to three days on the vast Navajo reservation, and by translating draft-related announcements and documents into tribal languages.

Some Native Americans, and some white officials who acted as liaisons on reservations, were unsure how to respond to the draft. After all, mere decades separated Native communities in the 1940s from the vicious military campaigns of the late 19th century. Some pro-Nazi Americans even encouraged Native Americans to resist the draft. In this effort, they were encouraged by the Nazi regime itself, which had declared the Sioux to be Aryans. The effects of actions like these were limited at best. But sporadic, limited draft resistance did occur, and it did not require the assistance of pro-Nazi groups. The people of Taos Pueblo were concerned that registering for the draft might lead to their hair being cut. Scores of Seminoles fled to the swamps of Florida, rather than face the possibility of being drafted. One official responded by noting that since the Seminoles and the United States had not signed a peace treaty after the 19th-century war, Seminoles were likely to be categorized as conscientious objectors. All but a couple of Seminoles eventually registered for the draft.

Pia Machita, a Papago (Tohono O'odham) healer from southern Arizona, advised younger Tohono O'odhams not to submit themselves to the draft. Twenty-some followers fled with Pia Machita into the wilderness when au-

General Douglas MacArthur meeting with members of the Pima, Pawnee, Chitimacha, and Navajo tribes serving together in a U.S. Army unit in late 1943. Of 42,000 eligible Indians, about 25,000 were drafted and served in World War II.

thorities tried to have him arrested. He was finally captured in May 1941. Three Iroquois groups argued that their young men should not be subject to the draft, pointing toward the treaty relationship between the tribes and the United States as proof that the Iroquois maintained \sovereignty. In the case *Ex Parte Green* (1941), the Supreme Court ruled that treaty rights did not exempt one from the draft. As war loomed ever closer, most tribes experienced an upsurge in patriotism toward the United States. The Navajos and other southwestern tribes that had used the swastika for centuries as an emblem of friendship banned the symbol in 1940, noting it had "been desecrated recently by another nation."

Thousands of Native American men registered for the draft. Some traveled great distances and stood in long lines to do so. Forty-two thousand Indian men were eligible to be drafted, and by March 1941, the BIA had registered 7,500, mainly in the southwest. Eventually, approximately 25,000 of those eligible did serve in the U.S. military. Native Americans may have had a higher rate of military participation during World War II than any other ethnic or racial group in the United States—it is not possible to confirm this assertion, though people at the time seemed to believe it. The attack on Pearl Harbor and the experience of being drafted to serve in the U.S. military in majority-white units drew Native Americans and their white counterparts together emotionally and physically, in ways that would have a lasting effect on Native-American life and on the white perception of Native Americans in the 20th century.

LIFE IN THE MILITARY

For Native Americans in some parts of the country, or with dark skin, or those who happened to also have African ancestry, service was confined to African-American units. Their treatment and experience during the war was very different from that of other parts of the military. The penalty for resisting Jim Crow could be severe. In Virginia, some members of the Rappahannock tribe were told to report to an all-black office. They refused to go, claiming their Native-American status, and were sentenced to six months in prison for violating the Selective Service Act. Other southern tribes had similar issues, though they did not usually end in jail time. Dark-skinned Choctaws from Mississippi, and some North Carolina Cherokees, were drafted into black regiments, in spite of the fact that they were recognized by the BIA as members of distinct cultural groups. Other, lighter-skinned Native Americans served in white units.

The War Department did relax some of its earlier opposition to Indian distinctiveness when it allowed some groups—most notably Navajos—to attend special training camps where instruction in English complemented instruction in soldiering. The main motivation for this all-Navajo program was to facilitate the incorporation of Navajos into majority-white units.

Upon being drafted or enlisting, most young Indian men's experiences varied little from those of thousands of other young American men. For many Native Americans, camp life marked their first long-term, intensive exposure to white people and vice versa. Army records did not distinguish Native Americans from other soldiers, so it is difficult to trace every aspect of Native involvement in the war. Native Americans were perceived by whites as something of a curiosity, and their exploits were often written about in the press, occasionally accompanied by photographs of young men in military uniform wearing headdresses.

FIGHTING WORLD WAR II

The U.S. Army, as it prepared to fight in Europe, Africa, and Asia, was profoundly regional in nature. Young men began their military lives with people from their counties, states, and regions. So, in areas that had higher concentrations of Native Americans, Indians formed a larger percentage of military men. One such unit, the 45th Army Infantry Division, was built on the foundation of previous National Guard units from Oklahoma and New Mexico. This unit, which fought during World War I and was revived in 1941, was about 20 percent Native American. In World War I, the uniforms of the 45th featured a swastika. When they went to war in Europe in the 1940s, the swastika had been replaced by a Thunderbird.

Even before Native Americans deployed for combat duty, the press had already devised the overarching narrative of their service. Since the stereotype of Native Americans insisted that they were descended from proud warriors of the past, they were obviously well suited to the rigors of combat. Glowing press reports mentioned individual Indians' skills with bayonets and rifles as evidence of their racial characteristics. One military-themed magazine noted that "the red soldier is tough. Usually he has lived outdoors all his life, and lived by his senses; he is a natural Ranger. He takes to commando fighting with gusto. Why not? His ancestors invented it." Even Germans praised Native-American fighting abilities, though it is not clear whether this was simply a form of propaganda. One general noted that "the most dangerous of American soldiers is the Indian. . . . He is the only American soldier (one) needs to fear." Native Americans were perceived to be more suited to fighting than their non-Native counterparts.

This kind of treatment continued throughout the war and extended to groups from regions without strong warrior traditions, in the Midwest, Pacific northwest, and the former Indian Territory, Oklahoma. Individual non-Native soldiers played into the stereotype, invariably nicknaming the few Native Americans in the unit "Chief."

Few non-Native Americans, outside of certain regions, had ever seen or had extensive contact with Native Americans, and soldiers giving each other nicknames was a way of cementing a bond that had to last in the life-

Ira Hayes at Iwo Jima

Ira Hayes was born on the Pima (Akimel O'odham) reservation in Arizona in the 1920s, and he enlisted in the Marine Corps after Pearl Harbor, as did many Navajos from the nearby Navajo reservation. His motives for enlisting, and many of the details of his early life, are not precisely known, though a broad sketch is possible. The Pimas, in spite of harsh treatment at the hands of the federal government and conflicts over water and land rights, identified deeply with the United States. Hayes had served in the Civilian Conservation Corps–Indian Division (or CCC-ID) during the New Deal. One of his closest friends, a white Marine named Arthur Stanton, described Hayes's motives as stemming from a desire to live up to the example of his ancestors, who, Stanton said, "roamed the vast plains of the great West, proud and free." It is unclear if Hayes actually believed this, but it is possible that both Hayes and Stanton believed some nomadic, warrior spirit pervaded the Pimas, who had in reality been sedentary for hundreds of years.

In February 1945, Hayes and other Marines battled their way to the summit of Mount Suribachi, an extinct volcano on Iwo Jima. Six Marines raised the flag there, and the image was captured by photographer Joe Rosenthal. The iconic shot rapidly became one of the most-reproduced photographs of the war. Realizing the bond-selling possibilities of the image, the Marines sought out the six individuals involved, only to find out that three of them had died in the fighting afterward. The survivors were whisked back to the United States. Hayes requested to remain with his unit, but was overruled.

Hayes and his fellow Marines toured the United States selling war bonds. Hayes was uncomfortable with his celebrity status and often responded to effusive praise by arguing that the men who died in the fighting were the real heroes. He won recognition from the National Congress of American Indians and the American Indian Veterans Association. After the war was over, Hayes hoped that his fame would fade and that he might be able to live a normal life in Arizona, but he was not so fortunate. To be sure, he was proud of his Pima heritage, and proud of his service, but he never considered himself a hero. He died in 1955 of exposure related to alcoholism.

Many Native Americans, both within and outside the military, still look to Hayes as a source of racial pride and a symbol of service to the United States.

Pima Indian Ira Hayes is depicted among the soldiers in the U.S. Marine Corps memorial sculpture in Washington, D.C.

A U.S. Marine Corps photo of Battle of Iwo Jima veteran Ira Hayes.

and-death situations posed by combat duty. By the 1940s, many white Americans were willing to extend some fellow-feeling to Native Americans. Far fewer would extend the same to African Americans, and the U.S. Army strictly segregated African Americans from the rest of the army (segregation extended to the women's auxiliaries and to the blood used for transfusions).

The combination of the largely stereotyped press coverage and the fact that the armed forces did not collect much useful data specifically about Native Americans (compared to African Americans, for instance) make it difficult to generalize about the overall experiences of Native Americans in combat. There were, of course, many great stories, some quite well known at the time.

The best-known stories may be those of Ira Hayes, who helped raise the flag at Iwo Jima, and the Navajo code talkers. But Ira Hayes's story, dramatic as it was, had little to nothing to do with race. It was publicized, in part, because of his race, but it is not terribly difficult to imagine other, non-Native soldiers performing the same courageous duty.

NATIVE-AMERICAN SOLDIERS
Joseph "Jocko" Clark, an Oklahoma Cherokee, attended the U.S. Naval Academy at Annapolis, and rose to the rank of admiral. General Clarence Tinker, an Osage, commanded air corps units in Hawaii before he was shot down in the Battle of Midway in 1942. Lower down the chain of command, ordinary soldiers—Native and non-Native alike—did extraordinary things when the situation demanded.

Ernest Childers, a Creek from Oklahoma, won the Congressional Medal of Honor for his heroism in the Allied invasion of Italy. Childers, a member of the 45th Army Infantry Division, broke his foot in April 1943 in an assault on German positions near the town of Oliveto. In spite of his broken foot, he managed to kill five enemy soldiers, capture another, and take out a German machine gun that had slowed American progress. While he recuperated from his injuries, he learned that his platoon was again under fire. Undaunted, he returned to battle and charged a German machine-gun nest, eliminating it.

Navajo Code Talkers

The Marine Corps began recruiting Navajo speakers in 1942 at the suggestion of a white civilian, Philip Johnston. Johnston was the son of a missionary in Navajo country and was aware of how few non-Navajos spoke the language. Johnston reported to Major James Jones in San Diego that even German anthropologists who had studied Navajo culture in the 1930s had ignored what they felt was a complex and frustrating language. The code, devised by Navajos and based on their language, impressed the military command, who approved the recruitment of nearly 30 Navajos and established the 382nd Platoon.

The code itself was remarkable. It was essential that the code be simple enough to understand in the heat of combat, and that it refer to specific aspects of modern military life, many of which were absent from Navajo reservation life. Two related codes emerged. One represented letters in the English alphabet with Navajo words, allowing the code to refer to specific islands that had no names in Navajo. The other, better-known code replaced military terminology with Navajo words (including some racial stereotypes). For example, "Japan" became *behnaalitsoiso*, meaning "slant eye." The United States was *nehemah*, or "our mother," and the Corps was *din-heh-ih*, or "clan." Other code words included *annasozi*, or "cliff dwelling," for "fortification"; *tsidi*, or "bird" for airplane; and *tsisi-be-wol-doni*, or "bird shooter," for "anti-aircraft gun."

As soon as the Navajos made it to Guadalcanal in 1942, the new code was put into use. The code talkers risked extreme danger—and not only because their huge radio packs made them targets for Japanese soldiers. On more than one occasion, code talkers were captured by Americans who assumed they were Japanese. Of the 450 who served, eight code talkers were killed in action. In the campaign for Iwo Jima, Navajo code talkers transmitted 800 messages flawlessly. The Navajo code was never cracked by Axis intelligence. The code was declassified in 1968, but long before that, Navajos had begun to take stock of their contribution to the American war effort. Individual code talkers reported feeling that they, as Navajos, had contributed something vital to the United States.

Navajo code talkers using a portable radio in December 1943 on the island of Bougainville.

Sergeant Nathaniel Quinton aided in turning back a German attack in November 1944, and superior officers reported that he killed or wounded 55 German soldiers in the process. He was later captured, but fought his way free, taking with him some maps detailing Germans positions. Herbert Bremner, a Tlingit, helped repulse a German attack in Holland; Houston Stevens, an Oklahoma Kickapoo, was aboard a landing craft that had been strafed by a German plane. He manned the machine gun mounted on the boat and managed to discourage another attack. Leonard Webber, an Idaho Shoshone, ran messages back and forth under fire in the island campaign in the Pacific.

Again and again, Native-American soldiers displayed bravery on the battlefield. As Kenneth Townsend, one of the leading scholars of World War II noted, though, these men "were typical of American soldiers in both theaters of war—not American Indian soldiers, but soldiers. Race commanded no role in displays of courage. . . . A warrior spirit did not propel these men into action." As most American soldiers did, they fought for their comrades, to do their duty, and to stay alive.

White soldiers were interested in Native-American religions in the field, and some Native Americans grew more familiar with Protestant and Catholic traditions. Native-American religions were one aspect of Native-American life that very few white people had any experience with or knowledge of. Indian communities blessed young men before they went to war, and Native medicine protected Native Americans on the battlefield. White soldiers were fascinated by tribal customs and viewed them as strange or exotic. As the war progressed, white soldiers began to take Native-American spirituality more seriously.

Native Americans fought alongside whites in regular army units, but many fought in the navy, where their exploits were not as well publicized, and some fought in special capacities, whether as Marines or members of the Signal Corps. In the Army Signal Corps, white officers recognized the utility of Native-American languages and began to train Native Americans as radio operators. From 1940 to 1942, Ojibwes, Pueblos, Oneidas, Sac, Fox, and Comanches served in the Army Signal Corps as radiomen. Their numbers remained small, however. Unlike the Marine Corps, the Army Signal Corps did not understand how useful Native language skills were to the war effort.

The Native-American war effort, just like the larger American war effort, was not exclusively male. Some 800 Native-American women joined women's auxiliary units such as the Women's Army Corps (WACs) and the Women Accepted for Volunteer Emergency Service (WAVES), while others worked as nurses. Even within the United States, Native-American women took on new roles, actively participating in civil defense and other activities.

THE HOME FRONT

World War II reshaped the United States as a whole, and Native America was no exception. In some ways, the Native-American home front was very much

This young Native American worked at the Atchison, Topeka, and Santa Fe Railroad yard in Winslow, Arizona, in 1943. As many as 40,000 Indians, one-quarter of whom were Navajo, worked in off-reservation war industries during World War II.

like the American home front as a whole. Families prayed for their loved ones' safe return from overseas, and communities performed religious rituals to reinforce their core beliefs. Women went into areas of employment and roles formerly reserved for men, and most Native-American communities got fully behind the wartime mobilization effort. As federal money was reallocated to fight the war, spending on the New Deal tapered off and finally ceased. The Civilian Conservation Corps and its Indian Division ceased operations. The shock to tribal communities from such funding drop-offs was more than made up for by the rise in off-reservation employment and higher wages that resulted. Native-American communities, however, had special relationships

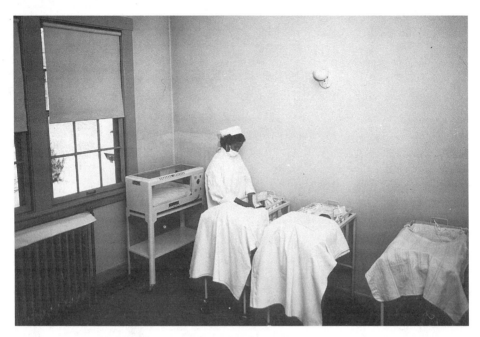

As white doctors and nurses left Indian hospitals during the war, some of their roles were eventually filled by Native Americans and a few African Americans, such as this black nurse caring for infants in the nursery of the Sante Fe Indian Hospital in New Mexico in 1951.

to the federal government and depended on congressional appropriations to a greater extent than other American communities. When this crucial source of funding was cut off, Native-American communities could suffer rapidly and many of the gains of the New Deal could be eradicated.

Native-American health services suffered dramatically during the war, and would take some time to recover. As doctors and nurses were diverted from Indian communities to serve the armed forces, Indian access to healthcare declined. Ninety reservation hospitals were in operation in 1940, and 13 of these had closed by 1944. One possible alternative to the diversion of white medical personnel was the hiring of African-American nurses, but this idea fell through when Native Americans realized the depth of racial prejudice among white reservation workers. Some communities, such as the Crows and Pueblos, took advantage of the decline in the number of white nurses to train more Native Americans as hospital ward attendants who might go on to become nurses once the war was over.

Forty thousand Native Americans left reservations to work in war-related industries in urban areas around the United States. Of these, 10,000 were Navajos. Many Navajo men found work building an army ordnance depot in New Mexico. Others worked in aircraft plants and shipyards. Of the 40,000 off-reservation workers, more than 10,000 were women. Boarding schools offered young women training in sheet metals, welding, and other essential skills for the war effort. Native-American women were not the only women who experienced drastic change in their status and role during World War II, but Native-American women were able to choose options for themselves that could scarcely be imagined in traditional communities. Choosing to leave a reservation was more than an act of self-liberation, though. It could also strain the bonds between people and their tribes, their ties to specific places, and their very cultural identity.

Cities with major defense industries, such as Los Angeles, Chicago, New York, and Detroit, saw their Native-American populations jump during the war. Often tribal members sought employment in the nearest regional center, then relocated to a metropolis once information was learned about where the highest wages could be earned. In this arena, Native experiences diverged substantially from those of African Americans, who were largely excluded from high-paying jobs, and then, after these jobs became open to them, were discriminated against in other ways.

Tribes with the capacity to do so contributed monetarily to the war effort. Some groups set aside funds for the purchase of bonds, while others held fundraisers. Pueblo dancers went on tour in 1943 and 1944 and used the hundreds of thousands of dollars they earned to purchase bonds. Other tribes participated in scrap metal drives. The war saw increased demand for Native-American agricultural products and livestock, along with a rise in the prices of those commodities, so some Native-American farmers and ranchers managed to do quite well for themselves during the 1940s. Overall, however, tribal finances and services declined over the course of the war.

CONCLUSION

The end of the fighting presented individual Native Americans, and the communities to which they belonged, with a significant choice. World War II had opened the path to acculturation and white acceptance in a way that other, earlier developments—from the Dawes Act to the boarding schools to the New Deal—had not. It might have been possible, if Native Americans so desired, to win full inclusion into the United States. However, making that choice necessitated leaving tribal communities and even tribalism itself behind, and Native Americans as a people had no desire to see this happen.

The united front that Native Americans had put up during the war, and the glowing reports of Indian accomplishments on battlefields around the world had led many legislators to conclude that Native Americans wanted total inclusion in all aspects of life in the United States. From the legislators' perspective, this would bring about an end of Indians' special status and the appropriations that derived from Congress as a result of this status. Some congressional leaders began to push for an all-out cessation, or termination, of the tribes as governmental entities, even as reduced services on some reservations threatened

Abandoned barracks from World War II at the U.S. Navy base at Fort Mears in the Aleutian Islands. Almost 900 Aleuts were forcibly removed from the Aleutian and Pribilof Islands and interned in camps in southeast Alaska, where 74 died.

The Aleutian Evacuation

Alaska was a territory of the United States when war with the Axis powers broke out in 1941, and some American military planners feared that a Japanese invasion might be able to roll up the Aleutian island chain, in spite of tough conditions, and thus possibly gain a toehold on mainland North America. As a result, considerable military resources were poured into the Aleutian Islands and into Alaska in general. The activity surrounding the mobilization brought federal dollars and workers into the territory, and significantly altered Native Alaskan and Aleutian ways of life.

The Aleut people suffered immeasurably as the result of a well-intentioned, but atrociously executed evacuation of their home islands. Though springing from a more positive motive than Japanese-American internment, the results were similar. After Japanese forces occupied Attu and Kiska, the U.S. Navy sent a ship to round up Aleuts against their will. Almost all Natives were required to leave, though some whites were allowed to stay. The Navy even broke families apart along racial lines. About 900 Aleuts were taken from their homes to unsanitary camps where they were quarantined by local residents. Children and the elderly suffered the harshest effects of the diseases that tore through the camps. Scores of Aleuts perished under such conditions. When they returned home, they found that their villages had been used to house military personnel, some of whom had vandalized their homes and appropriated their belongings. Some measure of justice was achieved in the 1980s, when Aleuts and Japanese Americans were both included in World War II redress measures signed by President Ronald Reagan in 1988. A $5 million trust fund was established, $1.4 million was designated to compensate for lost church property, and surviving Aleuts received $12,000 each.

a return to pre-Indian New Deal conditions. Furthermore, if Native Americans did not have a relationship with the federal government, they would risk being subjected to the worst impulses of state-level governments, many of which openly discriminated against Native Americans by refusing them the right to vote. Bolstered by their wartime experiences, Native Americans took on increasingly public, vocal roles to secure their rights as Americans. In 1944, the National Congress of American Indians was formed in Denver, Colorado, to achieve self-determination: Native Americans could chart an assimilationist or a tribalist course, but it was their choice to make.

The federal government continued to take a leading role in Native-American affairs after the war. Those who preferred to disband the tribes passed the Indian Claims Commission Act in 1946. In its original form, many tribal leaders supported it, eager to have a federal body hear their land claims. Congressional wrangling changed the character of the law, however, into something that would bring about a final reckoning between the tribes and the federal government, after which Native-American governments would cease to exist. After Harry Truman won the presidency in 1948, pressure mounted from both Democrats and Republicans to proceed with termination, a process by which the U.S. government sought to assimilate Native Americans into American society.

MATTHEW JENNINGS
MACON STATE COLLEGE,

Further Reading

Bernstein, Alison R. *American Indians and World War II: Toward a New Era in Indian Affairs.* Norman, OK: University of Oklahoma Press, 1991.

Calloway, Colin G. *First Peoples: A Documentary Survey of American Indian History.* Boston, MA: Bedford/St. Martin's, 2004.

Cole, Terrence M. "Jim Crow in Alaska: The Passage of the Alaska Equal Rights Act of 1945." *Western Historical Quarterly,* v.23 (November 1992).

Edmunds, R. David, Frederick E. Hoxie, and Neal Salisbury. *The People: A History of Native America.* Boston, MA: Houghton Mifflin, 2007.

Fixico, Donald L. *Termination and Relocation: Federal Indian Policy, 1945–1960.* Albuquerque, NM: University of New Mexico Press, 1986.

Kohlhoff, Dean. *When the Wind Was a River: Aleut Evacuation in World War II.* Seattle, WA: University of Washington Press, 1995.

Philp, Kenneth R., ed. *Indian Self-Rule: First-Hand Accounts of Indian-White Relations from Roosevelt to Reagan.* Logan, UT: Utah State University Press, 1995.

CHAPTER 8

The Civil Rights Era: 1950 to 1969

NATIVE AMERICANS FACED the immediate postwar years with many of the same emotions as other Americans. Many were proud to have served their country, and they looked forward to a future of peace and prosperity. But unlike most other Americans, Native Americans faced a major choice—whether to continue to strive for inclusion into life in the mainstream United States, or to press for rights as members of tribal communities. At the same time, Native Americans faced a special sort of threat from the federal government: the termination of their tribes.

The United States did not intend to eradicate Native Americans, but some politicians demanded a cessation of the relationships—some of them based on treaties signed in the late 18th century—between Native-American nations and the United States. Also in the aftermath of World War II, the U.S. government offered incentives to Native Americans to relocate from reservations to urban areas to search for employment. Termination and relocation were the twin pillars of U.S. Indian policy in the 1950s. Although a look at federal policy is too broad to encompass every single Native-American community, most communities had to deal with these dangers to their existence before the decade was out.

Because of these threats, and in the midst of the Civil Rights Movement of the 1960s, there was a wave of decentralized Native-American activism beginning in the late 1950s and running through the 1970s. This movement, which has been called Red Power, began to address the need for reconciling Native identity, in an era when few Indians lived as they had done a century earlier, and many had moved to cities. Native Americans wanted to modernize—that is, they wanted equal access to healthcare and education opportunities, they wanted the same standard of living as other Americans, and they wanted these things on their own terms, not doled out as a gift from a paternalist federal government. However, many of them also wanted to preserve, in some fashion, the old ways and Native traditions, whether that meant following Native religions, reviving cultural traditions, or learning the Native languages that had begun to die out.

In 1950, the U.S. census counted 357,499 Native Americans. This number represented an increase of 3.5 percent from the 1940 figure. Notably, the 1950 census was the last in which racial classifications were made by census takers. In 1960, and in every census thereafter, people have been able to self-identify racially (the system changed again in 2000 to allow people to self-identify as multiracial or to "check more than one box"). In 1960, the U.S. census recorded a Native-American population of 523,591. This astounding 46.5 percent increase seems less surprising in light of the changing methods of collecting information.

ROOTS OF TERMINATION

Though termination dominated the scene in the 1950s, termination-like policies had been floated by some legislators in the World War II era. In fact, the Indian Claims Commission, established in 1946, can be seen as a sort of final reckoning of Indian land claims, to be followed by the end of tribal status. Fortunately for tribal governments, so many tribes filed claims that the commission worked until 1978, by which time federal policy toward Native Americans had experienced major changes and had moved away from termination.

Republicans took control of Congress in 1946, and pushed hard for termination. Democrat Harry Truman won the presidential election in 1948, and though he battled with Congress when it came to African-American civil rights, he left the wrangling over Indian policy primarily to legislators. Indeed, one of the major narratives of U.S. Indian policy in the 1950s was the shift away from the presidential model (with Franklin Roosevelt, Harold Ickes, and John Collier dominating the scene) to more of a legislative-centered model.

Truman appointed Dillon S. Myer to the post of Indian Commissioner. Myer, a veteran of the New Deal and the director of the War Relocation Authority (which supervised the 120,000 Japanese Americans relocated from the West Coast during World War II), reasoned that it was time to move Native Americans "out of the shadow of federal paternalism and into the sunlight of full independence." Myer wholeheartedly approved of the 1924 Indian Citizenship Act, but thought the Indian Reorganization Act was poor policy because it set

Native Americans apart from the rest of society and exoticized them unnecessarily. Myer addressed the National Congress of American Indians (NCAI) in Bellingham, Washington, in 1950, and noted that on his watch the Bureau of Indian Affairs (BIA) would tend toward self-determination for Indians. As it turned out, Myer's vision of self-determination differed dramatically from that of the NCAI and many Native-American communities. Myer also established the federal policy of relocation. His rough treatment of some Native-American communities—Native Alaskans, for instance—began to convince many Native Americans that he did not have their best interests at heart.

In August 1953, two developments occurred that provided the legal framework for termination and convinced most Native Americans that termination would be extremely detrimental to their rights and tribal governments. The House of Representatives passed House Concurrent Resolution 108. Though the document was not binding, it was signed by President Dwight Eisenhower. It declared:

Whereas it is the policy of Congress, as rapidly as possible, to make the Indians within the territorial limits of the United States subject to the same laws and entitled to the same privileges and responsibilities as are applicable to other citizens of the United States, to end their status as wards of the United States, and to grant them all of the rights and prerogatives pertaining to American citizenship. . . .

It is declared to be the sense of Congress that, at the earliest possible time, all of the Indian tribes . . . located within the States of California, Florida, New York, and Texas . . . should be freed from Federal supervision and control and from all disabilities and limitations specifically applicable to Indians. . . .

The measure went on to list other tribes that were deemed ready for termination, such as the Flatheads, Klamaths, and Menominees. There was hardly any debate on, or even much public awareness of, the sentiments contained in H.C.R. 108. Most Americans—and their lawmakers—seemed more concerned with fighting in Korea, racial desegregation, and the Second Red Scare. Just a few days after Eisenhower signed the concurrent resolution, he signed Public Law 280. Public Law 280 extended state-level criminal and civil jurisdiction over Native-American communities in several states, including California, Minnesota, Wisconsin, Oregon, and Nebraska. What was striking about both Concurrent Resolution 108 and Public Law 280 was their lack of regard for Indian opinion and lack of Indian input. The U.S. federal government once again made clear that it was the final arbiter of American-Indian affairs.

CASE STUDIES IN TERMINATION: THE MENOMINEES
In June 1953, Senator Arthur Watkins, a Republican from Utah and a forceful advocate of termination, confronted Menominee leaders in Wisconsin.

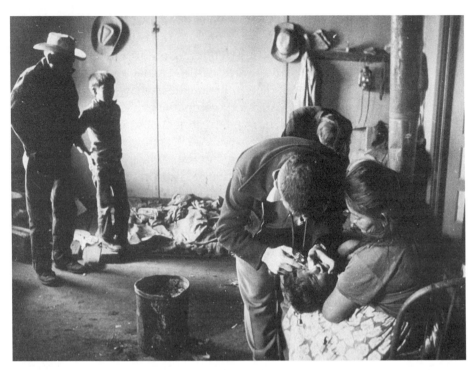

An Indian Health Service doctor making a visit to a Native-American household to check on the health of a small child in the 1950s. Termination meant tribes like the Menominees would lose access to federal services and Indian hospitals.

Watkins argued that the federal government had hindered Menominees and mismanaged their financial affairs, and that the tribe would do better managing itself. Congress, Watkins implored, would give up its hold on Menominee lands and pay the Menominees $1,500 each.

The Menominees were chosen for such an "honor" because they were perceived to be wealthy, with access to prime timberlands and a profitable sawmill. Their 3,000-plus members held over 230,000 acres collectively (but still under the auspices of the federal government). Watkins began the meeting by explaining the benefits of termination and then threatened to withhold the per capita payments unless Menominees voted for termination. The Menominees opposed termination, arguing that they were not as prosperous as Watkins and others claimed. A sizable portion of the tribe remained on welfare, and there were vast disparities in health and education levels between the Menominees and their white neighbors.

The Menominees had won an $8.5 million settlement against the federal government, and Watkins managed to block access to these funds unless the tribe supported termination. A slight majority of Menominees voted in favor of termination. Although the majority of the tribe quickly came to oppose it, the Menominee Termination Act became law in 1954, and the Menominees began their adjustment to life without federal recognition. Bureau of Indian Affairs schools became public schools. The Indian Health Service (IHS) hospital closed, and life became discernibly worse for most Menominees. Levels of education fell and levels of poverty increased through the 1960s, until finally, in 1973, after a hard-fought battle by activists, the Menominees' tribal status was restored.

CASE STUDIES IN TERMINATION: THE KLAMATHS

The Klamaths of southern Oregon were another tribe that was actually terminated. Though their original 1.9-million-acre reservation had been halved by a surveying error and various assaults, such as allotment, the Klamaths owned almost 600,000 acres of prime timberland, capable of producing as much as 3.8 billion board feet of lumber. The lumber business provided a basic income comparable to other Oregonians. Still, the Klamaths remained poorly educated and in poor health, and the reservation was wracked by alcoholism, as well as other diseases associated with poverty. The Klamaths, unlike the Menominees, featured a vocal faction in favor of liquidating the timberland holdings and breaking apart the reservation. Recognizing that the Klamaths might fall victim to unscrupulous land speculators or other such schemers, Congress allowed the Klamaths six months to finalize their tribal membership. Arthur Watkins also held up payment of a $2.6 million judgment from the Claims Commission until the Klamaths accepted the fact that they were to be terminated.

Nearly three-fourths of Klamaths agreed to take a one-time payment of $43,700 for their portion of the tribe's estate. As some tribal leaders had predicted to Arthur Watkins—who wanted to hear none of it, and often treated Native witnesses before his committee harshly—one after another Klamath used the money to flee bad conditions in rural Oregon for the seeming security of life in Portland or San Francisco. But $43,700 coupled with poor education and no job skills could only stretch so far, and within a matter of years, many Klamaths had traded rural poverty in the land of their ancestors for urban poverty in a sea of white faces.

Every terminated tribe suffered, but the Klamaths may have had it the worst of any Indian group. Some tribal members invested their settlements wisely, but many more did not. By 1989, three years after tribal recognition was restored, one in 100 Klamaths had college degrees, and about a third of Klamaths subsisted on less than $5,000 a year. Tribal lands, once rich with game and fish, had been placed into a national forest, managed for the benefit of non-Native hunters. There were high cultural costs as well. Community rituals and traditions disappeared as Klamaths dispersed. To complicate matters, the final termination settlement had established a date—August 13, 1954—when no more Klamaths would be enrolled (and shut out of future

Termination led to the loss of the Klamath's remaining 600,000 acres of timberland, which was much like this National Forest property in Southern Oregon.

disbursements). Within single nuclear Klamath families, some siblings could claim Klamath identity and reap the benefits, while younger brothers and sisters, born after the cut-off date, received nothing.

TERMINATION'S PEAK AND THE TURNING OF THE TIDE

The termination movement peaked in 1954, when many more tribes came up for proposed terminations. What was especially disturbing about this wave of terminations was that it mattered little whether tribal members approved or disapproved of termination. They simply had no say in the process. In some key ways, termination reflected the assimilationist goals of the disastrous policy of allotment, which had significantly diminished the Indian land base between the 1880s and the 1930s under the guise of helping "primitive" Native people along the path to "civilization" and cash crop agriculture.

Tribes terminated on Watkins's watch in 1954 included the aforementioned Klamaths and Menominees, the Alabama-Coushatas, and the Utes and Pai-utes in Utah and Oregon. In 1956, three Oklahoma tribes with tiny land bases were terminated (the Peorias, the Wyandottes, and the Ottawas). In 1959, the California Rancherias and the Catawbas of South Carolina were termi-nated. In 1962, the last termination took place, as the Poncas of Nebraska lost their tribal status. Most of the terminated tribes were eventually restored to their previous federally recognized status, but not without substantial emo-

Alice Jemison on Termination

Alice Jemison (1901–64) was a member of a prominent and powerful Seneca family. Jemison was an opponent of the Indian New Deal, and had even gone so far as to appear with far-right-wingers and Nazi sympathizers who shared her views on Indian affairs. She was not a fascist, rather she was devoted to the cause of treaty rights and the sovereignty of the Seneca Nation as defined by treaties. In 1948, Jemison gave a speech against a measure that would make New York State courts responsible for interpreting laws within the Seneca Nation, in essence, weakening tribal courts. The speech, which is excerpted below, demonstrates the link between the origins of termination in the 1940s and the more militant moves of Indian activists in the 1960s. It was delivered before the Senate Subcommittee on Interior and Insular Affairs. The measures passed, and for a time, Iroquois affairs were under the jurisdiction of the state of New York.

In proposing legislation for the Six Nation Indians of New York State, this committee is dealing with Indians who have been in constant contact with the white race since colonial days, and who played a very significant part in the early history of our country. . . . [George] Washington, in his wisdom, recognized us as human beings, and under the same principles of the Constitution of the United States entitled to the same rights and privileges, the pursuit of happiness. These treaties guaranteed the boundaries of vast tracts of land, and these lands were to remain ours until we decided to sell to the United States.

The Indians have progressed under this system. They have taken their own time in doing it. They have kept their shares of the treaties. They have never made war against the United States. . . . In the First World War when it was not legal to draft Indians our boys volunteered, and in this last World War we did not resist the draft, and out of a total number of approximately 2,700 Seneca Indians who occupied two reservations in New York State, there were approximately 500 Indians serving in the recent World War.

We did this because this is our country and we love it. We did this because we recognized this Government as being our Government as much as it is the Government of every State in this Union.

We too have contributed to the development and progress of this country. Now these bills have been introduced which by their very nature would violate every provision of our treaty for self-government. No Indian asked for the introduction of these bills. I don't know who asked that these bills be introduced. I do know that down through the years there has been a constant effort to remove the Indians from the little land that they do now own either to other lands or to force them to live under the laws of the white man.

We have kept our shares of the treaties, and we are here to ask that you keep yours. . . . So long as we are peaceful we should be left alone to enjoy what little rights we do now have, and the rights of which we are sure.

tional and financial upheaval. Termination reduced Indian land holdings, cost 11,000 people their clear, federally recognized identity as Native Americans, and cut off federal services for about three percent of federally recognized Native Americans. All of the tribes that were terminated before the program was unofficially retired in the 1960s suffered.

The motivation to end termination as federal policy came from a dedicated group of activists working at the National Congress of the American Indian (NCAI). NCAI leaders, including D'Arcy McNickle, Helen Peterson, Ruth Muskrat Bronson, and Joe Garry met in Washington, D.C., early in 1954 to determine how best to respond to the threat posed by termination. Garry's request for participation made the nature of the challenge clear: "the supreme test for our strength and our will to survive, as Indians, is now before us."

Led by Garry, and signed by representatives of 43 tribes from 21 states and the territory of Alaska, the emergency meeting drafted and approved a Declaration of Indian Rights and sent it to President Eisenhower. The document rejected termination in strong terms, calling it a "one-sided approach to free the government of responsibilities and obligations guaranteed in treaties and agreements with them." Here was rhetoric that Watkins and other terminationists would be hard pressed to ignore. Rather than setting Indians free, their pet policy was seen to be setting the federal government free from obligations demanded of it by treaties.

To drive home the point, many signers of the document stayed in Washington for the termination hearings on the Flathead reservation, D'Arcy McNickle's home. The Flathead termination failed due to a combination of high-level activism and grassroots lobbying of the Montana congressional delegation. Along with the newly rejuvenated NCAI, Congress began to hear from other, largely non-Indian groups such as the American Civil Liberties Union, the American Legion, the General Federation of Women's Clubs, and the National Council of Churches. Congressional support for termination weakened, and bills that would have terminated the Colvilles of eastern Washington and the Florida Seminoles were rejected. In the 1954 midterm elections, Democrats won control of Congress, and their support for termination was lukewarm at best. The tide was turning against termination, finally, though more tribes would still be terminated. It was also, unfortunately, too late for the Klamaths and the Menominees.

ATTACKING THE NATIVE LAND BASE

A frustrating accompaniment to the attack on tribal sovereignty and treaty rights was a renewed assault on tribal lands in the 1950s. Such assaults were often cloaked in good intentions, but tribes were rarely adequately consulted or compensated for losses that crippled their economies and damaged the ties of community.

A 1952 photograph of an Elbowoods, North Dakota, dance lodge, which was built by the Mandan, Hidatsa, and Arikara people in 1921. When it was submerged during the completion of the Garrison Dam in 1953–54, it was one of the last surviving Indian dance lodges in the country.

The Missouri River flooded in 1943 after a rapid snowmelt, prompting the Army Corps of Engineers to look for a solution. The solution they hit upon involved six large dams on the Missouri River, including Garrison Dam on the Fort Berthold Indian Reservation in North Dakota. The Fort Berthold Reservation, which dated to the 1851 Treaty of Fort Laramie, originally encompassed about 12 million acres. The Affiliated Tribes (Mandan, Hidatsa, and Arikara) watched the reservation shrink from these 12 million acres to fewer than one million, about half of which were not owned by Indians. The Affiliated Tribes opposed the dam project, but were powerless to stop or modify as the federal government was particularly insensitive to Indian rights and deaf to Native-American voices. Some members of the Tribal Business Council, most notably Chairman George Gilette, wept openly as the secretary of the interior, J.A. Krug, signed the contract that sold the tribes' most productive agricultural land—155,000 acres of it—to the United States to be submerged forever beneath the waters of Lake Sakakawea (named in honor of Sacagawea—the young Shoshone woman who traveled with the Lewis and Clark Expedition from 1804 to 1806).

The project devastated Fort Berthold. Twenty-five percent of the reservation, including much of the most productive land for farming and ranching, was underwater. Towns that once existed in close proximity were split apart by the newly enlarged Missouri River and reservoir. Population centers were forced to relocate. Farmers who had previously supported their families left to seek wage labor in the surrounding region or became welfare recipients. There were also untold consequences to animal species in the Missouri River Basin. In 1993, representatives from 28 affected tribes formed the Mni Sose Intertribal Water Rights Coalition. Mni Sose argued that although the tribes should have seen some benefit from the destruction of so much of their homelands, they did not. Their utility bills remained comparatively high, and their influence in river policy remained weak, in spite of treaty rights that were not forfeited.

All told, the Pick-Sloan plan, as the project was known, inundated hundreds of thousands of acres on Indian land in the Dakotas, including significant portions of the Fort Yates, Standing Rock, Cheyenne River, Lower Brule, Crow Creek, and Yankton Reservations, in addition to the Fort Berthold Reservation. The dam project did significantly reduce the danger of flooding in predominantly white areas lower down the Missouri, but this security came at a high price: another black mark on the United States' treatment of Native Americans.

In the northeast, a similar situation played out. Mohawk people relinquished territory when the St. Lawrence Seaway was constructed, beginning in September 1954. In return, many communities were forced to relocate, and many of the region's people, Native and non-Native alike, were left to deal with increased levels of industrial activity and pollution. In the 1960s, Seneca leaders fought hard against the Kinzua Dam project on the Allegheny River in northwestern Pennsylvania. In doing so, they stood on the 1794 Treaty of Canandaiugua, which stipulated that Seneca reservation lands would never be disturbed or claimed by the United States. The eventual flooding of 10,000 acres forced the relocation of many Senecas, including the remains of the Revolutionary War–era leader Cornplanter.

THE DECLINE OF THE NATIVE-AMERICAN FARM

By 1960, fewer than 10 percent of Native Americans worked as farmers, a 35 percent decrease from pre–World War II numbers. While white family farmers lagged behind the factory farms, they at least had access to revolutionary agricultural equipment like modern fertilizers and pesticides and state-of-the-art tractors—the gains of which are often underestimated. In contrast, most Native-American farmers lagged decades behind white farmers—less likely to have been given loans to purchase equipment, less likely to have accumulated the capital through other means, and, in general, less likely to have a long history of raising crops for market. While this was also true of white farmers in communities like those of the Amish or the Mennonites, the economic needs of those communities were different, and in the sense that they had few impoverished people among them, they could be consid-

A portrait of an elderly Iroquois farmer in upstate New York in the 1960s. Farming and cattle ranching decreased rapidly among Native Americans after World War II, and fewer than 10 percent were farming by 1960.

ered relatively prosperous—simply a different kind of prosperity from that of Middle America. In contrast, Native families that had previously worked the land as subsistence farmers—growing what they needed for themselves, with little left over for the market—were no longer able to survive economically. In many cases, the poor quality of their land left them nutritionally wanting, forcing them to purchase some of their food from the store or to suffer from malnutrition. The need for the store meant a need for cash; the need for cash meant a need for other lines of work.

By 1964, the median income of Native-American farmers was $1,800 a year, compared with $5,710 a year—three times more—for white farmers. Cattle farming in particular suffered, and Indian-owned cattle farms died off, as more Natives leased their lands to white cattlemen (or other farmers) who could qualify for the loans necessary for modern agricultural endeavors. Because of its seasonal nature—meaning the labor must be done in one part of the year in order to reap rewards in a later part of the year—commercial farming was driven by loans, whether sharecroppers owing a debt to the company store, or modern farmers putting up their future harvest as collateral on the loans to make that harvest possible.

Because of their relative lack of collateral, and official or unofficial racial discrimination policies at most banks, Native-American farmers were exceptionally unlikely to qualify for agricultural loans, making them all but ineligible to participate in the agricultural industry. Leasing their lands instead—usually at a pitiful amount—provided a small income, while letting the owner pursue other employment opportunities where his ethnicity might not prove such a burden.

RELOCATING NATIVE AMERICANS

The federal government actively promoted the removal of Native Americans from reservations to America's urban centers in the 1950s. Relocation was an outgrowth of World War II–era Native-American success. Native Americans had shown themselves capable of industrial employment and adjustment to life in majority non-Native cities during this crucial era. As pressure mounted at the congressional level to do away with Indian tribes altogether, lawmakers and others concerned with Indian affairs sought some way to move Native peoples away from reservations, where employment was scarce, to big cities, where employment was plentiful. As early as 1948, Navajos were encouraged to leave their reservation land for employment in Salt Lake City, Denver, and Los Angeles. Special job placement offices were set up in each of these cities to help the Navajos secure permanent employment after World War II.

Although relocation began before Dillon Myer took office, and he was one of the primary architects of the program as it took shape in the 1950s, it did not take full effect until after he had been replaced by Glenn L. Emmons as commissioner of Indian affairs. Relocation shared some of the same goals as termination, boarding school education, and even the Dawes Act of the 1880s. It sought to weaken tribal affiliations and move Indians toward full inclusion in American society, and so was essentially assimilationist in nature. It also had as one of its goals the erasure of communally held reservation land from the American landscape.

Initially, Native Americans were skeptical of the program and hesitated to sign up for it. However, Native Americans were curious about life off reservations, and many eventually signed up for the program. Native Americans who had experienced life off reservations, perhaps as soldiers during World War II or those who had moved for war-related jobs, returned to reservations with stories about stores, movie theaters, and other exciting aspects of life in big cities.

Once a Native American signed on for relocation, the applicant chose a city and was put in contact with someone in that town. An officer from the Bureau of Indian Affairs met the relocatee on his or her arrival and directed the purchase of some basic household goods. One of the leading scholars of relocation, Donald Fixico, points out that adjusting to life on a schedule was not easy: "living by a strict timetable was a new experience for almost all relocated Indians." The BIA's relocation officers also steered their charges toward houses of worship and grocery stores. The BIA covered the first month's rent and transportation to and from work. BIA officers did provide some job placement services and counseling in a more limited way and checked up on the relocatees for nine years. At that time, the relationship between the Indian and the BIA came to an end.

Young males were primarily the ones who signed up for relocation. Many were frustrated with the lack of opportunity available on reservations, which were sinking further into poverty for much of the 1950s, while the rest of American society was moving into an era of unprecedented prosperity. Young men might move to the city, try to establish themselves, and then move their families from the reservation to join them. Some relocatees, though assuredly a minority, had already earned some college credit. These individuals had a relatively easy time of joining the burgeoning postwar middle class. Other relocatees were not nearly so fortunate.

INDIAN CHICAGO

The first Native Americans to relocate to Chicago came in 1952. From 1952 to 1959, over 4,900 Native Americans moved to Chicago. A plurality (37 percent) were from Native-American communities in the upper midwest, nearly a third came from the northern Plains, and 13 percent and 12 percent came from Oklahoma and the southwest, respectively. Lakotas and Ojibwes accounted for approximately half of all relocatees to Chicago between 1952 and 1959. There were some important distinctions, cultural and otherwise, in the experiences of the two tribes. The vast distance between the northern Plains and Chicago ensured that Sioux trips home were rarer, while the relative ease of travel between Ojibwe country and Chicago allowed some Ojibwes to consider Chicago as a sort of temporary home. One historian who studied the phenomenon even suggested that Ojibwes adapted the move to Chicago and back into older migration patterns in search of food or wage labor.

Chicago was a vibrant (and occasionally tense) multiethnic and multiracial patchwork during the middle of the 20th century. Though some areas of overlap existed, and the older Chicago was being transformed by major changes in the American economy, the city's ethnic groups continued to live in discernible enclaves and to take jobs in specific occupations that were attached to one's racial identity. Native Americans were confronted with something of a problem in this regard, since they did not have the numbers necessary to dominate a neighborhood.

Education and job training were the most pressing problems, and adjusting to life in the busy, rigid world of Chicago was difficult. Still, most Indians in Chicago managed a modest increase in prosperity during the 1950s. They used their wages to purchase the consumer goods that dominated the American economy: televisions, cars, radios, and household appliances. Housing also posed a problem. The YMCA on the city's Near North Side was fine for single young men, but not for families. As some Chicago neighborhoods' white residents left when African-American residents moved in, the BIA took advantage of the low rents in these transitional neighborhoods to place Native-American families there. Urban renewal projects, which displaced large numbers of poor African Americans and concentrated them in projects such as the Robert Taylor homes, had the added consequence of displacing Native-American families that had recently moved into neighborhoods. Though nothing on the order of white–black tension, Native–black tension did exist in some communities.

BIA publicity to promote relocation was glowing, and often depicted happy scenes of middle-class life in cities and suburbs. The reality was much more complicated. Native Americans faced cultural shock and were often paid low wages. BIA agents had a habit of securing seasonal or temporary work for Native Americans, who then had difficulty finding new work after the initial jobs were completed. Relocation also grew to be quite expensive, to the point that some of its supporters began to question its cost effectiveness. Some policy makers even eyed economic development on reservations themselves, but that was not undertaken in any meaningful way during the 1950s.

Until its gentrification in the early 21st century, Uptown, on Chicago's North Side, was a primary center of Native-American life in Chicago. High rents and racially discriminatory real estate practices combined to keep Native Americans out of most Chicago neighborhoods. Conditions in Uptown were not good, and many Indians lived in dilapidated or otherwise unsuitable housing, but in terms of all the housing options available to Native Americans in the United States, Uptown apartments were at least acceptable. Indians were never as concentrated in Chicago as they were in Minneapolis or smaller urban centers close to reservations, but there were enough in some neighborhoods to give those places a distinctly Native-American "feel."

THE AMERICAN INDIAN CENTER OF CHICAGO

The All-Tribes American Indian Center of Chicago (later the American Indian Center) was the first of its kind in the United States. At the center, Native

Americans from around the country came together to organize and com-memorate what set them apart from the American population as a whole—their status as descendants of the original inhabitants of North America. The center's constitution read:

We, the American Indians of Chicago, in co-operation with our non-Indian friends, do hereby affiliate ourselves and our common interests, in a civic and cultural organization to be known as the All-Tribes American Indian Center of Chicago, to promote fellowship among the Indian people of all tribes living in metropolitan Chicago, and to create bonds of understanding and fellowship between Indians and non-Indians in this city; to stimulate the natural integra-tion of American Indians into the community life of Metropolitan Chicago; to foster the economic and educational advancement of Indian People; to en-courage membership in artistic and avocational pursuits; and to preserve and foster arts and crafts and Indian cultural values.

The All-Tribes American Indian Center worked to fulfill its mission by hosting powwows, athletic contests, and dinners. It encouraged cross-tribal understanding, as well as racial pride in a broadly Native-American identity.

The American Indian Center of Chicago was founded in 1953 and moved to this headquarters building in 1966. As of 2010, it was the oldest continuously operated urban Indian organization in the country.

THE CHICAGO CONFERENCE

In 1960, University of Chicago anthropologist Sol Tax proposed an update of the Meriam Report, which in 1928 had collected and analyzed data on Native-American living conditions and the effects of federal policy. Tax's idea was to involve the Indians themselves in this update, and he secured initial funding from the Scwartzhaupt Foundation for this purpose. In part because of the federal hydroelectric and flood control projects that had led to the seizure of a great deal of Indian land, the National Congress of American Indians (NCAI) responded favorably to Tax's idea, as well as to his proposal that Indians from non-federally recognized nations be allowed to participate, which aided the movement to grant recognition to those nations.

After a year of preparation and smaller regional meetings, the American Indian Chicago Conference (AICC) met in Chicago in June 1961, with 500 Indian delegates from 90 different tribes and other communities, discussing pan-Indian issues facing the United States.

The conference produced a landmark policy statement, the Declaration of Indian Purpose, which called for a reversal of the federal government's termination of past treaties and the closure of various Bureau of Indian Affairs (BIA) offices; better healthcare, economic development, and educational opportunities for Native Americans; and strengthened protection of water rights, among other issues. The AICC essentially jump-started the Native-American activism of the 1960s and resulted in the creation of the National Indian Youth Council (NIYC).

Because young Indian activists perceived the NCAI as too mainstream, too stodgy, the NCAI's endorsement of the AICC was not encouraging to them. Several young activists did attend the Chicago conference and were instrumental in including "the inherent right of self-government" in the declaration, but decided to form their own body to pursue their interests. A subsequent meeting in Gallup, New Mexico, later that summer resulted in drafting a constitution and bylaws for the National Indian Youth Council, an incorporated charitable organization.

Taking cues from civil disobedience movements around the world, the NIYC became instrumental in organizing protests during the 1960s and beyond, including "fish-ins" in Washington State, when state and local authorities refused to acknowledge the fishing rights granted by federal law, and a 1964 march on Washington's capital city of Olympia. To a greater extent than the NCAI, the NIYC reached out to the African-American Civil Rights Movement, sending Indian representatives on southern Freedom Rides and Martin Luther King's celebrated 1965 protest in Montgomery, Alabama.

RED POWER

Just as the African-American Civil Rights Movement was in part a response to segregation (and to white attempts to preserve it), but was really about

The Indian Civil Rights Act

Though African Americans made the greatest strides and enjoyed the most publicity in this area, civil rights were a multiracial concern in the 1960s. In 1961, the U.S. Senate took up the task of evaluating the state of Native-American civil rights, with particular concern for the fact that tribal governments were not beholden to the U.S. Constitution, which led in many cases to human rights abuses of reservation citizens. A 19th-century Supreme Court decision had established that Congress had the authority to impose laws on Indian reservations, and so for six years the matter was taken up in hearings, culminating in the passage of the Indian Civil Rights Act of 1968 (ICRA).

The ICRA protected the rights of all persons from the acts of tribal governments and applied many of the protections of the Bill of Rights to reservation residents while attempting to preserve tribal sovereignty. For instance, accused criminals were not required to be provided with an attorney, which would have been a financial burden on tribal governments; similarly, although Congress is forbidden to establish a state religion, tribal governments are allowed to establish an official religion for the reservation. However, the right of an individual to worship as he pleases is protected by the ICRA; so, too, are freedoms of speech, press, assembly, equal protection, due process, and privacy (including the Bill of Rights' protection against unreasonable search and seizure).

With the passage of the ICRA, it was quickly established that Indian tribal governments could now be sued, just like state, local, and federal governments. The federal court hearing the case of *Dodge v. Nakai*, the first such case, in which the plaintiff sought an injunction against the Navajo Tribal Council, decided that if Congress had granted federal civil rights to those subject to tribal governments, those governments' sovereignty could not protect them from suit in federal court. A number of suits followed in the ensuing years.

broader issues, the Native-American Civil Rights Movement, or Red Power movement, was a response to the federal policies of termination and relocation in the 1950s. The Red Power slogan at the time was used specifically by younger Native activists like those of the NIYC, in symmetry with the militant Black Power wing of the African-American activists; in further symmetry, they dismissed older, often more conservative activists as "Uncle Tomahawks."

While Americans of all ethnicities spent much of the 1960s and 1970s wondering "what does it mean to be an American?" or "what does it mean when I say I'm Irish?", the question "what does it mean to be an Indian?" was asked in the context of cultural and actual battles that had been fought for 400 years.

That context included a new interest in Native Americans among whites, as evidenced by the institution of Native American Studies programs at universities and the advent of revisionist histories that reconsidered the role of indigenous American peoples in the story of the continent. The NIYC, for instance, published a newspaper for its organization called *ABC: Americans Before Columbus*, which not only had the half-playful, half-clever sound of so much activist language, but emphasized the idea of "Americanness" predating the arrival of whites.

Though the NIYC criticized them—some of the criticism amounting to the accusation that they had been waiting for President John F. Kennedy to bring harmony to the reservation, and then gave up hope when he was assassinated—the National Congress of American Indians became much more proactive in the mid-1960s, appointing Vine Deloria, Jr., its executive director in 1964. In the three years he served, membership increased from 19 tribes to 156 tribes, saving the organization from bankruptcy—due not simply to Deloria, but also to the increased interest in Native Americans and Red Power.

VINE DELORIA, JR.

Vine Deloria Jr.'s grandfather was the Reverend Philip Deloria, also known as Tipi Sapa, an Episcopal priest (one of the first Sioux to be ordained) as well as a Nakota Sioux leader. Vine Sr. was an Episcopal deacon and missionary; his sister Ella was an anthropologist who studied under Franz Boas and Margaret Mead and published many important works on the Sioux Nation.

Vine Jr. graduated from Iowa State University with a general science degree, spent two years in the Marines, and returned to school for both a theology degree (from the Lutheran School of Theology in Rock Island, Illinois) and, after his tenure with the NCAI, a law degree from the University of Colorado. Well-educated, well-spoken, and devoted to both his faith and his people, Deloria was an important figure and writer in the Red Power movement. His 1969 book *Custer Died for Your Sins: An Indian Manifesto* was not the first of its kind, but it benefited from its evocative title, his unique perspective as a third-generation theologian of a "white" religion (which, by all rights, made him a figure of respect and authority from a conventional white perspective), and his skill with words. The book opens vividly:

One of the finest things about being an Indian is that people are always interested in you and your "plight." Other groups have difficulties, predicaments, quandaries, problems or troubles. Traditionally we Indians have had a "plight." Our foremost plight is our transparency. People can tell just by looking at us what we want, what should be done to help us, how we feel, and what a "real" Indian is really like. Indian life, as it relates to the real world, is a continuous attempt not to disappoint people who know us. Unfulfilled expectations cause grief, and we have already had our share. Because people can see right through

Jay Silverheels and Tonto

Few cultural phenomena have captured the imagination of Americans the way television did in the 1950s. For Native Americans, the options for participating in this new development were limited. Some television programs and Hollywood films featured Native-American characters, but many of these were white men in "red face." They occasionally portrayed one-dimensional victims of white aggression, but more often they portrayed one-dimensional perpetrators of violence against unsuspecting, virtuous whites. One character who defied these perceptions was Tonto.

Tonto was a leading character in the 1955 western movie, *The Lone Ranger*, and in the extremely popular television show of the same name, which ran from 1949 to 1957. The show focused on the exploits of the masked title character, but Tonto also played a significant role. The show portrayed the Lone Ranger and Tonto as roughly equal and dependent on one another, but Tonto was still a stereotype of sorts, the "good" Indian who was helpful and kind, in stark contrast to other Indians who were not so good-natured.

Tonto was played by Jay Silverheels, a Mohawk actor who struck several significant blows for Native Americans in Hollywood. Silverheels was born Harold J. Smith on the Grand River Reserve in southern Ontario in 1912. His earliest successes came as an amateur boxer, but he was working in Hollywood by 1937. His career spanned several decades and various media, but Silverheels had difficulty escaping the typecasting that accompanied his greatest fame as Tonto. Even in the 1960s and 1970s, complex, engaging roles for Native Americans were rare.

In the more radical days of the 1960s, Jay Silverheels and Tonto provided an easy target for Red Power activists, who perceived Tonto as an "Uncle Tomahawk," fawning over his masked leader, and eager to help out white people whenever possible. Silverheels himself defied such categorization. In the 1960s, he helped form the Indian Actors Guild. The Indian Actors Guild lobbied writers, producers, and directors for more appropriate roles and encouraged Native-American actors to pursue their aspirations. Silverheels was the first Native American to receive a star on the Hollywood Walk of Fame, in 1979. When he died the next year, he was cremated and his ashes were returned to the Grand River Reserve.

us, it becomes impossible to tell truth from fiction or fact from mythology. Experts paint us as they would like us to be. Often we paint ourselves as we wish we were or as we might have been.

The more we try to be ourselves the more we are forced to defend what we have never been. The American public feels most comfortable with the mythical Indians of stereotype-land who were always THERE. These Indians are fierce, *they wear feathers and grunt. Most of us don't fit this idealized figure since we grunt only when overeating, which is seldom.*

To be an Indian in modern American society is in a very real sense to be unreal and ahistorical. In this book we will discuss the other side—the unrealities that face us as Indian people. It is this unreal feeling that has been welling up inside us and threatens to make this decade the most decisive in history for Indian people. In so many ways, Indian people are re-examining themselves in an effort to redefine a new social structure for their people. Tribes are reordering their priorities to account for the obvious discrepancies between their goals and the goals whites have defined for them.

This book was one of the earliest to present an overview of contemporary Native-American issues, and did it as events were unfolding—it was published right around the time that the Indians of All Tribes decided to occupy Alcatraz.

THE OCCUPATION OF ALCATRAZ

On November 20, 1969, about 100 Native Americans occupied and claimed possession of Alcatraz Island, located in San Francisco Bay, California, famous for being the home of a federal prison until 1963. The island remained continuously occupied by as many as 300 Indians until June 11, 1971—nearly two years. Joining the Natives at Alcatraz for a few days or weeks became a sign of solidarity for many members of AIM and other Native-American self-determination activists. Though the later Wounded Knee incident is better remembered today for its drama; the occupation of Alcatraz was the most vivid and powerful action of the Red Power movement, despite the lack of response to the manifestos issued by the members of the occupation.

The justification for the Alcatraz occupation was the 1868 Fort Laramie Treaty and related federal legal precedent that allowed Indians to reclaim land that had been appropriated from them, once the government no longer needed it. In the late 1960s and early 1970s, 50 federally owned properties were identified that had fallen into disuse, demonstrating that lack of necessity. Alcatraz was the best known and the most prominent. Once the most famous federal prison, it had been closed in 1963. Indian activists had occupied it for a few hours in 1964, using the occupation as an opportunity to file a claim to retake the land to found an all-Indian university. The attorney general denied the claim; Alcatraz had not gone unused long enough to demonstrate a lack of need. In 1969, when the island was still vacant, the long-term occupation began. The occupying group called itself Indians of All Tribes, emphasizing that this was an Indian occupation, not a tribal-specific occupation. Shortly into the occupation, the activists invited Indians from any tribe in North America to a meeting of what they called the Confederation of American Indian Nations. In addition to the university proposed earlier, they hoped to use the occupation to bring about the creation of an Indian cultural center on Alcatraz that would serve as a major meeting place for Indians of all tribes, as well as a museum and a place of worship. The activists stressed pan-tribal cooperation and did not single out any one issue as the object of protest; rather, the cause was that of greater Native control over their own destiny—American-Indian self-determination.

During most of the occupation, the most prominent voice of Alcatraz was Richard Oakes, a San Francisco State University student and member of the Mohawk nation. Numerous Native-American and other interested groups not directly connected to the Alcatraz occupation expressed their support, including student groups, university Native-American Studies programs, and other activist groups. Letters from all over the country, from Americans of all ethnicities, were sent to the White House supporting some or all of the occupants' requests (or "demands" as some news reports put it, implying the otherwise-unused island was being held hostage). Outside supporters, in a show of solidarity, helped to provide food, clothing, medical supplies, and cash. In an age when many of the most famous demonstrations were marked by violence from one side or the other, the Alcatraz occupation remained largely peaceful.

In 2006, this graffiti dating from the occupation of Alcatraz could still be seen on the island. Alcatraz had been vacant for six years when Native Americans began their occupation in 1969.

The occupation began optimistically, and as the number of occupants grew, an informal school was assembled to teach occupants' children, and committees were formed to address health and food needs. The occupants even started a local newspaper. A dozen or so men were appointed as the local security force, glibly referred to as the "Bureau of Caucasian Affairs"; they were criticized in later years as having been too aggressive in their efforts to make sure that Alcatraz did not become home to illegal drug use.

The federal government opted to wait, watch, and see how the occupation transpired. As time waxed on, media attention wandered and the occupation's population dwindled, in part because of disagreements over leadership and the inability to see any of the occupation's requests met. In May 1970, the government cut off water and electricity to Alcatraz, and most of the leadership left the island after fires destroyed several buildings (the media reported with skepticism the accusation that outsiders, government or otherwise, had set the fires). By the time the federal government sent in marshals to end the occupation, there were only 15 occupants remaining.

Still, the importance of Alcatraz should not be understated, despite the greater prominence of armed conflicts like Wounded Knee. The Alcatraz occupation stimulated public discussion among Americans of all races, and provided a focal point to demonstrate mainstream American support for Indian self-determination. It continued to be spoken of in high regard throughout the following decade.

THE FOUNDING OF THE AMERICAN INDIAN MOVEMENT

In time, the broader, decentralized Red Power movement would be overshadowed by the American Indian Movement (AIM), which was founded in 1968 in Minneapolis, Minnesota, by a small group of urban Chippewas. While other Indian activist groups took their inspiration from the early days of the Civil Rights Movement, AIM was more directly inspired by the Black Panther Party that had recently been formed in Oakland, California.

Originally a local movement, AIM was founded in self-defense to patrol the streets of Minneapolis and "police the police." There was a long history of police brutality against Native Americans in Minneapolis, with Indian bars routinely harassed, Indian brawlers were arrested while non-Indians were told to go home and sleep it off, and so on. Many people, including AIM cofounder Dennis Banks, have claimed that the Minneapolis police had a quota of Indian arrests to make each month to demonstrate their preservation of law and order. Many of these arrests never led to prosecutions—witness statements weren't taken, evidence wasn't taken, interrogation was minimal, and the arrested Indians in many cases were released after a night or a weekend in jail. Often, many of the same individuals were arrested, week after week. Some weren't arrested—simply beaten at the scene of the alleged crime, or threatened with arrest or assault if they didn't return home.

House Made of Dawn

The Pulitzer Prize in Fiction winner for 1969, N. Scott Momaday's second novel, *House Made of Dawn*, is frequently assigned reading in schools today (and still read for pleasure). Momaday is a Kiowa writer, born on the Kiowa Reservation in Oklahoma to writer Natachee Scott Momaday and painter Al Momaday. The novel not only sealed his fame as a writer and reteller of Kiowa legend, it also helped spur the mainstreaming of Native-American literature. Sometimes called the Native-American Renaissance, the period from the late 1960s to the early 1970s saw authors like Louise Erdrich, Leslie Marmon Silko, and James Welch produce their early work, which found wide multiracial audiences. Concurrent with this surge in fiction was the maturation of Native-American Studies departments in universities, and attempts to re-historicize the white settling of the Americas from a Native-American perspective, or at least one less driven by Manifest Destiny and white privilege.

The "house made of dawn" is a perfect world of spiritual unity between the people and the land, which the protagonist, Abel's grandfather Francisco has tried to raise him to revere. The novel opens with Abel's return from World War II, a significant experience for many Native-American men sent overseas. The story of Abel's postwar life is marked by violence, partially inspired by the real story of a New Mexico state trooper killed by a Native American, and by Native-American beliefs and customs like the peyote ceremony (the novel was many white Americans' first introduction to peyote, in an age when hallucinogens of any kind were a novelty). As in many postwar narratives, one of its central themes is alienation, but this can be read not only as the alienation of the returning veteran, but also as the alienation of the Native American in an increasingly modern world that conceives of him as a part of the past that has been outgrown.

AIM established a street presence of sober, watchful Native Americans who monitored and in some cases photographed police actions in Indian neighborhoods. This protective action sometimes extended to warning people when squad cars were approaching, preemptively clearing out the bars so that there was no one there to arrest. In the first year after AIM's founding, unprosecuted arrests of Native Americans declined by 50 percent in Minneapolis, a figure even AIM's opponents would have trouble ascribing to anything but the group's prevention of police misbehavior.

During AIM members' visits to the Alcatraz occupation, Banks represented the occupants to the press on numerous occasions, and used the Alcatraz publicity to recruit for AIM. New chapters were started around the country, notably in San Francisco, Chicago, Cleveland, Milwaukee, and Los Angeles. In the 1970s, AIM would achieve national, and even international, prominence.

CONCLUSION

The 1950s were a decade of contrasts for Native Americans. Native-American communities continued to struggle to define themselves as distinct, self-governing entities, while federal policies like termination and relocation threatened their very existence. At the same time, the outright racism of past decades began to ease, and some Native Americans began to experience the benefits of America's massive consumer-driven economy in the 1950s. Still, by the end of the decade, the Native-American land base was in peril, and many Native Americans lived in concentrated, degrading poverty on reservations.

In the 1960s, with the Red Power movement and the occupation of Alcatraz, as well as the growing pan-tribal consciousness, Native Americans took crucial steps toward full equality, self-determination, and Indian civil rights, building on the successes of earlier decades. While the Civil Rights Movement for African Americans depended on the establishment of new rights and protections, what Native Americans wanted was the acknowledgment and enforcement of rights they had already been granted. It would be up to future generations to continue to attempt to secure Native Americans' rightful place in the United States.

MATTHEW JENNINGS
MACON STATE COLLEGE
BILL KTE'PI
INDEPENDENT SCHOLAR

Further Reading

Apted, Michael. *Incident at Oglala*. DVD. Los Angeles, CA: Miramax, 1992.

Banks, Dennis, with Richard Erdoes. *Ojibwa Warrior: Dennis Banks and the Rise of the American Indian Movement.* Norman, OK: University of Oklahoma Press, 2004.

Biolsi, Thomas and Larry Zimmerman. *Indians and Anthropologists.* Tucson, AZ: University of Arizona Press, 1997.

Calloway, Colin G. *First Peoples: A Documentary Survey of American Indian History.* Boston, MA: Bedford/St. Martin's, 2004.

Churchill, Ward and Wall Vander. *Agents of Repression.* Boston, MA: South End Press, 1988.

Crow Dog, Mary, with Richard Erdoes. *Lakota Woman.* New York: Grove Weidenfeld, 1990.

Davis, Mary B., Joan Berman, Mary E. Graham, and Lisa A. Mitten, eds. *Native America in the Twentieth Century.* New York: Garland, 1994.

De Leon, David. *Leaders from the 1960s.* Westport, CT: Greenwood Press, 1994.

Deloria, Vine, Jr. *Behind the Trail of Broken Treaties: An Indian Declaration of Independence.* New York: Dell, 1974.

————. *Custer Died for Your Sins.* Norman, OK: University of Oklahoma Press, 1988.

Edmunds, R. David, Frederick E. Hoxie, and Neal Salisbury. *The People: A History of Native America.* Boston, MA: Houghton Mifflin, 2007.

Fixico, Donald L. *Termination and Relocation: Federal Indian Policy, 1945–1960.* Albuquerque, NM: University of New Mexico Press, 1986.

Hendricks, Steve. *The Unquiet Grave.* New York: Thunder's Mouth Press, 2006.

King, C. and Charles Springwood. *Beyond the Cheers.* Albany, NY: State University of New York Press, 2001.

LaGrand, James B. *Indian Metropolis: Native Americans in Chicago, 1945–1975.* Urbana, IL: University of Illinois Press, 2002.

Matthiessen, Peter. *In the Spirit of Crazy Horse.* New York: Penguin, 1992.

Peltier, Leonard. *Prison Writings.* New York: St. Martin's Griffin, 2000.

Philp, Kenneth R. *Termination Revisited: American Indians on the Trail to Self-Determination, 1933–1953.* Lincoln, NE: University of Nebraska Press, 1999.

Rawls, James J. *Chief Red Fox is Dead: A History of Native America Since 1945.* Belmont, CA: Wadsworth/Thomson Learning, 2001.

Smith, Paul Chaat and Robert Allen Warrior. *Like a Hurricane: The Indian Movement from Alcatraz to Wounded Knee.* New York: New Press, 1997.

Thornton, Russell. *American Indian Holocaust and Survival: A Population History Since 1492.* Norman, OK: University of Oklahoma Press, 1987.

Weyler, Rex. *Blood of the Land.* New York: Vintage Books, 1984.

Wilkinson, Charles F. *Blood Struggle: The Rise of Modern Indian Nations.* New York: W.W. Norton, 2005.

CHAPTER 9

Activism and Conflict: 1970 to 1989

THE 1970s SAW the continuation and realization of the previous decade's pursuit of Native-American civil rights and self-determination, but while many of the gains of the 1960s were abetted by or even originated with the federal government, tensions became increasingly high now in Indian-federal relations. At their lowest ebb, this led to armed conflicts on a scale not seen since the 19th century's Indian wars, and widespread retaliatory harassment of reservation Indians. Even so, Native Americans continued to make great strides in improving their lives and their communities.

During the 1970s, another change came about in Native-American self-identification and cultural awareness. The U.S. census of 1980 recorded 1,366,676 Native Americans living in the United States, which represented an increase of 72.4 percent from the previous census in 1970. The 1980 census recorded that the largest number of Native Americans in any state were resident in California, followed by Oklahoma, and, in declining order, Arizona, New Mexico, North Carolina, Alaska, and Washington. The state with the highest number of Native Americans as a percentage of the overall population was Alaska, which was followed in declining order by New Mexico, South Dakota, Arizona, Oklahoma, Montana, North Dakota, Nevada, Wyoming, and Washington.

The reason for the massive rise in the number of Native Americans from the 1970 census to the 1980 census cannot be accounted for simply by a much higher birth rate. Most of the increase is made up by those aged older than 10 years and by those who were recorded in the 1970 census but not identified as Native Americans. This rise could not result from migration, as was the case with many other ethnic communities in the United States that had increased their numbers between 1970 and 1980.

The only possible cause was that far more people were identifying themselves as Native Americans than had been the case 10 years earlier. This clearly came from a major transformation in Native-American communities that coincided with a resurgence of political and historical consciousness throughout the United States. In 1983, American anthropologist Henry Dobyns, who in 1965 estimated the original Native-American population prior to 1492 as 10–12 million, revised this estimate to 18 million, showing that there had probably long been a large number of Native Americans who had not been counted accurately in population returns.

By the time of the 1980 census, many more people of all races in the United States and overseas began to recognize that the Native-American people had been badly wronged in the land seizures during the 19th century and in their other dealings with the U.S. government. Events in the 1970s, especially the Wounded Knee Incident, had much to do with this shift in cultural attitudes about Native Americans, and their growing visibility in American culture and politics in the 1980s.

SELF-DETERMINATION

The keystone of federal support of Indian self determination finally came in 1975, with the Indian Self-Determination and Education Assistance Act. Some of the groundwork was laid by the 1972 Indian Education Act, a congressional response to the Kennedy Report (Indian Education: A National Tragedy—A National Challenge), named for Senator Robert F. Kennedy, the chair of the Senate Special Subcommittee on Indian Education when the subcommittee's work began (after his assassination, his brother Senator Edward Kennedy cochaired the subcommittee with Walter Mondale).

The Kennedy Report had outlined the major challenges and educational deficits facing Native Americans in school, and after several years of discussion, the act was ready. As passed, the 1972 act consisted of four major parts: funding for public schools with Indian students, with additional funding for Indian-run schools; grants for Indian education, to be given to Indian groups, private nonprofit organizations, colleges, and state education departments; funding for adult education and job training; and the establishment of an Office of Indian Education and a National Advisory Council for Indian Education.

The subsequent 1975 act went significantly further, building on the educational opportunities created in 1972 with a grander scope. While there had been a tug of war between federal authority and tribal sovereignty, more often than not characterized by the former's disdain for the latter, the 1975 act was the result of years of discoveries by disparate agencies, task forces, and congressional committees that showed that the combination of the federal government's attitude toward Native Americans and the changes in modern life had created third-world living conditions in many of the country's reservations. This was evident not simply in terms of poverty levels, but also in terms of citizens' mistreatment by their governments, inability to participate in the advantages of modernity, and difficulty in "pulling themselves up by their bootstraps." While other acts in the 1960s and 1970s addressed one aspect or another of these problems, the 1975 act was one of the few to explicitly address the big picture. In essence it allowed tribes to create their own programs and infrastructure using federal money, rather than wait for the intercession of federal agencies to do it for them. If a new hospital was needed for the reservation, the tribe could petition the appropriate federal agency, fill out the paperwork, and receive the funding to build the hospital themselves.

Building a hospital yourself may not sound like an advantage over having it built for you, but not only is it quicker than waiting for it, you have more control over exactly how it is designed. This ability did much to undo the federal government's long history of paternalism—that is, treating Native Americans and their organizations as though they were children who could not be trusted to take care of themselves. With the 1975 bill, the federal government was not stepping in and remaking Native-American society; it was giving back some of the authority it had assumed, while retaining the responsibility that years of treaties had given it, and which recent congressional legislation had reaffirmed.

The 1975 legislation was followed by two more education-related acts—the Indian Education Assistance Act of 1975 and the Education Amendments Act of 1978—which further increased the funding for Native-American education, while placing a greater share of responsibility for planning local education initiatives in the hands of Native-American parents. Numerous Native Americans and organizations took advantage of the new opportunities offered to them; college enrollments rose steadily, budgets in Indian-populated school districts swelled, and healthcare and living conditions began to improve.

THE ALASKAN SETTLEMENT ACT

Self determination was an issue addressed in Alaska as well, where complaints over the use of land in the young state had been rampant for years. When the 1867 Treaty of Cessation—"Seward's Folly"—transferred the lands of Alaska from Russian to U.S. control, it put the local tribes under the same jurisdiction as other Native Americans. Subsequent acts explicitly extended to Alaskan Natives the same protections extended to other Natives. However, once Alaska was granted statehood in 1959, the actions of the state government did not reflect this policy, as it converted various plots of land into public land

The photo shows construction of a road in the Alaskan forest along the route of the future Trans-Alaska Pipeline in October 1969.

rather than tribal land, prohibited duck hunting on tribal lands, and proposed nuclear tests and the building of a hydroelectric dam—propositions that would be profitable for the state government, but that were opposed by Natives who felt the state lacked the authority to make these arrangements. Furthermore, when the Bureau of Indian Affairs (BIA) convened a meeting in 1966 to work out an arrangement that would address Alaskan Native concerns, it failed to include any Natives in the proceedings, prompting an outcry from Native groups, until the Department of the Interior imposed a land freeze, withdrawing public lands from appropriation and prohibiting the issuance of mineral rights without the petitioning of a federal court, until such time as Congress could pass a bill that would settle and clarify matters.

The presence of oil in Alaska and the rising costs of fuel impacted the formulation of this bill, even in the late 1960s. Few had any idea how bad the fuel shortage would become in the 1970s or in the next century. President Richard Nixon and other figures in the federal government wanted a trans-Alaskan oil pipeline, and native complaints over land use were the only substantial obstacle. While the federal government had a long and well-documented history of ignoring the rights it had extended to Natives when new factors arose, by the 1960s and especially the 1970s, the political consequences of cutthroat behavior were more severe. Perhaps in no other decade than the 1970s was the general public better disposed toward Native Americans in conflict with the federal government, as shown by the reaction to the Wounded Knee incident.

Five years after the land freeze, the resulting bill, the Alaska Native Claims Settlement Act, was signed into law on December 18, 1971. By this time the benefits of the oil pipeline were even more keenly desired and helped to motivate the settlement, which granted title of 44 million acres of Alaskan land to various native corporations, including 4 million acres of urban land, individual grants, cemeteries, and historic sites. An additional $962 million in compensation was given to the regional corporations, which were instructed to distribute 10 percent to all shareholders and 45 percent to village corporations and shareholders who did not live in villages. Although more generous than it might have been in previous generations, the settlement was not widely popular with Alaskan Natives, and there was some sentiment that their leaders had been swayed by the deep pockets of federal interests. Three hundred seventy-five million acres to which they believed they had the right were denied to them, in part due to the construction of the pipeline, and hunting and fishing rights were tightly constrained. Over time, 41 percent of Alaskan land was set aside as national parks, scenic rivers, and forest preserves—a move popular with the environmental groups so often allied with Native interests, but a half-measure at best from a Native perspective.

The "corporations" mentioned above were established by the act and organized between 1972 and 1974. The existing 12 regional Native associations of Alaska were used as the geographic basis of 12 Native corporations—for-profit corporations established to pursue Native business interests—while about 200 village corporations were created to cover Alaska's many smaller areas. Every person "of at least one quarter Alaska Eskimo, Indian, or Aleut blood" alive as of the bill's passing on December 18, 1971, was automatically enrolled in a regional corporation and given 100 shares of stock. This was the method used both to organize the land ownership and to distribute the cash settlement, which amounted to about $6,000 per person paid out in bits and pieces (another source of complaint) over the 10 years following the bill's passage.

The Kake salmon cannery in southeast Alaska was a Native-owned business managed by the Organized Village of Kake for almost 30 years. It closed in 1977, but was a forerunner of the large number of Native corporations created after the Alaska Native Claims Settlement Act.

As a creation of Congress, the act too often followed legislative logic rather than local logic: for instance, though a certain number of acres of land was granted to each particular corporation, it proved difficult for some of these corporations to actually secure enough land to satisfy those allotments during the lengthy and controversial land selection process that occupied much of the 1970s. Some regions simply weren't large enough, or didn't have enough uninhabited land available. As a consequence, three of the regional corporations petitioned Congress to renegotiate their parts of the agreement. The Cook Inlet regional corporation, for instance, was eventually granted oil and gas deposits and $100 million worth of federal properties.

The distribution of cash to shareholders still left a good deal of it in the hands of the corporations, some of which began in the mid-1970s to invest it in the private sector or to use it to fund business ventures, often joint ventures with established outside businesses positioned to benefit from Indian capital and (in some cases) natural resources. Thus, unlike many federal settlements with Natives in the past, the 1971 act actually encouraged greater interaction between native resources and the "mainstream" American economy—which, in light of some of the complaints about the act's politicization, was a beneficial wrinkle often overlooked.

THE AMERICAN INDIAN MOVEMENT IN THE 1970s

The most well-known Native-American activist group, the American Indian Movement (AIM), had been founded in the late 1960s, originally as a Minneapolis-based local organization inspired by the Black Panthers. The publicity surrounding the group of Indian activists occupying Alcatraz provided AIM cofounder Dennis Banks, who along with other AIM members joined the Alcatraz activists for a while, with the opportunity to recruit at the national level. By the end of the 1960s, local AIM chapters had opened throughout the country. One of the new recruits was Russell Means, an Oglala Sioux from the Black Panthers' home of Oakland, California. In 1970, at the age of 31, he was made AIM's first national director, and it was under Means that AIM achieved its greatest fame through a series of symbolically powerful protests and eventual armed conflict with the federal government.

The first such demonstration was the "countercelebration" of the Fourth of July, 1971. Means and a group of AIM members occupied Mount Rushmore, which had been seized from the Lakota Sioux in the aftermath of the Great Sioux War of 1876–77, despite having been granted to the Sioux in perpetuity by the Fort Laramie Treaty only a few years earlier, and which was part of the Black Hills held sacred by the Sioux. The mountain was ceremoniously renamed Mount Crazy Horse after one of the Sioux leaders who fought in the war and is revered by modern Native-American activists for his attempts to preserve traditional Indian ways of life in the face of American encroachment.

Dennis Banks, a cofounder of the American Indian Movement, confronting police officers at an antiwar protest in New York City in 1967.

That same year, on Thanksgiving, AIM members in Plymouth, Massachusetts, occupied the *Mayflower II*, a replica of the *Mayflower*, and painted it red to draw attention to Native-American concerns and to the tendency of so many white Americans to treat Indians as a part of the American past, not the American present or future. The following February, Means led a protest caravan of over 1,000 activists to Gordon, Nebraska, where an Oglala man named Raymond Yellowthunder had been beaten to death by two white men in front of many witnesses. Local authorities had not charged the men, but were eventually pressured to do so by the publicity; they became the first whites jailed in Nebraska for the death of an Indian. While the Alcatraz occupation in the late 1960s had brought significant mainstream American attention to the cause of Native-American civil rights, it had not resulted in tangible gains—none of the activists' requests had been granted. AIM, on the other hand, was now achieving real, demonstrable results, and its star rose quickly.

That summer—the summer of 1972—a newly energized AIM organized a caravan called "The Trail of Broken Treaties." The caravan traveled from place to place, picking up Indians from one reservation or community and another, until over 2,000 people from almost 100 reservations had joined the protest, which traveled to Washington, D.C., on November 3, the eve of the presidential election. They brought with them a platform of 20 points related to self determination and the reinstatement of various broken treaties, and they had arranged in advance to meet with representatives of the Bureau of Indian Affairs and the Department of the Interior (of which the BIA is an agency). When that meeting was denied them and they were given nowhere to convene, 400 of the 2,000 protesters, mostly AIM members, occupied the BIA building for six days, until the White House announced a public commitment to negotiating Indian rights. As with the Alcatraz occupation, the occupation ended with little violence (vandalism resulted in significant property damage to the BIA building), but the protesters were able to take copies of internal BIA records that cast the agency's policies in an unfavorable light when shared with the press.

LEAD UP TO THE WOUNDED KNEE INCIDENT

Perhaps nothing in Native-American history after World War II is as well known as the armed conflict between AIM and federal and state law enforcement at Wounded Knee. Although Alcatraz raised public support of Indian causes, Wounded Knee raised awareness and interest, driving new influxes of funding for the Native American Studies programs that had been founded in the 1960s and helping to guarantee that this new awareness was not a transient fad, as so many causes of the era proved to be. There continues to be a great deal of controversy surrounding the events of Wounded Knee and incidents that followed, and students interested in learning more should investigate a variety of sources and perspectives. After all, any time an armed conflict involves a government and its citizens, the history written is an uncertain one; arguments are still waged over how to write histories of the Civil War, whose participants are long-since dead and who fought for institutions much changed in the intervening time. This is not the case with Wounded Knee. Many of the participants are still living and influential, and because of this, many of the resulting conflicts remain unresolved.

To call it an "incident" is misleading at best, but the terminology has arisen to differentiate discussion from the 1890 Wounded Knee massacre of 200 Lakota Sioux by the 7th Cavalry. The 1973 conflict culminated in a 71-day armed standoff, the longest and largest-scale armed conflict in North America (between any parties, Indian or otherwise) since the 19th-century Indian wars. It began as an internal conflict at the Pine Ridge Indian Reservation, an Oglala reservation in South Dakota (and overlapping into Nebraska). One of the largest reservations in the country, it is bigger than some states in land area; it is also one of the poorest reservations, with high unemployment and suicide rates and one of the lowest life expectancies on this side of the globe.

From 1972 to 1976, Pine Ridge was run by tribal chairman Richard "Dickie" Wilson, widely disliked by many on the reservation and in the greater Native-American community. Wilson was derided as an "Uncle Tomahawk" who

Native-American Agriculture in the 1970s

Having begun a steady decline after World War II, Native-American agriculture continued to decline in the 1970s, when more than half the population lived in rural areas, but only 11 percent farmed the land (a slight increase from 1960, but an overall decline of more than a third since the start of World War II). An inability to get credit to fund agricultural operations and a lack of access to the gains of modern technology led many Indian land owners to lease their lands to white farmers at low rates. But in this decade, a new problem became chronic for those remaining Native farmers: water rights. Access to water is critical for farming, whether to irrigate crops or to feed livestock, and this is even more true in the arid areas in which so many Native farmers lived.

Though an early-20th-century Supreme Court ruling had guaranteed Native Americans the right to access water, Indian farmers in the west frequently had to go to court to see that ruling enforced, and not everyone had the time or other resources to wait for the court system's protections. Furthermore, it was not until 1976 that the Supreme Court ruled that the ground and subsurface water beneath an Indian reservation belonged to that reservation—only access to surface water like lakes and streams had previously been protected, and the growing water needs of white settlements had driven municipal governments to use those Indian water supplies for their own purposes. To this day, there is no clear ruling on whether water rights apply to the use of water only for crop irrigation—which has explicitly been protected—or for other uses, such as drinking and household water consumption, industrial uses, and provision for livestock.

cozied up to federal authorities rather than fight for Indian rights. Numerous reports, including the extensive 1992 documentary *Incident at Oglala*, have accused him of embezzling funds provided to the reservation by the BIA. During his four-year tenure, 50 Pine Ridge citizens were killed, many under strange or unclear circumstances—given Pine Ridge's population, this was more than double the national average.

One of the unsolved apparent murders was that of Ray Robinson, a civil rights activist who had worked with both Martin Luther King, Jr., and Jesse Jackson; his body had still not been found as of 2010. Other unsolved murders included a number of Wilson's enemies, and more and more Pine Ridge Sioux believed his security team was responsible. Answering directly to Wilson and funded by a $67,000 BIA grant, they were called the "GOON squad"—Guardians Of the Oglala Nation—and one former member has said that their armor-piercing ammunition was provided by the Federal Bureau of Investigation (FBI), which had become increasingly concerned about the potential for violence from AIM members and other Red Power activists. Members of the GOON squad even included BIA agents moonlighting for extra income. What has often been overlooked, however, is that Wilson initially supported AIM, but withdrew his support after the BIA occupation. Wilson claimed that he withdrew support because the theft of BIA documents would result in the loss of Indian lands, as the deeds no longer existed to prove their ownership; his opponents believed he simply did not want to lose the support of the federal government. Over the years, Wilson's hatred for AIM increased, as they remained a thorn in his side throughout his term of office.

SHEEP MOUNTAIN

One reason the federal government found it financially worthwhile to support Wilson was because of land claim disputes at Pine Ridge. The Department of the Interior had been embarrassed by Pine Ridge Indian opposition to an attempt to transfer an eighth of the reservation to the federal government— the Sheep Mountain Gunnery Range, which had been borrowed by the War Department during World War II to train soldiers. The return of the land had been indefinitely delayed, but the government had never officially taken ownership of it; and then, in 1970, a classified program revealed that Sheep Mountain included rich uranium deposits. Now, just as Native-American groups nationwide were making a concerted effort to hold the government to the terms of its treaties, and land claims were particularly prominent because of the then-ongoing Alcatraz occupation, the government had a motive to keep Sheep Mountain—and attempted to transfer it secretly to government control. Wilson's election followed shortly after this dispute heated up; the BIA grant and the firepower of the GOON squad were wildly disproportionate to what could have been expected a few years earlier. Although there is no "smoking gun" to prove that the federal government colluded with Wilson for the sake of an ulterior gain, as it did in so many foreign countries, the circumstantial evidence is highly suggestive.

The main opponents to the attempt to seize Sheep Mountain, and to Wilson's leadership, were the traditionalists of Pine Ridge, who wanted to maintain the old ways. A petition to the Justice Department to investigate the apparently politically motivated deaths at Pine Ridge failed, as did an attempt to impeach Wilson in February 1973. Although the BIA was compelled to initiate impeachment proceedings when the petition requesting them was turned in with more signatures than the number of votes that had brought him to office, the agency allowed Wilson himself to preside over the impeachment and sent 60 U.S. marshals for his protection. When the impeachment failed, Wilson forbade his opponents from meeting together within the confines of the reservation. An illegal emergency meeting four days later decided to request assistance from AIM, perhaps in part because National Director

Russell Means was himself Oglala. When Wilson refused to meet with Means, Wounded Knee, a small settlement on the reservation, was chosen as the symbolic site for a press conference about the problems on Pine Ridge. It suited AIM's genius for powerful, symbolic gestures like the Mount Rushmore occupation, and the publicity that already followed the group would bring outside attention to the reservation's situation.

WOUNDED KNEE 1973

AIM sent a caravan of 54 cars to Wounded Knee on February 27, 1973, and a smaller group to nearby Rapid City, from which it would be easier to coordinate media matters. The following morning, the Wounded Knee group discovered that the GOON squad and BIA police had erected roadblocks with the apparent intention of keeping them in town. Though AIM members later said they anticipated the roadblocks would be removed upon the arrival of the U.S. marshals and the FBI, who had been dispatched in case of violence, the marshals instead fortified the roadblocks, and by the end of the day, the federal forces had assigned an additional 250 marshals, multiple SWAT teams, and 14 National Guard armored personnel carriers to Pine Ridge. It resembled the sort of amassed force brought to bear against a serious, dangerous threat. General Alexander Haig, the vice chief of staff of the army who would later serve as Ronald Reagan's secretary of state, sent two colonels to Pine Ridge, experts in unconventional warfare (such as the guerrilla wars of South and Central America), to help coordinate the federal effort.

Most of the 200 AIM members had arrived unarmed, and in the face of such forces, armed themselves by breaking into a trading post and taking the guns that were for sale. As federal forces sealed the off-road perimeter, AIM consolidated its food supplies in case of prolonged cutoff from the rest of the world, though no one present guessed they would be in Pine Ridge for over two months. From the start, locals—and later, non-locals who had traveled to South Dakota—snuck past the perimeter (set up to prevent exit more than entrance) to bring in food, clothes, and first-aid supplies, prompting a five-state cordon around South Dakota. Supporters countered by arranging food drops from small privately flown planes, some of which were fired upon by federal troops. More than 2,500 Americans were arrested for giving aid to the trapped AIM members; few were ever prosecuted. An attempt to offer amnesty to Oglala traditionalists backfired when roadblocks were temporarily lifted on March 11, which they expected would result in an evacuation of Wounded Knee by non-AIM members (allowing for a more serious incursion against AIM, without concern for bystanders). Instead, Pine Ridge Oglala swarmed into Wounded Knee, proclaiming themselves the Independent Oglala Nation, separate from the Wilson government.

Two AIM members, Frank Clearwater and Buddy Lamont, were killed by federal gunfire during the periodic shoot-outs that occurred during the stand-

This sign supporting Leonard Peltier was photographed in Detroit in 2009. Peltier has been treated by many activists as a political prisoner, and his supporters have included Archbishop Desmond Tutu, the Dalai Lama, Amnesty International, and Nelson Mandela.

off. More than 500,000 bullets were fired by federal forces over the course of the 10 weeks, but they suffered no fatalities. One serious casualty was Marshal Lloyd Grimm, paralyzed by a shot in the back, believed to be friendly fire.

On May 3, the federal government conceded to meeting with Indian representatives to discuss the 1868 Treaty of Fort Laramie, which had been routinely violated, and to explore the establishment of a federal treaty enforcement commission. They also agreed to a three-day moratorium on arrests, beginning when the Wounded Knee AIM members surrendered their weapons, and to not interfere with the funeral ceremony and procession for Buddy Lamont. Only the funeral agreement was honored; the federal side reneged on all other points. Arrests began within moments of the cease-fire and eventually totaled 562 arrests (in addition to the 2,500 abettors mentioned above). Of the 562, only 185 were indicted; the rest had charges dropped or were released when grand juries failed to find the evidence sufficient for their arrest. Of the 185 indicted, only 15 were convicted. The charges that were successfully prosecuted were minor, like trespassing and interfering with the delivery of the mail.

Prominent AIM members were harassed with multiple charges that, although they could be beaten as the legal process took its course, tied up considerable time—and discouraged further activism. Russell Means, for instance,

The 1975 Pine Ridge Shootout

On Pine Ridge, recriminations after the events of 1973 were severe. Hundreds of AIM members and supporters were seriously injured in the next three years, and at least 69 were killed, with a number of disappearances that might inflate that number. In multiple cases, eyewitnesses reported GOON squad members as the assailants, but none were ever convicted. The FBI, which held jurisdiction over criminal investigations in Indian Country, was viewed by many Pine Ridge Indians as a hostile agency. Tensions boiled over on June 26, 1975, erupting in a shoot-out between AIM members, federal agents, GOONs, BIA police, and white vigilantes. The FBI was there in search of a Pine Ridge Indian named Jimmy Eagle, in the course of investigating an assault and robbery outside the reservation. Two FBI agents and one AIM member were killed. The resulting investigation has remained controversial. AIM member Leonard Peltier was arrested the following year, after being extradited from Canada, where he had been living in hiding after evading arrest in Denver.

In 1977, Peltier was convicted of both murders, principally on the basis of a signed affidavit by a local and allegedly mentally ill woman who claimed to be his girlfriend and an eyewitness; when she subsequently attempted to testify for the defense, planning to say that the FBI had intimidated her into composing the affidavit, the judge barred her testimony on the grounds of mental incompetence. Numerous other problems with the federal case have been pointed out: for instance, that Peltier never drove a red truck, which the FBI initially described in its all-points bulletin; that all the eyewitness testimony was later recanted; that there were problems with the ballistics tests performed on the murder weapon (years later, FBI records revealed that the ballistics report had in fact determined that Peltier's firearm could not have been the murder weapon, and that this report was withheld during trial); and that the prosecution was inconsistent even about what it accused Peltier of doing. At his trial, the prosecutor described him as the murderer of two agents at point-blank range. In the appeal, the prosecution described him as one of several shooters, perhaps because of the aforementioned ballistics report.

After the shoot-out, the FBI regularly patrolled Pine Ridge with 250 agents, conducting searches without warrants, interrogating locals, and allegedly opening fire multiple times. At the end of the summer of 1975, Dickie Wilson signed the paperwork to transfer title of Sheep Mountain, which includes Pine Ridge, to the Department of the Interior, which designated it as an annex of the Badlands National Monument; a subsequent act of Congress made the transfer official. In the intervening time, Wilson had been defeated in election by Al Trimble, whose tribal government filed a lawsuit against the federal government. A compromise was reached: Pine Ridge was granted the right to reclaim the surface land, but the mineral rights—and the uranium—would be the permanent and exclusive domain of the U.S. government.

was charged with 37 separate felonies for his part in the Wounded Knee incident; his bail was set at $125,000, and by the time he had been exonerated on all counts three years later, the National Lawyers Guild had spent more than $1 million on his defense. In a sense, the federal government may have gotten what it wanted: many AIM leaders were for years either tied up in lawsuits, in hiding to evade charges, or in prison. After AIM leader Jack Trudell spoke out against the government in a February 11, 1979, speech delivered in front of the FBI building and focusing in part on the mishandling of the Leonard Peltier case, his Nevada home caught fire late that night, killing his wife, their children, and his mother-in-law. Fearing that AIM had become too prominent and simply provided targets for Indians' enemies, Trudell dissolved the movement's national office and titles; since then, it has persisted as a group of like-minded, but independent local chapters.

NATIVE AMERICANS AND CONGRESS

The increasingly contentious atmosphere in Indian-federal relations led to the 1975 establishment of the American Indian Policy Review Commission (AIPRC) by an act of Congress. The bill was drafted in the immediate aftermath of the Wounded Knee fiasco by an attorney working for Senator James Abourezk (D-SD), the chairman of the Senate Interior Subcommittee on Indian Affairs. Like the Chicago Conference in the 1960s, the AIPRC was intended to update federal Indian policy and began with an overview of the policy and existing Indian-federal relationship, led by three senators, three members of the House of Representatives, and five Native Americans. Abourezk chaired the commission.

Task forces were assigned to 11 areas: trust and the Indian-federal relationship; tribal government; federal administration and Indian affairs; jurisdictional matters; education; health; reservation and resource development; urban and rural non-reservation Indians, a growing group; Indian law; terminated and non-federally recognized tribes; and alcohol and drug abuse. After two years, the task forces' various investigations were presented to Congress on May 17, 1977, in the form of a two-volume, 923-page report consisting of the collected data and summaries and analyses thereof, and 206 recommendations pertaining to policy, procedure, and future legislation. One of the overarching themes of the report was that the relationship between Native-American tribes and the federal government should be grounded in principles of international law as well as one in which weaker governments accepted the protections of the stronger government, creating an obligation on the part of the American government which had, at best, been inconsistently honored. Chief among the commission's recommendations was the formal recognition of these two ideas.

As a result of the AIRPC's recommendations, the position of BIA Commissioner was upgraded to an assistant secretariat within the Department

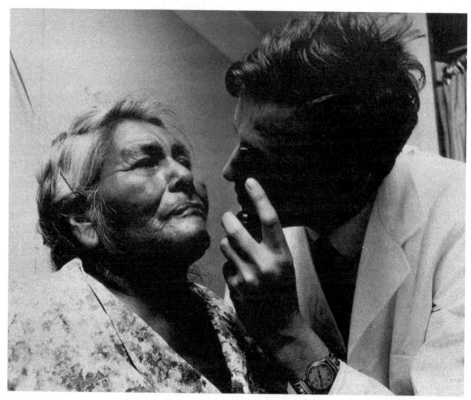

The 1975 American Indian Policy Review Commission was charged with studying Indian-federal relations and the status of Indian affairs, including health. This Pima Indian woman in Arizona was undergoing an eye examination from a National Institutes of Health doctor in the mid-1980s.

of the Interior, and both houses of Congress adjusted the structure of their committees with respect to Indian affairs. In the spirit of acknowledging the sovereignty of tribal governments, Congress adjusted the tax relationship between tribes and states, which was instrumental in the later phenomenon of reservation casinos. The Department of Education created a special Office of Indian Education. New procedures were set out for tribes seeking formal federal recognition, long a contentious issue.

Perhaps most significant among the legislation that followed the AIRPC's report was the American Indian Religious Freedom Act (AIRFA) and the Indian Child Welfare Act. The AIRFA was a reversal of the American approach to Native-American religion, which long predated the founding of the United States. Even those early Americans who did not see themselves as missionaries obligated to convert savages and heathens looked down on Native religious practices, and as the Indian wars drew to a close with the advent of the 20th century, the federal and state governments promoted assimilation—"Americanization"—of Indians by prohibiting their religious practices,

The *Martinez* Decision

The 1968 Indian Civil Rights Act (ICRA) guaranteed certain civil rights to the subjects of tribal governments, and in so doing, it was determined by the federal courts that tribal governments were not sufficiently sovereign to prevent them from being sued in federal court. For 10 years, many such lawsuits were brought against tribal governments—few of them pertaining to the issues, such as denial of due process, which had inspired the ICRA, perhaps for the simple reason that those who had grown up on the reservation were not used to such rights. Instead, suits dealt with such things as corrupt or unfair election procedures, prison facilities, property disputes, discrimination, and the requirements imposed on those seeking to vote or to run for tribal offices. One of these cases, *Santa Clara Pueblo v. Martinez*, was appealed to the U.S. Supreme Court, which thus heard its first ICRA case in 1978.

Contrary to all expectations, the Court ruled 7–1 that the ICRA did not in fact waive tribal governments' sovereign immunity to lawsuits, and furthermore that tribal officials could not be sued either (that is, not for their actions in that official capacity). In a decade when the abuses of tribal governments such as Dickie Wilson's at Pine Ridge had been so much publicized, the *Martinez* decision was seen as a significant blow to Indian civil rights. The tribal courts have become more important as a result, as they are the principal—and often the only—venue to which a Native American can appeal when tribal government has violated his rights.

in whole or in part. In 1934, U.S. law, outside the constitutional proscription against Congress's establishment of a religion and the Supreme Court's interpretations thereof, finally acknowledged an unrestricted freedom of religion on reservation land.

Other prohibitions continued, however, including the banning of peyote and the lack of access to many sacred sites no longer located on Indian land. Passed in 1978, AIRFA for the first time established a clear federal policy of protecting the right to worship with as few restrictions as possible. Peyote, for instance, is still a controlled substance, but may be legally purchased for religious use. Over the next year, a report required by AIRFA was prepared, showing hundreds of instances of laws that abridged Native worship rights; however, contrary to the intent of AIRFA, few actions have been taken to undo those laws, and 10 years after its passage, the Supreme Court ruled that AIRFA was only a "policy statement" that created neither rights nor cause of action. Disputes over worship rights continue to this day.

Other legislative gains for Native Americans in the 1970s included congressional action that enabled the Indian Claims Commission to find in favor of the Sioux from whom the Black Hills had been taken, awarding the tribe $17.5 million plus interest (the Supreme Court upheld the decision on appeal, but some 30 years later, the money had not yet been disbursed).

LEGAL RULINGS IN THE 1980s

Native Americans won a number of important legal judgments in the 1980s. Fishing rights for many Native Americans in the Pacific Northwest and the Great Lakes were confirmed during the 1980s. In 1981, U.S. District Court Judge Noel Fox's 1979 decision in favor of the rights of Native Americans to fish commercially in the Great Lakes was reaffirmed. Two years later, a January 25, 1983, decision in the U.S. Court of Appeals for the Seventh Circuit in the case *Lac Courte Oreilles Band of Lake Superior Chippewa Indians et al. v. Lester P. Voight et al.*, known as the Voight decision, upheld the rights of the Chippewa people of Lake Superior "to hunt, fish and gather" in lands they held in northern Wisconsin.

However, not all the decisions were in favor of Native-American rights. In 1981, *Montana v. United States* went to the U.S. Court of Appeals. The Crow Tribe of Montana sought to prevent hunting and fishing within their reservation by anyone who was not a member of their tribe, but Montana sought to regulate hunting and fishing, and the decision came down in favor of the state of Montana. The case established two conditions for tribal authority over issues such as regulation of activities of non-Indians on tribal lands. One was that there must have been an agreement between such parties and the tribe, and the other allowed tribal regulation when the activities affected the safety and security of the tribe.

Another major legal development in the 1980s was also over land rights, and again the findings were largely against Native Americans. In multiple cases, the Yakima tribe in Washington State cited their original treaty with the United States by which the reservation was given to the Native Americans for their "exclusive use and benefit." Furthermore, it stated that "no white man [shall] be permitted to reside upon the said reservation without permission" from the tribe. In spite of the original treaty, many non-Indians had bought land, and over the years through inheritance and sales, much land had ended up in the hands of non-Indians. In *Brendale v. Confederated Tribes and Bands of Yakima Indian Nation*, Justice John Paul Stevens accepted the rights of the Yakima people over Brendale, who had planned to redevelop his land. In a reversal, Justice Byron White in *Wilkinson v. Confederated Tribes and Bands of Yakima Indian Nation* rejected the Yakima rights and found in favor of Wilkinson. In the final judgment, Justice Harry Blackmun in the *County of Yakima v. Confederated Tribes and Bands of Yakima Indian Nation* found that the Yakima did not have the rights over some of their lands.

CASINOS AND GAMBLING

There were other court battles and laws that transformed the nature of Indian reservations. The Indian Mineral Development Act of 1982 allowed the mining of reservation land. The hope was that reservation authorities could become financially self-sufficient by allowing mining. However, a number of other reservations decided to embark on the establishment of gambling facilities on reservations. The first group of Native Americans to become involved in gaming was the Seminole tribe in Florida, starting with high-stakes bingo games in 1989. This soon ended up in the courts. The *Seminole Tribe v. Butterworth* Supreme Court decision ruled that Native-American reservations had the right to operate gambling facilities, even if this was in contradiction of the civil statutes of the relevant state authority. This decision was contested in *California v. Cabazon*, but the Supreme Court upheld the decision that the Cabazon tribe, who lived in southern California, were able to open a high-stakes bingo game and card-playing facility on their land in spite of California state laws.

As casinos and gambling facilities started opening on many reservations, the Indian Gaming Regulatory Act of 1988 was passed by Congress. This affirmed the rights of Native Americans to conduct gaming on their own lands, but only after negotiation with state authorities. An exception was in Alaska, where the Native Alaskans had tribal lands, but these were not technically reservations (except those of the Tsimshians). As a result, Alaskan Native tribal governments also did not have the power to collect local taxes from business operations conducted on their land. And gaming transformed many reservations. When President Bill Clinton invited Native-American and Native-Alaskan tribal leaders to the White House in 1994—for the first time since 1820—he wrote that some had become so wealthy from gaming that they flew to Washington, D.C., in their own planes, while others were barely able to afford the trip.

NATIVE AMERICANS IN POLITICS

In 1981, a Native American, Tom Fredericks of the Mandan-Hidasta tribe, was temporarily appointed assistant secretary for Indian Affairs in the Department of the Interior; he was then replaced by Kenneth Smith of the Wasco tribe. Ross Owen Swimmer of the Cherokee tribe then took over the same post in 1985.

Born in 1943, Swimmer had gained a bachelor of arts degree and then a doctorate in jurisprudence from the University of Oklahoma; he became principal chief of the Cherokee Nation of Oklahoma in 1975. In 1983–84, he was cochairman of the Presidential Commission on Indian Reservation Economies, and remained as principal chief of the Cherokees until 1985. When Swimmer resigned to move to the Bureau of Indian Affairs, he was succeeded by his deputy, Wilma Mankiller, who became the first female principal chief of the Cherokees. She served in that position for 10 years. Within the Native-American communities, Swimmer remains a figure of some controversy because of his hope that he might be able to end the rule of the Bureau of Indian Affairs over the lives of the Native Americans. Swimmer was replaced late in 1985 by Ed Brown of the Pascua Yaqui tribe.

The 1980s saw the emergence of a number of other politicians with Native-American heritage, the most well known is Alfred Charles "Al" Sharpton (1954–). He is best known as an African-American Pentecostal and later Baptist preacher, but he also has Cherokee Indian ancestry. A leading campaigner for civil rights, he hosted a radio talk show and was also a candidate in the primary for U.S. Senator from New York in 1988, 1992, and 1994, as well as for the Democratic nomination for the U.S. presidency in 2004. Another activist of African-American and Native-American (Cherokee-Creek) ancestry was Rosa Parks (1913–2005), who in 1955 refused to give up her bus seat to a white man in Montgomery, Alabama, and started what became the Montgomery bus boycott, taken as the start of the modern Civil Rights Movement. In 1980, she inaugurated the Rosa L. Parks Scholarship Foundation; in February 1987, the Rosa and Raymond Parks School, named after Rosa and her late husband, was opened in their honor.

Another well-known Native-American politician was Ben Nighthorse Campbell (b. 1933), who was of Cheyenne ancestry, born in Auburn, California. He had served with distinction in the U.S. Air Force in Korea, and from 1983 until 1987 was a member of the Colorado State House of Representatives in Denver. In 1986, he was elected to the U.S. House of Representatives and served until 1993, when he began his service as U.S. senator from Colorado. He retired from the Senate in 2005. A rancher, horse trainer, and designer of jewelry, he is one of only a few Native Americans to have served in Congress.

Philip "Phil" C. Bellfy (1946–), from the Chippewa tribe had risen to national prominence in 1977 when he was arrested for trespassing after he refused to remove his hat upon entering the Michigan State capitol building in Lansing. In 1988, he was a Workers' League candidate for presidential elector for Michigan. Michael James Lowrey (born in 1953 of Cherokee ancestry) was active in the American Civil Liberties Union; in 1980 and again in 1984, he was a citizens' candidate for presidential elector for Wisconsin. He was also active in the National Organiza-

Ben Nighthorse Campbell of Colorado in 2007.

tion for Women. Tom Cole (b. 1949), of Chickasaw Indian heritage worked on the staff of Mickey Edwards in the U.S. House of Representatives, from 1982 until 1984, and then served as the state chair of the Oklahoma Republican Party from 1985 until 1989. He was a member of the Oklahoma State Senate from 1988 until 1991, and later served as secretary of state of Oklahoma and member of the U.S. House of Representatives.

In Alaska, Native Americans involved in politics included William L. Hensley (b. 1941), who was elected to the Alaska State Senate in 1970, served as a member of the Democratic National Committee from Alaska in 1984, and also was a delegate to the Democratic National Convention in the same year.

In 1988, Russell Means of AIM also ran for the presidential nomination of the Libertarian Party. He gained further exposure from acting in a number of films beginning in 1990, including *The Last of the Mohicans* (1990), *Natural Born Killers* (1994), *and Pocahontas* (1995). He published his autobiography *Where White Men Fear to Tread* in 1995.

A CULTURAL SHIFT

During the 1970s, a change in attitudes toward Native Americans led to a growing interest in and understanding of Native-American life and culture among Americans of all races. For example, in June 1976, the 100th anniversary of the Battle of Little Big Horn, historians openly challenged the "legends" that had surrounded George Armstrong Custer. Custer was no longer seen as an embodiment of "true" American values of heroism and self-sacrifice, and by the 1980s, he was no longer viewed as a brave soldier who died heroically, neither by most people within the United States nor by those overseas.

During the 1980s, the lead-up to the commemoration in 1992 of the 500th anniversary of the arrival of Christopher Columbus in the Americas led to intense debate in the United States and throughout the Americas. Columbus, who had been celebrated in the 400th anniversary in 1892, was no longer held to be as much of a great hero by 1992. It was also established by medical historians that the Spanish brought malaria to the New World. Other changes stemmed from scholars' attempts in the late 1970s to reassess the complex roles played by 19th-century Native-American figures such as Sitting Bull (c.1834–90), Crazy Horse (c.1849–77), and Chief Joseph (c.1840–1904) of the Nez Perce.

The 1980s then ushered in a new wave of books looking at Native-American history and society. These included important reference books such as William Brandon's *The American Heritage Book of Indians* (1984), Colin F. Taylor's *Encyclopedia of North American Tribes* (1988), Carl Waldman's *Atlas of the North American Indian* (1985) and *Encyclopedia of Native American Tribes* (1988), Jack Weatherford's *Indian Givers: How the Indians of the Americas Transformed the World* (1988), and Bill Yenne's *The Encyclopedia of North American Tribes* (1986).

In addition to the many books celebrating the lives of Native Americans, there were other ways in which they were recognized. Except for a U.S. postage stamp showing Pocahontas in 1907 to commemorate the 300th anniversary of the establishment of Jamestown, it was not until 1968 that a named Native American—Chief Joseph—appeared on a postage stamp. Then, in 1977, a set of four stamps were issued showing Pueblo art. In 1980, the post office issued not only a set of stamps showing Indian masks, but also featured Crazy Horse and the Cherokee scholar Sequoyah in a series of stamps celebrating famous Americans. A number of other stamps featuring Native Americans and Native-American art followed in the 1980s and 1990s. The appearance of Native Americans on postage stamps was symbolic of the growing recognition of the contributions of Native Americans in U.S. history.

LITERATURE

Until the 1970s, most of the books on Native Americans were not written by Native Americans. There was some change during the 1970s that saw Simon Ortiz's *A Good Journey* (1977) and Duane Niatum's *Digging Out the Roots* (1977) appear; and early in the 1980s, Niatum, of the Klallum, wrote *Songs for the Harvester of Dreams* (1981). In 1981, the Laguna Pueblo writer Leslie Marmon Silko's collection of short stories and poetry, *Storyteller*, helped tell more of her story, after she had already gained national attention for her novel *Ceremony* (1977). Born in Albuquerque, New Mexico, in 1948, Silko had been educated at the University of New Mexico and wrote about her heritage—part Pueblo Indian, part Mexican, and part Caucasian. In 1969, in her first published story, "The Man to Send Rain Clouds," she had identified as Native American, and by 1980, she was already the subject of a biography by Per Seyersted. Her *Storyteller* brought together poems, legends, and photographs, alongside stories that helped give readers an insight into Native-American values, which she used in her later novel *Almanac of the Dead* (1991). Silko also wrote a screenplay for Marlon Brando, who had made headlines in 1973 by not appearing to collect his Oscar for his performance in film *The Godfather*, but sending in his stead an activist for American Indian rights known as Sacheen Little Feather, who read a statement denouncing the treatment of Native Americans.

A cousin of Silko's, Paula Gunn Allen, born in 1939 of mixed Laguna/Sioux and Lebanese ancestry, worked at the Native American Studies program at the University of California, and became the editor of *Studies in American Indian Literature: Critical Essays and Course Design* (1983), which helped popularize Native-American literature further. Allen's search for her identity from a feminist perspective featured heavily in her novel *The Woman Who Owned the Shadows* (1983), and she also explored this in nonfiction in *The Sacred Hoop: Recovering the Feminine in American Indian Traditions* (1986). Allen wrote much poetry including *Shadow Country* (1982) and *Skins and Bones:*

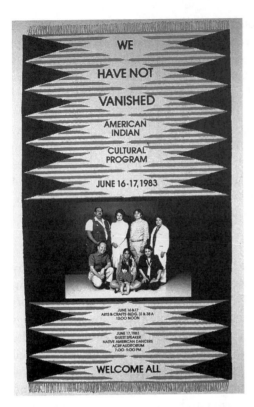

WE
HAVE NOT
VANISHED
AMERICAN INDIAN
CULTURAL PROGRAM
JUNE 16-17, 1983

JUNE 16&17
ARTS & CRAFTS-BLDG. 31 & 38 A
12:00 NOON

JUNE 17, 1983
GUEST SPEAKER
NATIVE AMERICAN DANCERS
A CRF AUDITORIUM
7:00-9:00 PM

WELCOME ALL

This poster for a 1983 cultural event called "We Have Not Vanished" suggests the changing self-image of Native Americans and their and growing presence in mainstream culture.

Poems 1979–87 (1988). Another feminist viewpoint appears in Janet Campbell Hale's (Coeur d'Alene) *The Jailing of Cecilia Capture* (1985), which centers on an alcoholic woman protagonist. Another feminist novel is Luci Tapahonso's (Navajo) *One More Shipwreck* (1981).

The Blackfeet writer James Welch, in his novel *Fools Crow* (1986), managed to describe the plight of the Blackfeet people in northwestern Montana in the 1870s. It was followed by Anna Lee Walters of the Pawnee, who wrote *Ghost Singer* (1988) about the U.S. government's policies in the 19th century. The disintegration of Native-American society that Barney Bush (Shawnee) had covered in his *My Horse and a Jukebox* (1979) was continued in *Inherit the Blood* (1985).

Rex Weyler's history *Blood of the Land* (1982) outlined government attitudes toward the Native-American movement, and Ray Youngbear (Mesquakie) included contemporary realism in his poetry collection *Winter of the Salamander* (1980). There was also the novel *Love Medicine* (1984) by the Ojibwa (Chippewa) writer Louise Erdrich, in which she described her people in North Dakota. These themes continued in her next two books, *Beet Queen* (1986) and *Tracks* (1988). Erdrich's husband Michael Dorris, who claimed Modoc ancestry, wrote *A Yellow Raft in Blue Water* (1987) about three generations of women on a Montana reservation. Dorris also wrote of his own children—before his marriage to Erdrich, Dorris had been the first unmarried man to adopt a child in the United States—in *The Broken Cord: The Family Ongoing Struggle with Fetal Alcohol Syndrome* (1989). Also of great importance is his *A Guide to Research in Native American Studies* (1984).

A number of poignant autobiographies appeared in the 1980s, many of which wove family stories and traditions into the account of the author's life. A few of these autobiographies are Percy Bullchild's (Blackfeet) *The Sun Came*

Down: The History of the World as My Blackfeet Elders Told It (1985); Florence Edenshaw Davidson's (Haida) *During My Time: Florence Edenshaw Davidson, a Haida Woman* (1987); John Fredson's (Gwich'in Athabascan) *Stories Told By John Fredson to Edward Sapir* (1982); Belle Herbert's (Athabascan) *Shandaa: In My Lifetime* (1982); and William Least Heat Moon's (Osage) *Blue Highways: A Journey Into America* (1982). By 1994, it was possible for Arnold Krupat to edit *Native American Autobiography: An Anthology*. Besides books, there were also new Native-American newspapers; *The Lakota Times*, first published on July 9, 1981, later became *Indian Country Today*.

FILM AND MUSIC

In Hollywood and the film industry in general, there had long been Indian actors and actresses. However, most of these played anonymous roles in westerns. In his autobiography *Songs My Mother Taught Me* (1994), Marlon Brando wrote that the film industry had "systematically misrepresented and maligned American Indians for six decades." The publicity that Brando gave to the Native-American cause in 1973 and other earlier support by Jane Fonda and others had helped establish good relations between Native Americans and many U.S. actors.

Although there were many instances where non–Native Americans played the parts of tribal chiefs and other Native Americans in films, these had become fewer and fewer during the 1970s—Trevor Howard in *Windwalker* in 1980, Robby Benson in *Running Brave* (1982), and Kevin Dillon in *War Party* (1989) being notable exceptions. Gradually a number of Native Americans started to play major roles. Filmmakers casted Native Americans including Tantoo Cardinal (Nootka) in *War Party* (1989), George Clutesi (Nootka) in *Spirit of the Wind* (1980), Charlie Hill (Oneida) in *Harold of Orange* (1983), and Michael Horse (Apache/Zuni) in *The Legend of the Lone Ranger* (1981). Graham Greene (Oneida), born on the Six Nations Reserve near Ontario, Canada, appeared in *Running Brave* (1983), *Revolution* (1985), and *Powwow Highway* (1989); he was later nominated for an Oscar for Best Performance by an Actor in a Supporting Role in *Dances with Wolves* (1990).

There were also a number of Native-American film producers such as Maggi Banner (Hopi and Tewa), who made *Coyote Goes Underground* (1989). Among the many others were Arlene Bowman (Navajo), *Navajo Talking Picture* (1986); Gil Cardinal (Metis), *Fister Child* (1986) and *The Spirit Within* (1988–91); Carol Geddes (Tlingit), *Doctor, Lawyer, Indian Chief* (1986); Bob Hicks (Creek and Seminole), *Return of the Country* (1984); George P. House (Gros Ventre) and Larry Little Bird (Santo Domingo Pueblo), *I'd Rather Be Powwowing* (1983); Alexie Isaac (Yupik Eskimo), *Yupiit Yuraryarait* (1983) and *Eyes of the Spirit* (1984); and Carol Korb, *Shenandoah Films* (1983 onward).

In the world of music, Eartha Mae Keith (1927–2008), known as Eartha Kitt, who was of mixed African-American and Native-American (Cherokee)

A protestor holds a sign reading "Eartha Kitt speaks for the women of America" during a 1968 antiwar protest. Kitt was able to make a comeback with her singing career in the 1980s.

ancestry, made a comeback in the 1980s. Kitt had been a famous singer and actress (as "Catwoman") in the 1960s, when Orson Welles described her as the "most exciting woman in the world." However, Kitt was blacklisted after telling First Lady Lady Bird Johnson about her opposition to the Vietnam War in 1968. It was not until 1984 that she was able to make a return to the music charts with "Where Is My Man," a disco song that became the first certified Gold Record in her career.

NATIVE AMERICAN ATHLETES

Native-American games such as lacrosse and shinny have long been played by many non-Native Americans, along with many other sports such as archery and horseback riding, which developed hunting and warfare skills. However, few Native Americans participated in mainstream U.S. sporting pursuits and, in part to counter this, in 1972 the American Indian Athletic Hall of Fame was established on the campus of Haskell Indian Junior College. Many of those inducted had long since died, but during the 1980s, there was a continual attempt to help document sporting champions both alive and deceased. In 1981, George P. Lavatta (Shoshone-Bannock) became an honorary inductee for his work for the Hall of Fame itself, and in the following year, Turner Cochran, the curator of the hall, was also made an honorary inductee for his work establishing the Hall of Heroes, which became the Hall of Fame.

In 1984, Haskell Indian Junior College celebrated the 100th anniversary of its founding.

That same year a large powwow was held during the Los Angeles Olympics to commemorate Olympic athlete Jim Thorpe, who had won two gold medals at the 1912 Olympics in Stockholm in the decathlon and the pentathlon. There was also a Jim Thorpe Longest Run, when relays of Native Americans ran from the lake of the Onondaga Nation in New York State to Los Angeles, California. Great controversy existed because Thorpe's medals had been revoked because of a claim that he had violated his amateur status by accepting expenses for playing in Minor League baseball. Thorpe went on to play professional football and baseball. In 1982, the International Olympic Committee had finally reinstated his amateur status, and at the end of the Jim Thorpe Long Run, his medals were returned to his family.

NATIVE-AMERICAN ART

In the realm of art, there had long been an interest in Native-American pottery, evidenced by the 1977 series of U.S. postage stamps of Pueblo art and the 1986 series of Navajo rugs. There had been relatively little change in style over centuries, with many Native-American artists continuing to use the same materials and patterns that their nation, and sometimes their own families, had used for generations. For example, Dextra Quotskuya from Arizona carried on a six-generation-long tradition of making pots, and Maria Martinez had been making pots for seven decades. However, there were now also many others who reused traditional patterns and imagery, but incorporated them with new styles, sometimes using Western art media and techniques.

R.C. Gorman, known as the "Picasso of American Indian artists," had served in the navy during the Korean War and then became influenced by the murals painted by Mexican artists Diego Rivera and David Siqueiros. He established his own gallery at Taos, New Mexico, and wrote his autobiography, *Radiance of My People* (1992), followed by a biography of his father, *Power of a Navajo* (1996). Michael Naranjo (Santa Clara Pueblo) was a veteran of the Vietnam War who lost his right hand in combat, then turned to art, establishing the Touched by Art Fund that has done much to help disabled people, especially but not restricted to veterans.

In 1990, the U.S. Congress passed the Indian Arts and Crafts Act, which helped in the promotion of Native-American artwork and handicrafts and protected against counterfeit or imported goods and deceptive marketing practices. One of the most important developments during the 1980s that has helped preserve Native-American culture and history was the establishment of the Museum of the American Indian within the Smithsonian Institution. Strongly supported by Ben Nighthorse Campbell, it was established with the support of an act of Congress in 1989. It operates in three facilities—the National Museum of the American Indian on the National Mall in Washington,

D.C. (which did not open until 2004), the George Gustave Heye Center in New York City, and the Cultural Resources Center in Suitland, Maryland.

CONCLUSION

The 1970s and 1980s saw the gradual erosion of paternalism, the idea that Native Americans did not have the capability to govern themselves and needed the assistance of the U.S. government. An increase in the Native American population contributed to a greater awareness of Native-American issues. Such legislative acts as the 1975 Indian Self-Determination and Education Assistance Act helped pave the way for the acceptance of Native Americans as a self-sufficient people. With advances in the areas of politics, art, literature, and athletics, Native Americans finally became more assimilated into mainstream American society. However, relations between the U.S. government and Native Americans remained strained, and groups such as the American Indian Movement (inspired by the Black Panthers) were established to promote Native American claims.

BILL KTE'PI
INDEPENDENT SCHOLAR

Further Reading

Apted, Michael. *Incident at Oglala*. DVD Narr. by Robert Redford. Los Angeles, CA: Miramax, 1992.

Banks, Dennis, with Richard Erdoes. *Ojibwa Warrior: Dennis Banks and the Rise of the American Indian Movement*. Norman, OK: University of Oklahoma Press, 2004.

Biolsi, Thomas and Larry Zimmerman. *Indians and Anthropologists*. Tucson, AZ: University of Arizona Press, 1997.

Braine, Susan. *Drumbeat . . . Heartbeat: A Celebration of the Powwow*. Minneapolis, MN: Lerner Publications, 1995.

Brando, Marlon. *Songs My Mother Taught Me*. London: Century, 1994.

Brandon, William. *The American Heritage Book of Indians*. New York: Dell, 1984.

Churchill, Ward and Wall Vander. *Agents of Repression*. Boston, MA: South End Press, 1988.

Crow Dog, Mary, with Richard Erdoes. *Lakota Woman*. New York: Grove Weidenfeld, 1990.

Davis, Mary B., ed. *Native America in the Twentieth Century: An Encyclopedia*. New York: Garland, 1994.

Deloria, Vine, Jr. *Behind the Trail of Broken Treaties: An Indian Declaration of Independence*. New York: Dell, 1974.

————. *Custer Died for Your Sins*. Norman, OK: University of Oklahoma Press, 1988.

Grossman, Mark. *The ABC-CLIO Companion to Native American Rights Movement*. Santa Barbara, CA: ABC-CLIO, 1996.

Hendricks, Steve. *The Unquiet Grave*. New York: Thunder's Mouth Press, 2006.

Hirschfelder, Arlene B. and Martha Kreipe de Montano. *The Native American Almanac: A Portrait of Native America Today*. New York: Macmillan, 1993.

Hirschfelder, Arlene B. and Beverly R. Singer, eds. *Rising Voices: Writings of Young Native Americans*. New York: Scribner, 1992.

Josephy, Alvin M., Jr. *500 Nations: An Illustrated History of North American Indians*. New York: Alfred A. Knopf, 1994.

Kavasch, E. Barrie. *EarthMaker's Lodge: Native American Folklore, Activities, and Foods*. Peterborough, NH: Cobblestone, 1994.

————. *A Student's Guide to Native American Genealogy*. Phoenix, AZ: Oryx Press, 1996.

King, C. and Charles Springwood. *Beyond the Cheers*. Albany, NY: State University of New York Press, 2001.

Klein, Barry T. *Reference Encyclopedia of the American Indian*. West Nyack, NY: Toll Publishers, 1993.

Lester, Patrick D. *The Biographical Directory of Native American Painters*. Norman, OK: Oklahoma University Press, 1995.

Matthiessen, Peter. *In the Spirit of Crazy Horse*. New York: Penguin, 1992.

Peltier, Leonard. *Prison Writings*. New York: St. Martin's Griffin, 2000.

Smith, Paul Chaat and Robert Allen Warrior. *Like a Hurricane: The Indian Movement from Alcatraz to Wounded Knee*. New York: New Press, 1997.

Snipp, C.M. *American Indians: The First of this Land*. New York: Russell Sage Foundation, 1989.

Waldman, Carl. *Atlas of the North American Indian*. New York: Facts on File, 1985.

————. *Encyclopedia of Native American Tribes*. New York: Facts on File, 1988.

Weatherford, Jack. *Indian Givers: How the Indians of the Americas Transformed the World*. New York: Crown, 1988.

Weyler, Rex. *Blood of the Land*. New York: Vintage Books, 1984.

Whitehorse, David. *Pow-Wow: The Contemporary Pan-Indian Celebration*. San Diego, CA: San Diego State University, 1988.

Wilkinson, Charles F. *Blood Struggle: The Rise of Modern Indian Nations*. New York: W.W. Norton, 2006

CHAPTER 10

Native Americans Today: 1990 to the Present

AMERICA TOOK NOTICE in November 2009 when the Sicangu Lakota Nation (Lower Brule Sioux) purchased a Wall Street investment bank. The tribal council made the deal in hope of generating income for a people who faced 40 percent unemployment on their South Dakota reservation. Potential profits from the venture were slated to be reinvested in local infrastructure and educational opportunities for that nation's youth. While many tribal members were suspicious about the secret details of the transaction, most were in favor of finding innovative methods to overcome long-term poverty and political marginalization.

Lakotas were unique in their methods, but not in their aims. Over the last several decades, Native Americans and Alaska Natives in the United States have made great strides in taking control of their economic, political, social, and cultural destinies. They have witnessed marked population recovery, increased sovereignty on their lands, economic development, and a cultural renaissance.

While Indians as a group were on a footing they had not enjoyed for at least a century, their communities were still plagued by the effects of American colonialism: poverty, disease, political uncertainty, and racial discrimination. For Native Americans, the years after 1990 offered hope for the future, but this hope was tempered by issues from the not-so-distant past.

POPULATION RECOVERY AND MODERN DEMOGRAPHY

Native-American and Alaska-Native populations in the United States have shown remarkable growth in the last several decades. In the broadest sense, they now number about 4.5 million individuals. While Indians live in all 50 states, the greatest populations are west of the Missouri River. In raw numbers, California (with over 300,000 Natives), Oklahoma, Arizona, New Mexico, Washington, and Alaska are homes to the largest indigenous communities. Alaska Natives account for over 16 percent of that state's population. Indians in New Mexico, South Dakota, Oklahoma, Montana, and North Dakota—states with numerous reservations—all account for between five and 10 percent of total populations.

In many respects, the present numbers are a triumph. After generations of persecution and land loss, indigenous populations declined to all-time lows around 1900. Recovery began in earnest around 1930, when the total Native population reached 362,000, and since 1970, when the population was 827,000, their numbers have risen dramatically. U.S. Census Bureau figures for 1990 (2,045,000) and 2000 (2,476,000) demonstrate the growth of people claiming Native American and Alaska Native as their main ethnicity.

This growth was largely the result of high fertility rates and improved health and healthcare. These numbers also represent a trend toward increased self-reporting due to growing Native pride. In recent years, this self-respect extended into another set of statistics that allowed census respondents to identify multiple ethnicities. Consequently, in 2000, another 1.6 million Americans claimed to be part Native American or Alaska Native. This yielded a total of 4.1 million individuals with some Native background. The U.S. Census Bureau estimated that this number had increased to 4.5 million by 2007, roughly 1.5 percent of the U.S. population.

Most of these people lived in cities. While reservations were still significant in Indian life, 64 percent of all Native Americans resided off reservation in 2000. Large-scale movement away from reservations began in earnest during World War II. Residents were pushed away by lack of economic opportunities. They were pulled into cities by access to jobs and the possibility of gaining better educations for their children. Presently, Los Angeles, Phoenix, and Chicago have the largest clusters of Native peoples, but most western metropolitan areas have significant Indian enclaves, as do many cities in the Midwest and northeast. The trend is toward greater urban numbers in the future.

Today, Indians still face poverty in their newer homes, but, as a general rule, they enjoy higher incomes and better educations than their relatives on reservations. These levels of comparative prosperity still fall far short of the incomes and educations of the majority culture. Additionally, city life has created an urban/rural split among some tribes. Those raised or residing off reservations often have been considered less "Indian" than those remaining on reservations.

The Duwamish tribe built this longhouse and cultural center in 2009 in West Seattle, Washington, to help maintain the tribe's traditional connection to the area.

Despite this general attitude, established urban communities are serving as new homes for cultural retention and revitalization. Urban dwellers often base their social lives around American Indian Centers in their communities. Most of these were founded in the 1960s and 1970s, and there are over 60 of them scattered around the United States. Most cities with significant Native populations have established centers. These spaces allow Indians to gather in a place where they are the majority; the centers also serve as clearinghouses for government and private agency services.

Despite changing emotional connections to Indian identities and new urban life ways, modern Native Americans continue to face dramatic economic and social challenges. In 2000, 920,000 of those identifying as Indians lived below the official poverty level. Family income was $13,000 less than the national average in 2005. Access to healthcare was often limited, and the Indian Health Service—responsible for serving about 1.9 million American citizens—was chronically underfunded and understaffed. Consequently, human immunodeficiency virus and acquired immune deficiency syndrome (HIV/AIDS), adult-onset diabetes, tuberculosis, and suicide levels were unacceptably high both on and off reservations. Residents of Pine Ridge and Rosebud Reservations in South Dakota had life-expectancy rates about the same as people living in Haiti—a troubling statistic for a country as wealthy as the United States.

This member of the Montana Indian Firefighters helped control devastating fires on the Flathead Reservation near Missoula, Montana, in August 2000. The Federal Emergency Management Agency joined in to provide assistance to fire victims after the fires were declared a federal disaster.

SOVEREIGNTY AND AMERICAN POLITICS

In addition to poverty issues, Native Americans in 2010 were still fighting to define their political and legal standing in the United States. Simply defined, sovereignty means that tribal law on reservations is supreme. Tribal sovereignty in the United States, however, has never been absolute; this is largely because the U.S. Constitution fails to include Indians. Consequently, their legal matters are mired in red tape as 389 treaties, 51,000 statutes, 2,000 federal court decisions, 500 attorney general opinions, 141 tribal constitutions, and 112 tribal charters might need to be considered. Without full constitutional protection, Congress and the president still are able to dictate policies to Native governments with a legal status best defined by the U.S. Supreme Court about 180 years ago. In *Cherokee Nation v. Georgia* (1831), the Court ruled that Indians on Indian land were part of "domestic dependent nations." While they were not subject to the laws and jurisdictions of individual states, they were not independent nations. They are still subject to federal laws and executive orders that are often alien to Native cultures.

Policies tend to change with each new Congress or presidential administration. In the 1990s, the federal government generally promoted self-governance and civil rights on reservations. President Bill Clinton, near the end of his first term, directed all agencies within the federal government to operate in a "sensitive manner respectful of tribal sovereignty." Congress was of similar mind in 1994 when it enacted the Native American Free Exercise of Religion Act. Finally, in 2000, the Bureau of Indian Affairs issued an apology for past harms done to Indian nations. The George W. Bush administration, however, proved less interested in Indian affairs and decidedly less popular among Native Americans—a population that tends to vote Democratic. President Bush was roundly criticized for ignoring treaty provisions, encouraging natural resource development on Indian lands despite local opposition, failing to address pressing social needs, and not respecting established government-to-government relationships. Candidate Barack Obama achieved mass support among Indians, promising to establish "nation-to-nation" relationships and to listen to Native voices while in the White House. As of 2010, President Obama's young administration was still viewed positively across Indian Country.

Citizens of Indian nations would prefer to be incorporated into the United States on their own terms. In recent decades, they have made significant progress in regaining tribal control of Native spaces. To aid these efforts, yearly sovereignty symposiums have been held since 1994. These have since become important forums for discussions about Indian culture, spirituality, social issues, and tribal law. The 2009 symposium theme was "Land, Wind, and Water." Sessions tended to focus on legal issues including water law, criminal law, land inheritance, and gaming regulation; social issues, including Native-American healthcare, climate crisis, and energy solutions; and matters of education, including a session called "Language, the Arts and Cultural Preservation: The Linchpins Holding Peoples Together."

A Native Peoples for Obama campaign sign rests on a whale bone in Barrow, Alaska, the northernmost town in North America, on August 21, 2008, the day of a local campaign rally.

LANGUAGE PRESERVATION AND EDUCATIONAL OPPORTUNITIES

Native languages are artifacts of great importance to indigenous peoples. Language retention solidifies group belonging and preserves important connections to places. Speakers of Indian tongues generally take great pride in their distinct tribal identities. Additionally, the logic of language is just as important as the words. Many ideas central to Native identity are nearly impossible to express in English, now the first tongue of most Indians.

In general, the health of Indian languages is less than robust. Hundreds of them have disappeared since European or American contact. About 175 Native languages are still spoken in the United States, but this is less than half the number spoken in 1492. About 20 are quite vibrant, as they have been handed down from generation to generation and are still used regularly among tribal members. Most healthy languages belong to large nations—Lakotas and Navajos, for example. Navajos have so many speakers they are able to maintain radio station KTNN as an all-Navajo-language medium. Smaller tribes, such as Cheyennes and Hupas, also have hundreds of dedicated speakers.

Unfortunately, 89 percent of these surviving languages are in danger of vanishing. Defined by scholars as "moribund," the remaining 155 tongues are spoken primarily by older adults who have been unable to pass their languages on; often these speakers amount to less than one percent of tribal populations. While reasons vary for not speaking Native languages, many Indians were actively discouraged from using their languages by the American education system they encountered off and even on reservations. Some scholars estimate that at the present rate of decay, this large group of languages will disappear by 2050. In general, the fewer the number of fluent speakers, the less chance a language has to survive.

The work of language retention was eased by the passage of the Native American Languages Acts in 1990 and 1992. The 1990 act declared a federal policy to "preserve, protect, and promote Indian languages." The 1992 act made federal grants available for preservation programs. Innovative teaching methods have emerged since that time. Reclaiming the knowledge of "hesitant" speakers is just one of them. Hesitant speakers still exist in most Native cultures. These are individuals who had intimate contact with the language in their youth, but rarely used it as they matured and entered adulthood. To tap their expertise, language students and educators posit how a specific phrase or idea may have been expressed and then ask the speaker to verify or amend this information. Similarly, master/apprentice programs have been implemented that allow speakers—hesitant or active—to pair with students to gain Indian knowledge in a more traditional one-on-one format. Because of these and other innovations, some language survival and even revival seems likely in the 21st century.

Language programs may also prove a draw to help keep Indian students in school. Unfortunately, these students do not always fare well in the majority culture's education system. Only about 60 percent of Native Americans nationwide graduate from high school, and just three percent of those go on to earn their bachelor's degrees. In comparison, nearly 25 percent of the European-American population attends college—a road that generally leads to substantially higher salaries and wages in their adult years.

Significant steps have been taken to help curb these alarming dropout rates and achievement gaps. One successful method to keep younger people in school was the promotion of cultural and language programs on reservation schools and in other public schools that serve large Native populations. These programs came into being after

This woman belongs to the large Navajo Nation, whose language remains widely spoken. Out of 175 surviving Native languages in the United States, 155 are severely threatened.

the Self-Determination and Education Assistance Act of 1975 gave Indian peoples local control of their children's K-12 educations.

To build on this success, the Tribally Controlled Community Colleges Act was passed in 1978 to encourage higher education on reservations. Bolstered by a decade of success at Diné College on the Navajo Reservation, by 2009, 36 Indian colleges were in operation in 14 states. In concert, their dual missions of preparing students for success and preserving indigenous culture and language were made available to nearly 20,000 students. Additionally, at least 50 mainstream universities offer Native language courses. Because of concerted efforts by Indians and educators, and major changes in governmental policies, many of the 155 threatened languages could survive.

IDENTITY ISSUES

Even if some Native-American languages do disappear, other identity markers remain, and many Native Americans stay connected to tribal groups. Being indigenous in the 21st century, however, is often a complex issue. Individuals wrestle with ideas of being ethnically Native or belonging first to a specific tribe. Additionally, there are multiple legal barriers to being recognized as "Indian" or as a tribal member. The U.S. government has not acknowledged a number of indigenous groups; and their omission from federal roles has had

Indigenous in the 21st Century

A Native American woman named Tessa K. Trow wrote the following on her feelings about trying to maintain Native identity in the face of severe social and economic problems:

Native Americans come from beautiful, resourceful cultures that have undergone unremitting change and suffering throughout the years. As a result of that change, being Native American in the twenty-first century comes with many hardships and difficult decisions; it means overcoming health problems stemming from social and economic hardships, overcoming poverty and lack of government recognition or assistance, as well as facing and mending distorted identity issues emanating from centuries of attempted erasure.

Statistics show that the overall health of Indians is poor which is due in part to their struggling economies and lack of government assistance. In the early 1990s, rates of alcoholism and tuberculosis infection were both more than four times higher among Native Americans than among the general American population. There is a common association between Native Americans and the prevalence of alcoholism yet what is disregarded is that it stems from their lands, life ways and cultures being destroyed by the United States government who replanted them and consequentially erased their identities—condemning them to small designated areas while stealing their natural resources.

Alcohol was introduced by foreigners and it has become a way of coping with devastating histories and modern poverty. Diabetes stems from the introduction of bread and processed foods. They eat these foods because rights to hunt are now often limited and their lands used for gathering vegetable foods have been stripped from them.

One of the biggest problems impeding Native Americans' road to recuperation is their struggling economies. The disturbing fact is that nearly 26 percent of Native Americans remain below the poverty line even in the twenty-first century. This provides ample explanation for the high number of violent or accidental deaths that plague children aged eighteen years or younger. It was reported in 2000 that about 6,000 young Indians belonged to one of 520 reservation gangs. Choosing that route to escape makes sense considering how colossal their obstacles are.

To be a Native American youth in the twenty-first century means discovering your identity and determining how to fit in between two very different worlds: the reservation and the modern world outside of it. Either they stay true to their culture, which has been greatly scarred and partially erased, or they leave the reservation where they are more likely to find a job but are even more likely to be negatively discriminated or lose their heritage.

adverse social and financial effects. Even among recognized tribes, individuals must sometimes prove their right to belong. While the tribes have the final say on who joins them, the methods for making those decisions are often imposed by outside standards.

Modern pride in having Native heritage has created a strong "pan-Indian" identity that emerged in urban areas in the late 1950s, and the idea was strengthened by the political activism of the 1960s and 1970s. This concept continues to be important, and it is perhaps best expressed by the Gathering of Nations Pow Wow motto: "Mexicans, 'Central Americans,' 'Native Americans,' & 'First Nations People,' are One Race, One Nation, One People!" In essence, many indigenous peoples celebrate relationships that go beyond the tribe as they try to connect with all tribal peoples to promote the common cause of greater self-determination.

Connecting with other Indians, however, does not replace the tribe in 21st-century America. Pan-Indianism tends to strengthen Native identities, and that often connects individuals more strongly to their own people. As of 2010, the Bureau of Indian Affairs (BIA) recognized 564 distinct tribes in the United States. But there are over 190 bands and tribes of Native Americans and Alaska Natives that are not recognized by the federal government. Without formal recognition, the federal government does not consider members of these groups to be "Indians." Consequently, they are denied benefits reserved for Native peoples. While some tribes are content with this relationship, most seek federal recognition to further the welfare of their citizens.

TRIBAL MEMBERSHIP

Recognized tribes have their own internal membership requirements, and some individuals wishing to be part of a nation fail in their efforts. Most famously, poet Wendy Rose, author of *The Halfbreed Chronicles,* considers herself Hopi, but has no standing in that tribe. As a result, she is not regarded as "Indian" by the federal government. Rose grew up hundreds of miles away from the reservation, but she identifies with her father's Hopi ethnicity and feels rejected by her mother's non-Indian people. Despite having 50 percent Hopi blood, the Arizona nation traces lineage through the mother's side, and it does not recognize Rose.

Rose and other observers agree that the tribes are and should be the final authority on membership. Even this responsibility, however, is tinged by American colonialism as tribes often rely on federal standards to ease the membership process. The BIA defines an Indian as "someone who has blood degree from and is recognized as such by a federally recognized tribe or village and/or the United States." While the federal government does not endorse a single standard for membership, "blood quantum" has become the norm for most tribes. To become a tribal member, applicants must document their lineage and prove that at least one-quarter of their blood relatives came from the specific tribe they wish to join. They can do this by analyzing birth certificates, death certificates, and probate records to find connections to people mentioned in early reservation enrollment records.

Blood quantum has replaced cultural knowledge as the preeminent way of determining membership in the 20th and 21st centuries. Although use of this equation began to emerge in the 1930s, this method is still criticized as "un-Indian" by some Native Americans who recall a time when common acknowledgment, demonstrating proper tribal behaviors, or adoption were the main measures of national belonging. Other critics claim blood quantum for Indians is discriminatory. While there are 12 "races" officially noted by the U.S. Census Bureau, American Indian is the only one that requires special documentation. Still, its use remains critical in Indian Country, where tribal membership through blood quantum often dictates federal and tribal benefits, as well as the right to share any profits generated by Indian gaming.

CASINO GAMING

Over the last two decades, gaming ventures on reservation lands have transformed Indian Country. Those who support gaming have suggested that gambling is part of many nations' deep cultural traditions. For some Native peoples, gaming has brought significant economic improvements. Other individuals and nations have claimed that modern forms of gaming have no place in Native spaces, and the unequal distribution of wealth from its profits is harmful to many tribes.

Despite such conflicting views, gambling on reservations has exploded in recent years and will likely remain around for a long time. The Seminole tribe of Florida forced federal action after they opened a high-stakes bingo parlor in 1979. This action provided a popular entertainment outlet for residents and visitors to the Miami metropolitan area. Its early years of operation were mired by legal challenges, but the Indian Gaming Regulatory Act (IGRA) settled these issues in 1988. The act created three classes of gaming: Class I gaming includes traditional activities such as hand games or stick games that generally serve ceremonial and social functions; Class II games are generally low-stakes affairs such as bingo and lotto; Class III gaming is essentially casino gambling. The National Indian Gaming Commission was established to oversee the fledgling industry.

Gaming spread rapidly across Indian Country after the IGRA was passed. By 1997, 142 tribes in 24 states had Las Vegas–style casinos. In 2009, there

The MGM Grand Casino at Foxwoods in Ledyard, Connecticut, in 2008.

Landless Tribes

Axle Olson, a member of the Little Shell Tribe of Montana, describes the experience of the 150 tribes in the United States that lack reservations. These tribes suffer from a lack of government services that other tribes have, and are usually not able to acquire federal recognition to improve their situations.

Tribal identity is central to Indian people in the twenty-first century. A person's tribe is their past, present and future; it is an Indian's home community. Still, Native peoples must navigate federal, state and tribal politics to function. The federal Bureau of Indian Affairs recognizes more than 500 "tribes." Tribes that are federally recognized work hand and hand with the U.S. government on a regular basis. They are eligible for various services, including, but not limited to medical treatment, food stamps, assistance with car insurance and supplies for a new job. Many tribes also receive money to establish income generating businesses such as casinos. Tribes use those profits to build schools and health care services. Most recognized tribes have reservations. Reservations are run by tribal governments giving the Natives a feeling of self control. A Native can always fall back on their reservation.

It is harder for Indians without land. There are 150 groups without reservations who have sought but failed to acquire federal legal status. In some states these tribes rely heavily on state programs and grants. Tribes will interact in a number of ways with state governments, and they can often get medical and food stamp services offered by states. Unfortunately, federal services are better.

I belong to one of these federally unrecognized groups. Personally, I can trace my lineage back in my Little Shell Tribe of Montana over eight generations. We are Chippewa Cree and related to the Rocky Boy Tribe of Montana and the Turtle Mountain Band of North Dakota. Unlike out relatives, we currently do not have a land base or access to federal programs. Consequently, we have been seeking federal recognition for decades. In 2009, Congressmen Denny Rehberg of Montana, introduced HR 3120, a bill to get federal recognition for Little Shell Chippewa. Although not yet law, the bill states that Little Shells were party to an 1863 federal treaty and mentioned in the 1934 Indian Reorganization Act. Consequently, federal recognition should be restored, and 200 acres of land should be awarded to us as a land base.

Most Natives take pride in being Native American, and their tribe and lands are part of their identities. A reservation is a place where Natives are at home. The reservations will have most resources tribe members need. They are, in essence, small communities for Natives to live and prosper.

were 510 gaming establishments—casinos, slot parlors, bingo halls, and poker halls—scattered around 33 states. Indian tribes in other states are trying to get new gaming establishments approved; these businesses range from the modest to the extravagant. The Las Vegas Paiutes, for instance, keep seven slot machines at their Snow Mountain Smoke Shop. The Mashantucket Pequot Tribal Nation, on the other hand, owns and operates Foxwoods Resort Casino in Connecticut. This complex houses 7,400 slots and 388 table games, a convention center, numerous hotels, and several entertainment venues. In total, it is one of the richest operations in the world.

Although few nations can hope to match Foxwoods, gaming has been seen by many as a route to economic self-sufficiency. Successful operations provide employment for tribal members and other individuals living in the vicinity. The profits of casinos are remitted to tribal members as annual payments and reinvested into tribal foundations that provide educational aid and serve as a source of capital for home ownership and business construction. Indian tribes also have the funds to pursue legal remedies against past and present wrongs done to them. Even for tribes lacking casinos, legal precedents created through other cases have provided some relief from past wrongs.

Gaming is not without its critics. Some scholars have suggested that regulations put into place to police gaming are detrimental to tribal sovereignty. Instead of Indian independence, new layers of legal controls have emerged. Additionally, some members of the majority culture have become increasingly antagonistic toward Indians because they are receiving special treatment. Gaming revenues have led to decreases in federal and state funding for social services that many Indian communities still need badly. More pragmatically, some Indians have noted that the economic benefits of gaming have not been universal. Because many tribes live on reservations far from urban centers, their operations have not been particularly lucrative. Tribal gaming generates $15 billion annually, but 20 percent of tribes see 80 percent of the profit. In the 21st century, then, a small number of very rich Indians have emerged, while many have remained deeply impoverished. Although all enterprises contribute to tribal economies, most Indian nations will need to find other mechanisms to ease financial pressures.

RESOURCES AND ENVIRONMENT

Many Indian nations have other resources available to them, and they have discussed the pros and cons of developing energy reserves. Nearly 33 percent of the low-sulfur coal deposits in the western states, half of all uranium deposits, and 20 percent of all known U.S. oil and natural gas reserves are on Indian lands. Mining and drilling these resources would—at face value—allow Indians with remote reservations to generate income that their casinos often have not. However, a history of resource exploitation and a desire to preserve environmental integrity make mining and drilling difficult propositions.

A Kalispel Perspective on Casino Gaming

Kalispel Tribe member Salina Nenema has seen the economic benefits of casino gaming first-hand. Residents of the Kalispel Reservation north of Spokane, Washington, experienced extreme poverty in the 20th century, with an average annual income of only $1,400 per person in 1965. With the construction of the tribe's casino in 2000 on trust land purchased specifically for establishing a gaming business, the Kalispels have seen their living standards rise dramatically. The Kalispels have not only been able to gain access to loans, pay for higher education, and preserve tribal heritage, but they have also contributed significantly to the surrounding region, as Nenema relates below:

The Kalispel Reservation consists of a small, remote strip of land adjacent to the Pend Oreille River, in northeastern Washington. These traditional lands provide little or no economic benefits or resources to survive on. So Kalispel people lived in poverty. That all changed with the approval of tribal gaming. The ability of the Kalispel Tribe of Indians to successfully integrate their culture and community life into the twenty-first century is due, in large part, to the ongoing success of the Northern Quest Casino.

This casino opened its doors for business in December of 2000, after successfully negotiating and then purchasing trust land off of the original reservation. Kalispels are one of three Indian Tribes in the nation to acquire new trust land in order to conduct casino operations. The casino's success is based, in part, on its location in Airway Heights, a community that is part of the Spokane metropolitan area.

Life before the casino was a daily struggle. Today, gaming profits fund education, housing, a Natural Resource Department, better health care, and a new Wellness Center. For me, a Kalispel Tribal member, benefits include a loan to purchase a home for me and my immediate family in Spokane, Washington, another loan to purchase a more reliable vehicle, full funding of my college education, and a trust fund for my son that he cannot get until he turns eighteen years of age.

The Kalispel people were always proud but now everyone holds their heads up high. Today, the tribe is a self-sufficient entity with their own business enterprises. Profits provide funding to keep traditional values alive; Kalispel language is documented now, so it will never be lost. Kalispels are good neighbors and they donate well over $1 million a year to charities, provide the city of Airway Heights with money for police cars and pay the city a yearly amount of money. Additionally, the casino employs many community members that are not Kalispel. Today, the tribe is truly a sovereign nation that is self-empowered to determine the use of resources. And for that I am truly grateful to those who have worked so hard to make tribal gaming a reality.

Spokane Nation's SHAWL Society—Sovereignty, Health, Air, Water, and Land—was in 2010 dealing with an environmental nightmare left behind by decades of uranium mining on their reservation. The Midnite Mine was discovered by Spokanes, but operated by a private company between 1955 and 1986. The mine in its heyday represented a needed source of jobs on a reservation that suffered 75 percent unemployment. Tribal members discovered the lasting health legacy of mining uranium only after the facility closed. Lupus and cancer rates are exceptionally high—partly the result of dust from the mine being carried home to miners' families before the dangers of radiation were clearly understood, and partly due to inadequate cleanup by the mine operator.

Over 33 million tons of radioactive slag litter the reservation, and the main pit remains exposed and partially filled with water. Many of the creeks nearby are badly polluted, and subsistence hunting and fishing activities are compromised as a result. Spokane Nation hired lawyers to sue the mine operator, but the corporation proved too large for them to fight. By 2009, the federal Environmental Protection Agency (EPA) had brought suit, but the case was still without resolution as of 2010.

NAVAJO NATION RESOURCES

Similarly, there are over 520 abandoned uranium mines on Navajo land. While these can cause many of the same problems as those on the Spokane reservation, coal mining and coal power generation garner most concern among Navajos. As of 2010, the tribe was divided on the issue of mining, coal burning, and even the existence of global warming—a by-product of energy production and consumption.

For many Navajo leaders, tapping energy resources has been a necessity on a reservation that cannot support all of its residents through more traditional herding and ranching activities. While many jobs have been generated through mining, there has been internal and international conflict about coal production for over 50 years. Rich deposits were found in 1951 on Black Mesa, a place sacred to Navajos and their Hopi neighbors. Consequently, many Indians opposed disturbing the area. Those in favor of development faced an issue of resource ownership as the boundaries between Hopi and Navajo countries were fixed by federal authorities without consulting either nation.

Ultimately, both tribes claimed ownership of the coal. To mine, internal dissent needed to be quieted and arrangements made with Hopi Nation. To add insult to injury, the mining company's leases were negotiated by the Department of Interior, and both nations were paid far less than market value for the coal. Ultimately, resource exploitation left a bitter taste in many Navajo mouths.

Half a century later, the Navajo Nation gained greater control of its resources and its own environmental policies, and it was in the business of burning coal to produce electricity. Its people were still divided over coal. Some favored resource use and job creation above all other concerns. They cited the suc-

Navajos have sought opportunities off the reservation, including military service, for decades. These Navajo men from New Mexico were serving with the U.S. Marine Corps in Iraq in 2005.

cesses of the Navajo Generating Station that began operations in 1975 and has been a consistent employer of hundreds of Navajos. A proposed and mostly constructed new generator—the Desert Rock plant—could employ hundreds more. Despite these benefits, other tribal members demanded environmental stewardship and respect for traditional life ways. They expressed well-founded fears that exploitation of Native lands would render them unfit for a number of cultural practices.

Navajos, like many Indian nations, have been divided about the development of their mineral resources. Because tribal government is financed through coal profits, the nation's president and council have wished to continue. Opponents have pointed out that coal's benefits have not been widely shared—most Navajos do not have access to these jobs, 30 percent of residents have no electricity in their homes, and damaged land has never been restored despite promises to do so. Additionally, the EPA and the tribal government have been at odds. The EPA has demanded that Navajos install costly scrubbers on their power plants to reduce carbon dioxide emissions. The tribal government has claimed these steps are unnecessary because global warming does not actually exist.

CULTURAL RENAISSANCE

Economic growth and Native pride have encouraged many Indians to seek better educations. Native Americans since 1990 have been very active and

Author Sherman Alexie speaking at a conference
in Los Angeles, California, in May 2009.

successful in defining themselves and their agendas in the educational system, the arts, and popular culture. This trend has created a fundamental shift in how Indians are represented, and images of stereotypical Indians prevalent throughout the majority culture through the 1960s have been disappearing, replaced by more complex and honest descriptions created by Indians themselves.

The growth of Native American Studies programs in higher education over the last several decades has been partly responsible for these changes. Scholarship about Indians was formerly confined to the discipline of anthropology and, until recent decades, was a discussion of vanishing, pre-modern cultures. As of 2010, there were over 100 multidisciplinary programs dedicated to American Indian studies at colleges and universities around the United States. Even more schools offered discrete courses in American Indian history and literature.

Many courses are led by Native professors who may be among the second generation of Indian scholars on college campuses. Philip Deloria, for instance, is the son of the Lakota historian Vine Deloria, Jr., who with English professor N. Scott Momady (Kiowa), began to make Indian history and literature vibrant and alive. The elder Deloria and Momaday were among the early significant players in changing intellectual views of Native peoples and their ideas. The younger scholars they trained, Native and non-Native alike, have continued this mission and have been joined by hundreds of others in the pursuit of honest interpretations of Native-American pasts and presents.

Native writers and filmmakers have been even more visible in modern America as their work has permeated contemporary popular culture. After a decade of watching films that were sympathetic to Native cultures—*Dances with Wolves* (1990), *Black Robe* (1991), and *Thunderheart* (1992), for example—filmmaker Chris Eyre (Cheyenne/Arapaho) teamed with writer Sherman Alexie (Spokane/Coeur d'Alene) to release *Smoke Signals* in 1998. This all-Indian production started an outpouring of work produced by large studios and independents alike. In concert, these newer films attempted to portray both the triumphs and tragedies of modern Native life. Above all, the characters are distinctly human and capable of both good and bad. Barely in their thirties when *Smoke Signals* came out, Alexie and Eyre owed a debt of gratitude to Native-American authors who paved the way for mass acceptance of their works. Wendy Rose's discussions about identity and "Indianness" and poet and musician Joy Harjo's (Muskogee/Creek) discussions of her own mixed ancestry were already winning awards 20 years before *Smoke Signals.*

CONCLUSION

The past and the present in Indian Country remain deeply connected, even as Native peoples work to redefine themselves in the 21st century. Sicangu Lakotas, for instance, may be poised to address many unresolved issues should their banking enterprise succeed. In addition to poverty abatement, they hope to address long-standing territory issues they have with the U.S. government. They are still fighting for adequate compensation for ceding the Black Hills, working to redefine water rights to the Missouri River for a number of Indian tribes, and lobbying to regain access to numerous sacred places held by non-Indian private land owners within Lakota ancestral lands.

Since 1990, Native peoples have made significant economic, social, political, and cultural strides. The general increase in their population pays tribute to these gains. Many problems remain unresolved, however, many issues appear solvable.

KURT E. KINBACHER
SPOKANE FALLS COMMUNITY COLLEGE

Further Reading

Calloway, Colin G. *First Peoples: A Documentary Survey of American Indian History.* Boston, MA: Bedford/St. Martin's, 2004.

Canby, William C., Jr. *American Indian Law in a Nutshell,* 3rd ed. St. Paul, MN: West Group, 1998.

Edmunds, R. David, et al. *The People: A History of Native America.* Boston, MA: Houghton Mifflin, 2007.

Fixico, Donald L. *The Urban Indian Experience in America.* Albuquerque, NM: University of New Mexico Press, 2000.

Fixico, Donald L., ed. *Treaties with American Indians: An Encyclopedia of Rights, Conflicts, and Sovereignty,* 3 vols. Santa Barbara, CA: ABC-CLIO, 2008.

Indian Country Today. Rapid City, SD: Native American Publishing CO. Available online, URL: http://www.indian country.com. Accessed December 2009.

Jackson, Deborah Davis. *Our Elders Lived It: American Indian Identity on the City*. Dekalb, IL: Northern Illinois University Press, 2002.

LaGrand, James B. *Indian Metropolis: Native Americans in Chicago, 1945–75*. Urbana, IL: University of Illinois Press, 2002.

National Alliance to Save Native Languages. Available online, URL: http://www.savenativelanguages.org/Alliance. Accessed December 2009.

Rosenthal, Judith W., ed. *Handbook of Undergraduate Second Language Education*. Mahah, NJ: Lawrence Earlbaum, 2000.

Wunder, John R. *"Retained by the People": A History of American Indians and the Bill of Rights*. New York: Oxford University Press, 1994.

Wunder, John R. and Kurt E. Kinbacher, ed. *Reconfigurations of Native North America: An Anthology of New Perspectives*. Lubbock, TX: Texas Tech University Press, 2009.

Abenaki: A subdivision of the Algonquin tribe.

aboriginal inhabitants: Term used by Thomas Jefferson in his Second Inaugural Address in an effort to promote a more humane policy toward Native Americans.

Adena: A group of tribes sharing a similar burial system that inhabited the Eastern United States from 1000 to 200 B.C.E.

Alaska Native Claims Settlement Act of 1971: Transferred 44 million acres of land into the hands of regional native corporations.

Algonquin: The Native-American tribe that inhabited the valleys of the Hudson and Delaware rivers.

Apache: The group of culturally related tribes originating in the American southwest.

assimilation: The process of growing into one's surrounding culture after belonging to another culture that is starkly different.

atlatl: A notched stick used to propel a spear, providing greater leverage than simply throwing a hand-held spear, achieving greater range and force.

Blackfoot: Tribe that inhabited the state of Montana.

Burke Act of 1906: Allowed reservation officials the option of issuing Indians certificates of competency as a means of ending treaty periods before their designated expiration time.

calumet: Peace pipe.

Cherokee: A nation of tribes originating in the American southeast.

comanchero: Traders and gun-runners, often of mixed Native American-European ancestry in the southwestern United States; often operating as outlaw bands.

Dawes Act: Act that, among other things, opened "surplus" Native-American land to railroad development.

Declaration of Indian Purpose: A public statement made at the American Indian Chicago Conference that demanded better treatment for all Native Americans.

full-blood: Ethnic purity with no mixed lineage.

Ghost Dance: A religious movement that peaked among Native Americans in the 1890s that incorporated a circle dance as its main religious symbol.

Havasupai: Tribe originating in the Grand Canyon area.

hogan: A Navajo Indian dwelling.

Hopi: A group of 12 Native-American village communities speaking the same language, located in northeastern Arizona, entirely surrounded by the Navajo Reservation.

Hopewell tradition: Phrase describing the common characteristics shared by a number of tribes inhabiting the rivers of the northeastern United States, during the time period 200 B.C.E. to 500 C.E.

indeb: A Native-American phrase meaning "we are dead now," or, less literally, "all hope is lost."

Indian Civil Rights Act: Extended many provisions of the Bill of Rights to apply to those who lived on Native-American reservations.

Indian Removal Act of 1830: Law that affected 100,000 Native Americans under which the U.S. Army forcibly relocated peoples from the southeastern United States to lands in the Indian Territory, now Oklahoma. Most were marched overland, although Seminoles from Florida were transported by ship from Tampa to New Orleans, then upriver to a later overland march.

Indian Reorganization Act of 1934: Congressional act granting increased rights to Native Americans, including a reversal of a provision of the Dawes Act that privatized certain lands owned by Native Americans.

Indian Self-Determination and Education Assistance Act of 1975: Established the Office of Indian Education and a National Advisory Council for Indian Education.

Iroquois: Word meaning "people of the longhouse."

Iroquois Six Nations: Confederacy composed of the Seneca, Cayuga, Onondaga, Oneida, Mohawk, and Tuscarora people.

Kachina: The invisible, god-like force of the Pueblo people. Also, kachina dancers, masked members who dress up as representation of the kachina spirits for religious ceremonies; also, kachina dolls, wooden dolls representing kachinas, given as gifts to children.

kiva: An underground chamber common to the Pueblo people, used for sacred ceremonies.

Lenape: A group of several organized bands of Native American people also known as the "Delaware Indians."

Massachusett: Tribe that inhabited the Boston area.

matrilineal: System of lineage used by some tribes that followed the mother's blood line instead of the father's.

Meriam Report: A 1926 government report detailing the horrid economic conditions a sizable sum of the Native American population was forced to endure.

Mohegan: Tribe that settled in the Connecticut area.

Narragansett: A tribe that controlled the western area of Narragansett Bay in Rhode Island at its peak.

Nunna daul Tsuny: Cherokee phrase meaning "the trail where they cried."

Pamunkey: A tribe that settled in Virginia and would later become subservient to the Powhatan tribe.

Pan-Indianism: Philosophy espousing unity of all Native-American tribes regardless of location or affiliation.

Paspahegh: A subservient tribe to the much more powerful Powhatan tribe.

Pennacook: Tribe that inhabited the Merrimack valley of New Hampshire and Massachusetts.

Penobscot: Tribe that inhabited Maine.

Pequot: Tribe that inhabited most of Connecticut.

Peyote Road: Phrase applicable to the Native American Church, a religious organization that advocated the consumption of peyote to induce spiritual journeys.

Pocumtuc: Tribe that inhabited the areas of western Massachusetts.

potlatch: A formal feast practiced among the Native American people of the north Pacific coastal areas, that both displayed the wealth of the host, and served to redistribute wealth to the participants.

Powhatan: Tribe that settled in Virginia and would later become a supreme leader of a confederacy of tribes.

powwow: A gathering.

pueblo: An apartment-like dwelling made from adobe or stone. The term also applies (when capitalized) to the peoples who lived or presently live in such structures in northern New Mexico, southern Colorado, and northeastern Arizona. Some 21 pueblo communities exist today, of which Taos, Acoma, Isleta, Laguna, and Zuni are well known today. The Pueblo people speak different languages, including Tewa, Tewi, Towa, Keres, and Zuni.

Red Power: Phrase coined by Vine Deloria to describe the growing pan-Indian movement of the late 1960s.

Red Progressives: Political group formed in the 1920s that advocated the improvement of Native-American living conditions, led by several Native American spokesmen including Dakota Sioux Charles Alexander Eastman.

sachem: In the Algonquin language, a great chief.

sagamore: A great leader or chief.

Shawnee: Tribe originating in the eastern United States that was forced to resettle in Oklahoma.

terra nullis: Latin for "empty land."

tipi: A traditional, conical Native-American dwelling.

tomahawk: A traditional hatchet.

travois: Transport device consisting of a litter of sticks that could be dragged behind a harnessed dog, or later, behind a horse, for carrying cargo or women and children.

Vision Quest: A personal undertaking usually by an adolescent that involves a spiritual quest using the devices of prayer, fasting, or other substances.

Wampanoag: A tribe located primarily in southeastern Massachusetts and Rhode Island.

wampum: Small cowrie shells used both in religious ceremonies and as a form of currency, when strung together.

wigwam: A traditional, domed Native-American dwelling.

Wounded Knee: Phrase that applies to both a massacre orchestrated by American troops in 1890 in which nearly 150 members of the Lakota Sioux were killed, and an incident in 1973 when organizers of the American Indian Movement occupied a small village in South Dakota and held it under its control for 71 days.

Index note: Page references in *italics* indicate figures or graphs: page references in **bold** indicate main discussion.

Y

Z

PHOTO CREDITS. Federal Emergency Management Agency: 182. Flickr/Rita Huang: 194. Flickr/kptyson: 157. Flickr/Steve Masiello: 188. Flickr/Barack Obama: 183. Flickr/Old Shoe Woman: 51. Flickr/Zol87: 139. iStockphoto.com: 12, 43, 46, 52, 185. Library of Congress: 6, 15, 16, 23, 25, 27, 28, 32, 33, 35, 42, 44, 49, 53, 63, 64, 66, 68, 69, 70, 71, 77, 78, 81, 82, 83, 84, 85, 95, 97, 98, 102, 104, 105, 119, 122, 133, 155, 174. National Archives and Records Administration: 88. National Library of Medicine: 90, 120, 128, 165, 172. National Oceanic and Atmospheric Administration: 10. Photograph ©Milton Rogovin 1952–2002. Courtesy Center for Creative Photography, University of Arizona Foundation: 135. Smithsonian Institution: 8, 55. U.S. Army: 112. U.S. Department of the Interior: 110. U.S. Fish & Wildlife Service: 154. U.S. Marine Corps: 116, 117, 193. U.S. Navy/Robert Cole: 169. Wikipedia: 3, 7. Wikipedia/Vlad Butsky: 130. Wikipedia/Kenny Corbin: 162. Wikipedia/Christopher Hollis: 115. Wikipedia/Joe Mabel: 181. Wikipedia/Tewy: 145.

Produced by Golson Media

President and Editor   J. Geoffrey Golson
Layout Editors   Oona Patrick, Mary Jo Scibetta
Author Manager   Susan Moskowitz
Copyeditor   Barbara Paris
Proofreader   Mary Le Rouge
Indexer   J S Editorial